Warwick University Caribbean Studies

The Commonwealth Caribbean in the World Economy

Ramesh Ramsaran

MACMILLAN CARIBBEAN

© Ramesh F. Ramsaran, 1989

All rights reserved. No reproduction, copy or transmission of this publication may be made without written permission. No paragraph of this publication may be reproduced, copied or transmitted save with written permission or in accordance with the provisions of the Copyright Act 1956 (as amended). Any person who does any unauthorised act in relation to this publication may be liable to criminal prosecution and civil claims for damages.

First published 1989

Published by *Macmillan Publishers Ltd*
London and Basingstoke
Associated companies and representatives in Accra, Auckland, Delhi, Dublin, Gaborone, Hamburg, Harare, Hong Kong, Kuala Lumpur, Lagos, Manzini, Melbourne, Mexico City, Nairobi, New York, Singapore, Tokyo.

ISBN 0−333−49867−4

British Library Cataloguing in Publication Data
Ramsaran Ramesh F.
 The Commonwealth Caribbean in the world
 economy.— (Warwick University Caribbean
 studies)
 1. Caribbean region. Commonwealth countries.
 Economic development
 I. Title II. Series
 330.9182′1

ISBN 0−333−49867−4

HC
155
.R17
1989

Cover based on a painting by Aubrey Williams presented to The Centre for Caribbean Studies, University of Warwick.

Series preface

The Centre for Caribbean Studies at the University of Warwick was founded in 1984 in order to stimulate interest and research in a region which is only now beginning to receive academic recognition in its own right. In addition to the publication of the papers from annual symposia which reflect the Centre's comparative and inter-disciplinary approach, other volumes in the series will be published in disciplines within the arts and social sciences.

This is the first volume in the series to focus on economics – in this case the economy of the Commonwealth Caribbean. Trapped in patterns of monoproduction during the colonial period, producing tropical plantation products for European and North American markets, trade and investment flowed from colony to metropolis and vice versa with few inter-Caribbean contacts. The failure to federate on independence perpetuated this pattern with a gradual shift towards the United States which has now become the dominant trading partner of most of the English-speaking Caribbean.

Dr Ramsaran's study examines the options open to Caribbean mini-economies and monoproductive systems, and the constraints under which they operate. With the decline of traditional exports and increasing competition from larger tropical producers new expedients have been sought such as tourism, off-shore finance facilities and assembly-type industries, but these create a network of new problems. Often a warping of social structures occurs and the cure may at the time seem worse than the disease. This book analyses the particular problems of 'development' in dependent middling economies which are too rich to qualify for concessional aid but are too poor in natural resources to diversify. It challenges many assumptions and, set within a wide framework, will provide a challenging analysis both for Caribbean specialists and and for those concerned with the general problems of small economies.

Prof. Alistair Hennessy
Series Editor

Warwick University Caribbean Studies

Andrew Sanders
The Powerless People – The Amerindians of the Corentyne River

Editors: Jean Besson and Janet Momsen
Land and Development in the Caribbean

Kelvin Singh
The Bloodstained Tombs – The Muharram Massacre in Trinidad 1884

David Nicholls
From Dessalines to Duvalier – Race, Colour and National Independence

Editors: Malcolm Cross and Gad Heuman
Labour in the Caribbean – From Emancipation to Independence

Harry Goulbourne
Teachers, Education and Politics in Jamaica, 1892–1972

Neil Price
Behind the Planter's Back – Lower Class Response to Marginality in Bequia Island, St Vincent

Douglas Hall
In Miserable Slavery – Thomas Thistlewood in Jamaica, 1750–86

Ramesh Ramsaran
The Commonwealth Caribbean in the World Economy

Editor: M. Gilkes
The Literate Imagination – Essays on the Novels of Wilson Harris

Miguel Barnet (Editor: Alistair Hennessy)
Runaway – The Autobiography of Estaban Montejo

Contents

	General notes	viii
	List of acronyms	ix
	List of tables	xi
	Introduction	xiii
CHAPTER 1	Recent trends and developments in the world economy	1
CHAPTER 2	The economy of the Commonwealth Caribbean in transition	25
CHAPTER 3	Major sectors of the Commonwealth Caribbean economy in a world context	56
CHAPTER 4	Offshore finance – The Caribbean connection	95
CHAPTER 5	Trade and economic relations	115
CHAPTER 6	Factors influencing Commonwealth Caribbean production structure and trade policy	144
CHAPTER 7	Aspects of the integration experience in the Commonwealth Caribbean	165
CHAPTER 8	External performance, capital movements and the growth of the foreign debt	180
CHAPTER 9	The international monetary system and Commonwealth Caribbean countries	210
CHAPTER 10	The framework of development: Some theoretical perspectives	247
CHAPTER 11	Small states and development strategies: Some further issues	261
CHAPTER 12	Concluding observations	286
	Index	289

To my nieces,
Asha, Patty, Sharon, Indra and Pamela

Acknowledgements

It is difficult to undertake a work of this nature without assistance of various kinds. My greatest intellectual debt is perhaps to some of my past students at the Institute of International Relations who, through their questions, their curiosity and their interest, have helped to fashion the structure and content of the work. The study is an attempt to meet certain needs. The encouragement of some of my colleagues both at the University of the West Indies and overseas institutions played an important part in helping me to complete the task. The comments of anonymous readers of the manuscript are gratefully acknowledged, as are those of Dr Paul Sutton. The burden of typing the various drafts was shouldered by Jackie Roberts, Jeanne Callender and Taimoon Stewart, and to them I am eternally indebted.

Ramesh F. Ramsaran

General notes

1 All money figures used in this study (except where otherwise stated) refer to US dollar values.
2 The term 'Commonwealth Caribbean' as used here generally refers to the thirteen members of the Caribbean Community (CARICOM). These are as follows: the Bahamas, Barbados, Guyana, Jamaica, Trinidad and Tobago, Belize, Antigua and Barbuda, Dominica, Grenada, Montserrat, St Kitts-Nevis, St Lucia, St Vincent. The last seven are members of the Organisation of East Caribbean States (OECS). The Bahamas, Barbados, Guyana, Jamaica and Trinidad and Tobago are often referred to as the More Developed Countries (MDCs) while the OECS and Belize are seen as the Less Developed Countries (LDCs). The Bahamas, as indicated, is a member of the Caribbean Community but is not part of the Common Market arrangements.

List of acronyms

AASM	Associated States of Africa and Madagascar
ACP	Africa, Caribbean and Pacific States
ALCAN	Aluminium Ltd. in Canada
ALCOA	Aluminium Company of America
CARIBCAN	Caribbean Canada
CARICOM	Caribbean Community
CBI	Caribbean Basin Initiative
CIPEC	Intergovernmental Council of Copper Exporting Countries
CORCO	Commonwealth Oil Refinery Company
DAC	Development Assistance Committee
DEMBA	Demerara Bauxite Company
DRS	Debtor Reporting System
EC	European Community (formerly EEC)
ECLA	Economic Commission for Latin America
EDF	European Development Fund
EFTA	European Free Trade Association
EIB	European Investment Bank
EPZs	Export Processing Zones
FDIC	Federal Deposit Insurance Corporation
FPDI	Foreign Private Direct Investment
FSCs	Foreign Sales Corporations
GATT	General Agreement on Tariffs and Trade
GSP	Generalised System of Preferences
HFCS	High Fructose Corn Syrups
IBA	International Bauxite Association
IBF	International Banking Facilities
IBRD	International Bank for Reconstruction and Development (World Bank)
ICSID	International Centre for the Settlement of Investment Disputes
IDA	International Development Association
IFC	International Finance Corporation
IMF	International Monetary Fund

ISCOTT	Iron and Steel Company of Trinidad and Tobago
ITO	International Trade Organisation
LDCs	Less Developed Countries
MDCs	More Developed Countries
NICs	Newly Industrialising Countries
OAS	Organisation of African States
OECD	Organisation for Economic Co-operation and Development
OECS	Organisation of Eastern Caribbean States
OPEC	Organisation of Petroleum Exporting Countries
SDRs	Special Drawing Rights
STABEX	Stabilisation of Export Earnings Scheme
TNCs	Transnational Corporations
UN	United Nations
UNCTAD	United Nations Conference on Trade and Development
WINBAN	Windward Islands Banana Growers Association

List of tables

1.1	Growth in world exports (current values) for selected periods	8
1.2	Growth of world production and trade, 1963–1985	10
1.3	Regional composition of world trade, 1948–85	12
1.4	Real rates of return on corporate capital, by country, 1962–76	16
1.5	Real growth of GDP, 1965–1985	18
1.6	Growth of population, GNP, and GNP per capita, 1955–80	21
2.1	Selected data on a select group of countries in the world economy	28–9
2.2	Distribution of GNP by countries grouped according to size of aggregate GNP, 1985	31
2.3	Distribution of GDP by countries grouped according to per capita GNP, 1985	32
2.4	Exports of goods and non-factor services (X) and imports of goods and non-factor services (M) as a % of GDP at current market prices	35
2.5	Commonwealth Caribbean: Sectoral contribution to GDP at current factor costs, 1963 and 1984	46–7
2.6	Contribution of manufacturing to GDP (factor cost) in real terms for selected countries, 1970–85	48
3.1	Prices of selected commodities, 1950–85	58–9
3.2	Proportion of total acreage under sugar cultivation in sugar exporting countries, 1958	66
3.3	Sugar and by-products as a percentage of total domestic exports	67
3.4	Sugar production, 1950–85	69
3.5	Banana exports from the Windward Islands, 1954–85	72–3
3.6	Stop-over visitors by country of residence, 1984	87

5.1	Growth of Commonwealth Caribbean trade, 1955–84	118–19
5.2	Commonwealth Caribbean: Major exports as a % of total domestic exports, selected years	122–3
5.3	MDCs: Composition of imports, selected years	124
5.4	OECS and Belize: Composition of imports, 1955 and 1983	125
5.5	Commonwealth Caribbean: Direction of trade, 1984	129
8.1	Public and publicly guaranteed long-term debt, 1970 and 1984	185
8.2	Fifteen biggest debtors at end of 1985	188–9
8.3	Commonwealth Caribbean: Selected data on external debt, 1970 and 1985	198–9
8.4	Total resource flows to developing countries by major types of flow, 1950–84	202–3
8.5	US direct investment position abroad: selected countries, 1982–85	206
9.1	Commonwealth Caribbean: Financial standing in IMF's general department at 30 April, 1986	212
9.2	Growth and composition of total world reserves, 1970 to 1986	236
11.1	UN Members grouped according to population size	262
11.2	Data on selected NICs	283

Introduction

One of the salient features of the post-war world has been the political disintegration of the European-based empires and the emergence of a large number of countries as independent nations in the international community. From the original 51 members in 1945, the membership of the United Nations had grown to 159 by October, 1986. The first British colony in the Caribbean to attain its constitutional independence was Jamaica in 1962. This was followed by Trinidad and Tobago also in 1962, Guyana and Barbados in 1966 and the Bahamas in 1973. In the ten years that followed, Belize and the members of what is now known as the Organisation of Eastern Caribbean States (OECS) also sought and gained independent status. The one exception was Montserrat which remains a British colony. The size of this island state (population 12 000) continues to test the imagination with respect to the kind of political arrangement possible in the light of the concerns of the British Government, the desires of its inhabitants and the fears of its neighbours.

Given the size of these countries and their limited resources there were questions about their ability to sustain themselves economically, and to survive in a world dominated by large states. The big question that was being asked during the 1960s and 1970s and to some extent is still being asked is, can these states be economically viable? A few of them have been able to attain growth rates that are higher than larger developing countries, but this does not answer the question, which some incidentally do not consider relevant. Whether or not the question of economic viability is relevant, the fact is small states face certain peculiar constraints which may not permit them to follow the same development paths pursued by the large industrialised nations.

The word 'development' itself may connote something quite different for a small state than for a large country. The kind of structural transformation to which large states can aspire as they attempt to overcome problems of poverty, may not be possible for a small country constrained by its small physical size and population, limited natural resources and paucity of skills. Not surprisingly, many of them are forced to live by their wits, specialising in activities which might be considered abnormal or unorthodox. In many cases the economic legacy of colonialism has been specialisation in a narrow range of activities which generally have declined in the post-independence years as a result of internal problems and market loss in the metropole. As traditional activities have waned, new ones such as tourism, assembly-type industries, free trade zones, casino gambling, tax haven services, offshore finance, offshore medical schools, etc., have emerged to provide jobs and foreign exchange. The need for economic survival makes the removal of moral inhibitions and legal barriers an easy matter. In such circumstances, small states, particularly the micro ones can and often fall prey to 'con men', individuals and companies who obtain special concessions that may impinge on the sovereignty of the country.

Unfortunately, many small countries have tended to frame development policy in a way that has ignored the implications of size. In the process, resources have not been put to their best use. Advantage has also often not been taken of the benefits which small size conveys in an international setting. On the other hand, little attempt is generally made by the large industrial countries to discriminate between large and small states in the implementation of trade and aid policies. There is often a great deal of contradiction between the expressed intentions of the rich countries and the policies they put into practice. A poor country, for instance, may be given aid to develop its exports, but having done so find itself facing trade barriers in the markets of the developed nations. Such barriers can persist even when the volume of such exports pose no threat to established industries in the rich nations. It is clear that in many areas of activity countries cannot expect special treatment because of their small size. Even in relations with such multi-lateral institutions like the IMF and the World Bank, small states have found it difficult to obtain special considerations even when the logic of their case is recognised. In important ways certain international organisations have become prisoners of their own rules and procedures, because the latter are favoured by the dominant members. In the same way, developed countries have failed to adjust their foreign policies and aid programmes to take cognisance of the changing international environment and the factors affecting the evolution of world political and economic relationships. Policies too heavily informed by narrow perspectives and reflecting essentially an ideological or security bias often do not have their desired effect. This is often compounded by a failure to understand the nature of the problem for which solutions are sought. No wonder questions are often raised about the real purpose of aid or trade concessions proferred by the developed countries. Ultimately, of course, a great deal of resources is wasted in the face of persistent poverty and suffering.

In the mid-1980s the prospects are that economic progress made so far could be lost. Real GDP in Trinidad and Tobago (which has the highest per capita income in CARICOM) dropped by over 30% between 1983 and 1986. In Guyana, too, real income fell by almost 25% between 1975 and 1985. Jamaica's experience has been similar, with total real income declining by 18% between 1974 and 1980. While some growth has taken place in recent years, the 1984 figure was still 12% below that of 1974. The elements necessary to sustain growth are clearly not there. Critical decisions affecting domestic economies are still largely outside national control. At the same time, population continues to increase at between 1% and 2% for most countries of the region. Unemployment is growing, particularly among young people, and now exceeds 20% of the labour force in most cases. In this situation social and economic instability is likely to increase. This in turn could have an adverse impact on foreign investment and the region's tourist industry, thus further exacerbating the economic situation. Since the Caribbean tends to be seen as one area from outside, social upheaval in one state is bound to affect the prospects of the others. There is, therefore, a compelling reason to intensify the collaborative approach to the region's problems.

In this study we look at the recent development experience of Commonwealth Caribbean countries and the relevance of international economic policies and institutions to their development efforts. These countries are not only 'developing', but are also small and have per capita incomes that place them in the middle income groups. This latter feature seems to be a curse in that it puts concessional aid beyond their reach — a type of aid which it is widely recognised they are most in need of, if they are to build on what they have already achieved, and if they are to avoid worsening their debt situation. Paradoxically, some of the very institutions and countries which advise poor states to rely on concessional finance are the ones whose policies tend to reduce the flow of such assistance.

This study is divided into twelve chapters. In the first we examine recent trends and developments in the world economy as a background to what follows. In the second we look at some of the structural changes that have taken place in Caribbean economies in recent years. The third puts major economic sectors in a world context. In the fourth the issue of Caribbean offshore finance is discussed in some detail. The fifth chapter puts into focus the changing pattern of trade and economic relations. Some relevant issues related to trade policies are taken up in chapter 6. In the seventh the

Commonwealth Caribbean integration experience is discussed against the background of the experience of groupings in other developing areas. The eighth chapter examines the balance of payments performance of Commonwealth Caribbean states and the problem of the foreign debt. In the ninth, questions pertaining to the reform of the international monetary system are brought into focus. Chapter ten concentrates on the general framework of development used in the Caribbean, while chapter eleven provides a discussion on issues of development strategy in small states. Finally, the twelfth chapter pulls together some concluding observations.

CHAPTER 1
Recent trends and developments in the world economy

Since the early post-war years, the configuration of the international economy has undergone a number of changes. The predominant economic position held by the US at the end of World War II has declined steadily.[1] Not only have the European countries and Japan, which were devastated by the War, recovered to become significant economic powers, but many new independent countries, largely poor, have entered the world stage. In this decolonisation process long-standing colonial economic arrangements have also been abandoned. The membership of international organisations has expanded correspondingly, even though the original charters in certain cases have remained largely the same. New groupings have emerged. With the disappearance of some of the basic premises on which the Bretton Woods international monetary system was founded, international monetary arrangements have also been forced to undergo change, and remain far from stable.

At the domestic level national economies have not only witnessed change in the structure of their output, but the process of growth and development has given rise to new problems. Several nations have significantly expanded their manufacturing capacity, while the service sector has increased its share of out-put in most economies. A few have been able to develop a remarkable export capacity. Agriculture's contribution to GDP, exports and employment since the 1960s has fallen in a large number of countries, both in the developed and developing world. For many countries, the ratio of trade to national income has increased. For instance, the share of exports (or imports) of goods and services in OECD GNP rose from about 13% in 1970 to about 20% in 1980.[2] In many developing countries the public debt (both internal and external) has increased significantly as governments have sought to borrow to finance consumption and investment. The external debt of developing countries is now a major international issue.

With the attainment of constitutional independence by politically dependent states, issues relating to social and economic development tended to assume greater importance in international fora. To deal with some of these problems, new institutions, both at regional and international levels were set up to complement existing organisations. The study of development and underdevelopment became a major preoccupation both in official and unofficial circles. One result of this was a proliferation of literature on problems of development. While many determinants of poverty were identified, there was a general recognition of the need for measures to accelerate the process of capital formation at the domestic level, and for the developed nations to provide financial and other assistance to supplement local resources and effort. The provision of aid not only became closely intertwined with the foreign policy process of the developed nations, often used at times as an instrument of leverage, but was also a strong influence on the political posturings and economic arrangements of poor states anxious to satisfy the requirements of aid-giving nations operating bilaterally or multilaterally. One reason frequently advanced in favour of political independence was that this would result in greater access to financial resources. The disappointment was not unexpectedly great when the quantum of aid did not match expectations, or when trade concessions were found to have little practical significance.

The increase in the number of independent developing countries, the growth in the development literature and frequent interaction in international fora have helped to foster not only an increasing understanding of the nature and scope of the development problem, but a growing cohesiveness among poor countries that often transcends political, economic, racial or religious differences as well as physical distance. By the early 1970s developing countries generally held the view that despite the growth of a greater measure of interdependence in the world economy, certain international organisations and arrangements were not functioning in the way they would like, and began clamouring for the establishment of a new world economic order. With the help of their intellectuals they had come to recognise the crucial link between the international environment and domestic conditions and performance. In this connection, specific proposals have been put forward for changes in the world trading system, the international monetary system and the framework for international investment and aid. The developing countries have argued that the 'old order' devised by the developed countries has been biased in favour of these countries.[3] While a number of developing countries have experienced impressive rates of growth in the post-war period (in some cases the rates have exceeded that of several industrialised nations), and life expectancy has increased in most of them, the problem of development remains a critical issue. Poverty is still manifested in many forms. Unemployment, unsatisfactory distribution of income and nutritional standards, and inadequate housing, health and educational facilities continue to be salient characteristics of those countries. The persistence of these problems demand a stronger national effort. It is widely felt, however, that the national effort would yield greater results if there is a more sympathetic international framework which recognises the needs and the peculiar problems faced by emerging nations. The latter feel that many of the industrial states as former imperial powers have a special responsibility to help in the development of poor states, as they themselves would have contributed to this poverty through neglect and exploitation.

Relations between developed and developing countries

With the growth in the number of independent developing states following the end of World War II, international economic and political relations entered a new phase. The newly independent countries, like those that were already on the world stage, varied widely in terms of physical size and population. Some derived their importance or attracted increased attention because of their strategic location, or because they possessed valuable mineral resources or raw materials. It is worth pointing out that by the time the post-war decolonisation process had begun, the foundations of important international organisations had already been put in place. Institutions like the IMF and World Bank which grew out of the International Monetary and Financial Conference of the United and Associated Nations (held at Bretton Woods, New Hampshire in July 1944) reflected largely Anglo-American thinking. Though the IMF Agreement was signed by forty-four nations (including some developing countries), the latter countries had virtually no influence in shaping the constitution of the IMF. Attempts by countries such as India and Ecuador to add a developmental function to the Fund's role were rejected.[4] It was felt that the International Bank for Reconstruction and Development (IBRD) should be the institution to be concerned with the problems of reconstruction and development. The IBRD's early efforts, however, were devoted to the reconstruction of Europe. 'It only became a development agency later, after the US Marshall Plan took the lead in financing the post-war recovery and the World Bank management found a new role for their agency.'[5] Even though two more institutions, the International Finance Corporation (IFC) in 1956 and the International Development Association (IDA) in 1960 were added to the IBRD, developing countries became increasingly disenchanted with the adequacy of these institutions as well as with the UN Economic and Social Council and GATT in dealing with the question of development. Pressures began to mount in the late 1950s and early 1960s for a new institution that could address itself to the inter-related problems of trade and development.[6] The developing countries saw the need for a specific new institution that would not be dominated by the concerns of the developed nations. Despite the desire of the Western industrial countries not to disturb the existing institutional status quo, the United Nations Conference on Trade and Development (UNCTAD) was formed in 1964. Though UNCTAD has done a tremendous amount of research on development issues and policies, the accomplishments of this organisation itself have been drawn into question in recent years, given its initial objectives.

With the intensive research that came to bear on problems of development from the early 1960s, and the increasing contact among developing countries in various fora, poor countries not only began to articulate their developmental needs more coherently, but increasingly began to take common positions on international issues. Group diplomacy began to assume significant dimensions. The 'battle lines' became more clearly drawn, but this was intended more to advance the cause of co-operation than to intensify conflict. In such circumstances terms like 'Centre' and 'Periphery', 'North' and 'South', 'First', 'Second,' and 'Third' World, while having obvious political connotations, were coined to point to certain economic realities in the global system, which international economic policy could not ignore. Developing countries are different in many ways, but the similarity of needs tend to transcend both geographical distance and other barriers. There are countries that are land-locked and have no access to the sea. Some are abysmally poor, facing very bleak prospects as a result of not having any valuable mineral or other natural resources in significant quantities. Some are island states or multi-island states. Countries differ in terms of levels of development and political arrangements. The factor of location makes some states more vulnerable than others. Almost all are characterised by dependence on a narrow range of activities for foreign exchange. For various reasons some states grew faster than others resulting in an increasing gap among some poor countries. This issue has led to calls for special policies to deal with the least developed of the developing countries.

With all these difficulties, there was a common perception in the early stages of the decolonisation process that it was necessary to mobilise the international community if poverty in all its various manifestations was to be overcome. The rich countries themselves recognised that development of the poor states would encourage the growth of international trade and investments, and thus contribute to a stronger economy. These two mutually reinforcing points of view formed the basis of the growth of multilateralism and international co-operation in the 1960s and 1970s. The principle of multilateralism in the conduct of international economic relations was, of course, strongly endorsed even before the War was concluded. It was widely accepted that if the world economy was to regain its vitality the bi-lateral practices that had emerged in the 1930s should be eliminated, and a more open trade and investment framework put in its place.

The removal of trade restrictions and the provision of aid to poor countries were the two important planks of the new multilateralism which was to be encouraged through such institutions as the IMF, GATT and the World Bank. Economic integration among groups of countries though implying a degree of trade discrimination was seen not to be inconsistent with the expansion of world trade. By the early 1970s, following the end of the first UN 'Development Decade', there was a great deal of disappointment among developing countries, not only with the aid effort of certain developed countries, but with the scope of access to the markets of the rich countries, and the flows of private capital. The concern over market access has persisted despite the adoption of generalised system of preferences (GSP) schemes by a number of industrial nations in the early 1970s to encourage the exports of manufactured and semi-manufactured products from the developing nations. Failure to stabilise international prices for commodities was also a source of disappointment. Then came the first oil shock of 1974 to be followed by another in 1979. Petroleum prices increased from an average of about US$2 a barrel in 1972 to around US$10 per barrel in 1974. By 1981–2 the figure had climbed to US$30. The result was a massive transfer of wealth from the oil importing developed and developing nations to the oil exporting countries. Between 1974 and 1981 the current account surplus of the oil exporting developing countries totalled US$424 billion. The deficits of the non-oil developing countries, however, amounted to US$444 billion, as compared to US$94 billion for the industrial nations.

The whole tenor of relations between developed and developing countries changed. The Organisation of Petroleum Exporting

Countries (OPEC) which since its inception in 1960 had served primarily as a forum for the exchange of information, discovered its tremendous power to influence prices in the 1970s. For purposes of international policy it became necessary to make a distinction between the oil exporting developing countries and the non-oil poor countries. While the latter felt the impact of the price increases on their balance of payments and their general development effort, they generally supported the principle of the right of poor countries to seek adequate remuneration for their exports, particularly those that were in the category of a wasting asset. The producers of other commodities no doubt saw in the OPEC approach an attractive method for dealing with the question of price instability. OPEC so far, however, has turned out to be a special case. In the context of the oil price increases, questions were to arise over the effort being made by the oil rich states to help the oil importing developing nations, and the general use that was being made of the newly gained wealth. The decline in oil prices since 1982 has brought some benefits to oil importing countries, but the global economy has not yet adjusted to the changed circumstances. The fact that some of the oil rich countries now find themselves in serious economic and financial difficulties has raised questions not only of economic management and development strategy, but also with respect to the ability of an economy with limitations in other areas to absorb a great deal of capital over a short period of time.

While generally there has been an increase in the size of the public sector in most developing countries, the expanded role of the state in oil exporting nations has been significant. The oil windfall during the 1970s encouraged governments to undertake a wide range of complex high cost projects with the aim of diversifying their economies. To do this, some took advantage of their enhanced credit rating and borrowed heavily in external markets. Money-centre banks flushed with liquidity from the recycling process lent willingly, in many cases without carefully weighing the risks involved. With the decline in oil prices in the early 1980s, and the inability of some major borrowers to service their debt, the scenario has changed drastically. With poor countries finding it increasingly difficult to raise money in international capital markets, and given the difficulties facing an expansion in exports, these nations now see a more urgent need for movement towards a new international economic order. They also recognise the necessity of accelerating South-South co-operation as a means of bringing this new order about.

The response of the developed countries of the north to the call for a New International Economic Order by developing countries of the south has been far from enthusiastic. The anticipated dialogue has remained largely a monologue. Many of the proposals put forward have received scant consideration, if not contempt. The northern countries have tended to view the call for a New Order with suspicion, arguing that many of the problems faced by southern countries are the result of policies at the domestic level and of corruption and mismanagement. The result is that the approach to problems in the international economy, and particularly those affecting developing states has lacked a systematic character. Tinkering and *ad hoc* or piecemeal solutions continue to be the order of the day. The southern countries themselves have contributed to this by their failure, in many instances, to articulate and implement policies at the domestic level which could make optimum use of limited measures, and to exploit adequately the possibilities for co-operation among themselves in various fields critical to their own development. In global terms, the international economy has performed well in certain areas, and this has no doubt contributed to the syndrome 'the old order has served us well, why change it?' Aggregate data, however, often do not reflect the problems of individual states, and one needs to interpret them with the care. In the following section we look at some recent developments in the world economy, particularly in the areas of trade and income.

For most of the post-war years world trade has grown at a fairly impressive rate. In current values world exports are estimated to have grown by an average rate of 12.5% between 1953 and 1980. Table 1.1 shows the growth rate of exports for groups of countries over particular periods. Here it can be seen that the growth of world commerce was not confined to the industrial nations, but that the developing countries and the Centrally Planned Economies also shared in the expansion. The growth rates for all groups were generally higher in the decade 1963–73, than in the previous decade, that is 1953–63. Trade continued to grow until 1980 when what turned out to be the longest recession in fifty years set in. The value of world exports declined in 1981, 1982 and 1983, but increased in 1984 and 1985 by 5.5% and 1% respectively. The figures relating to the developing countries for the period 1973–83 reflect the higher prices for oil. Even when the OPEC countries are excluded from the group, the export experience of the other developing countries still appears to be impressive. Even in the face of recession the value of exports from the Centrally Planned Economies continues to show an upward trend.

One can get a better indication of what has been happening in the world economy in recent years by looking at trade in terms of

Table 1.1 Growth in world exports (Current Values) for selected periods

Countries	1953–63	1963–73	1973–83	1980	1981	1982	1983	1984	1985
All countries	6.4[a]	14.1	12.1	21.5	−1.1	−6.6	−1.8	5.5	1
Developed market economies	6.8	14.6	11.0	17.7	−1.8	−6.3	−0.4	6.5	3.5
Developing market economies	4.1	13.6	15.1	32.6	−0.5	−11.0	−8.3	4.0	−5.5
Developing market economies[b]	2.9	11.9	14.9	24.0	9.1	−0.1	1.4	10.0	n.a.
Centrally Planned Economies	9.1	11.8	12.6	17.0	2.6	4.6	5.8	3.0	−1.5

n.a. not available

[a] All figures expressed as percentages
[b] Excluding OPEC countries.

Sources: UN Yearbook of International Trade Statistics, Various Issues; GATT, International Trade, Various Issues.

volume. By doing this one escapes the distortions introduced by prices and changes in the value of the US dollar. The decline in the dollar value of trade in 1981 and 1982 appears to be partly the result of a strong appreciation of the US dollar in this period.[7] Table 1.2 shows the average annual percentage change in the volume of world production and exports respectively. The growth in the volume of production (all commodities) which averaged 6% in the period 1963−73 dropped to 2% in the 1973−82 period. Between 1977 and 1979 the figure averaged about 4%. This fell to ½% in 1980 and 1% in 1981. Production declined by 2% in 1982, but increased by 2%, 5½% and 3% in 1983, 1984 and 1985 respectively. All sectors have been affected by the recent downturn, but the mining sector has been particularly hard hit. Between 1973 and 1982 the average rate of growth was ½% as compared to 5½% in the period 1963−73. After increasing by 4½% in 1979, there were four consecutive years of decline in this sector, followed by zero growth in 1984 and a drop of 2% in 1985.

Manufacturing production which experienced a growth rate of over 4% between 1977 and 1979 was also affected, the rate dropping to less than 1% between 1980 and 1982, but since then has averaged over 3%. After little growth in 1980 and 1981, and a decline of 2% in 1982, agricultural production has also increased at an average rate of over 3% since. The performance of all sectors in 1984 raised hopes that the recession of the early 1980s was ended, but the experience in 1985 indicated that the world economy may not yet be ready to resume the robust growth rates of the 1960s.

As far as exports are concerned, the volume increased by an average of 3% per annum in the period 1973−82, as compared to 8½% in the previous decade. From a growth rate of over 5% in 1978 and 1979 respectively, the volume of world exports dropped significantly in 1980 and 1981 and actually declined in 1982. This decline in the volume of world trade was only the third recorded in the post-war period.[8] The other two occurred in 1975 (3%) and 1958 (a little less than 1%). The trends in the volume of exports reflect the trends in production. The year 1984 recorded the highest growth rates for recent years in all sectors, but trade in agricultural and mineral products actually declined in 1985. Trade in manufactures, however, still grew at over 5% as compared to 5% in 1983 and 12% in 1984.

The fact that the volume of exports in the period 1963−73 grew at a rate almost three times that of the period 1973−82 can be explained by several factors. There is no doubt that in the former period cheap fuel costs, low inflation rates, increased foreign

Table 1.2 Growth of world production and trade, 1963–1985

	1963–73	1973–82	1977	1978	1979	1980	1981	1982	1983	1984	1985
Production[a]											
All merchandise	6	2	4½	4	4	½	1	−2	2	5½	3
Agriculture	2½	2	2	4	1	0	4	2½	0	5	2
Mining	5½	½	5½	−1	4½	−2	−2	−7½	−1½	0	−2
Manufacturing	7	2½	5	4½	5	½	½	−2	3½	7	4
Exports											
All merchandise	8½	3	4½	5½	6	½	3	−3	2	9½	3
Agricultural products	4	4	2	9	7	7	4	−1	1	4	−1
Minerals[b]	7	−2½	2	1½	5	−6½	−10	−6	−1	2	−2½
Manufacture	11	4½	5	5	5	5	4	−2	5	12	6

[a] Figures are average annual percentage change in volume
[b] Including fuels and non-ferrous metals
Source: GATT, *International Trade*, Various Issues.

investment and expanding commodity markets had a positive effect on the expansion of trade. These factors working in reverse may have had an opposite effect on growth during most of the 1970s. In addition, however, there were changes in certain fundamental conditions. 'By the late 1960s the opportunities for catching up with the technology of the US had been largely exploited by both Japan and Western-Europe, so one source of exceptional growth declined in significance. Another source − the shift of workers from low-productivity agriculture to high productivity manufacturing − had also largely been exhausted. A third source − trade liberalisation and reintegration of the industrial economies after World War II − though it had boosted growth for at least two decades, was no longer providing the stimulus it did earlier. Finally, the increasing share of service industries in GDP may have slowed the growth of GDP since the growth of productivity has traditionally been lower in services than in manufacturing.[9]

The external performance of the industrial nations has varied widely in recent years. While the current account balance of the US deteriorated from a surplus of $6.3 billion in 1981 to a deficit of $118 billion in 1985, Japan's surplus increased from about $5 billion to almost $40 billion in the same period. The persistently strong external position of this latter country in the context of the difficulties being experienced by its competitors has increased the pressures on it to open up its markets to a greater volume of imports. Non-tariff barriers are particularly strong in the Japanese market, and this has made it difficult for countries to sell to Japan on the scale they desire. Anticipating the threat of sanctions to its exports, Japan has sought to guarantee its share of foreign markets by entering into partnership arrangements with foreign firms anxious to share in Japanese technology and management expertise.

As indicated earlier, the expansion of world trade has affected both developed and developing countries. Increasing populations and incomes in the developing countries have provided an increasingly greater market for the manufactured goods of the developed nations. The decline of agriculture in many poor nations has also resulted in increased food imports from the developed countries. The economic expansion in the industrial nations in turn has tended to result in a greater demand for both raw materials and manufactured goods. The trade liberalisation process in the postwar period, however, appears to have had a more favourable effect on the developed nations. An examination of Table 1.3 shows that the share of the developed market economies in world exports increased from 63.6% in 1948 to 71.0% in 1973. In this period,

Table 1.3 Regional composition of world trade, 1948–1985

		1948	1963	1973	1978	1979	1980	1981	1982	1983	1984	1985
Developed market economies	X	63.6	67.5	71.0	67.2	65.3	63.3	62.8	63.3	63.3	64.1	65.3
	M	64.9	68.2	72.4	68.3	70.3	69.4	66.7	66.0	65.2	67.0	67.9
OPEC countries	X	5.4	6.1	7.3	11.2	13.3	15.2	14.4	12.2	9.9	8.9	8.1
	M	4.1	2.9	3.4	7.2	5.7	6.1	7.1	7.9	7.7	6.4	5.9
Other developing market economies	X	24.6	14.3	11.9	12.0	12.2	12.6	13.6	14.2	15.6	16.4	16.2
	M	25.2	17.2	13.2	14.4	14.6	15.5	17.0	16.5	16.8	16.6	15.5
Centrally Planned Economies	X	6.4	12.2	9.8	9.6	9.2	8.9	9.2	10.3	11.2	10.6	10.4
	M	5.8	11.7	11.0	10.1	9.4	9.0	9.2	9.6	10.3	10.0	10.7

X = percentage share in world exports
M = percentage share in world imports
Source: UN *Yearbook of International Trade Statistics*, Various Issues

OPEC's share increased slightly from 5.4% to 7.3%. The share of other developing market economies, however, declined from 25.2% to 13.2% between 1948 and 1973. The proportion relating to the Centrally Planned Economies increased from 6.4% to 9.8%. The increase in oil prices following the Arab-Israeli War of 1973 had a significant effect on the regional distribution of trade. The share of the developed market economies has declined from 71% in 1973 to around 64% in recent years. OPEC's share has correspondingly increased from 7.3% in 1973 to 15.2% in 1980. The proportion appears to have dropped in recent years, following the decline in the price of oil since 1981. OPEC's share in world exports dropped to 8.1% in 1985. Its share of world imports has also tended to fall in recent years, no doubt reflecting the reduced import capacity. Other developing market economies have accounted on average for 16% of world exports and imports respectively since 1983. This represents an increase of 4 to 5% since the early 1970s. The share of the Centrally Planned Economies in world imports and exports has been averaging around 10% in recent years. As far as individual countries are concerned, some (e.g. Japan) have increased their share in world exports, while others (e.g. the US) have lost ground. In the mid-1960s the Asian newly industrialising countries of Hong Kong, South Korea, Singapore and Taiwan accounted for less than 2% of world exports. In 1987 this is expected to increase to over 6%.

Trade issues in the 1980s

As indicated earlier, there has been a strengthening in the trading relationship between the developed and developing countries in the post-war period. The nature of this relationship has changed in many ways. In the 1950s and 1960s exports from developing countries consisted largely of un-processed minerals, food and raw materials. Growth in the developed countries was quickly reflected in increased imports of minerals and raw materials by the developing nations. This in turn resulted in greater foreign exchange earnings which enabled the primary exporting countries to import the capital goods needed for development. In this sense trade tended to be viewed as 'an engine of growth.'

Traditionally, the tariffs of the developed nations have been structured to encourage imports in raw, rather than processed, forms. This tended to discourage the expansion of manufacturing capacity in the developing countries. In most cases the companies engaged in the production of the commodities were vertically integrated enterprises with their head office located in one of the developed countries. In other words, these companies were not only engaged in the mining (or growing end) but in transport, refining and even distribution. Except where bulk made it uneconomical for the raw items to be shipped back to the refining centres, refining and processing capacity was generally located abroad. In the 1960s and 1970s many developing countries adopted a variety of measures to expand local processing and manufacturing capacity. In several developing countries manufacturing output forms an increasingly significant part of total output. Most of the products manufactured in developing countries can also be found in the market of the developed nations where economic expansion will not necessarily now lead to increased demand for imports from the developed nations. On the contrary, the production of many classes of manufactured goods at costs below those prevailing in the industrialised nations have led to the institution of many forms of controls aimed at curbing imports of manufactures from the developing countries. Despite the praise often heaped on the free market system, protectionist measures have increased in the industrialised nations.[10]

Until recently, there was a tendency to view protection in terms of trade measures alone such as tariffs and quotas. In practice protection can take a variety of forms such as direct subsidies or preferential taxes and credit treatment. These amount to indirect protection since they reduce production or sales costs. Such measures have been used in the developed countries to prop up certain specific industries such as steel, chemicals, motor vehicles and ship building. In Western Europe the share of public spending in the form of subsidies has been increasing. Another device (which incidentally violates the principles and rules of GATT) is the use of quantitative restriction in the form of 'voluntary' export restraints and orderly marketing agreements. Sanitary and packaging requirements have also been used to restrict trade. Restrictions now apply not only to the traditionally protected sectors such as steel, textiles, clothing and agriculture, but have also been extended to new sectors, such as automobiles and electronics. Non-tariff barriers account for most of the increase in protectionism that has taken place in recent years.

Non-tariff barriers affect trade from both developed and developing countries. Based on information on non-tariff barriers for 1984, it has been estimated that in the case of the United States 9.2% of imports from the industrial countries were subject to non-tariff barriers, as compared to 16.1% from the developing countries. For Japan the comparable figures were 12.4% for imports from the industrialised countries and 14.5% for imports originating in developing nations. For the European Community it was 21.7% for the latter group and 10.7% for the developed countries. In almost all the industrial countries the share of imports subject to non-tariff barriers has tended to increase in recent years.[11]

There are two aspects of the new protectionism that we need to consider at this point. Is the growth of obstacles to trade founded on genuine economic arguments, or is it mainly a political reaction to an economic issue? The second aspect is the likely implications of protectionism for world trade. Let us take the first. One of the weak arguments advanced by developed countries to keep out exports of other countries from their markets is that the lower costs of such exports results from unfair means, such as government assistance and payment of exploitative wages. As such, they could not allow cheaper imports to put workers out of employment or to allow living standards to fall in their own particular countries. The World Bank's World Development Report of 1984 argues that problems such as unemployment, inflation and slow growth in the industrialised countries has a great deal to do with the economic policies pursued.[12] Two policy-induced developments, it was felt, that deserved special mention were the 'increasing rigidity of the labour market and the resulting strong upward pressure on real wages', and 'the growth and pattern of public spending, taxation, and fiscal deficits'. The tendency for real wages to outstrip productivity was seen as a major cause of unemployment. In the face of this, many companies substituted capital for labour and capital-intensive methods of production tended to become widespread. This, however, has not been able to stem the slide in profitability in the corporate sector. With the exception of one or two countries, the real rates of return on corporate capital has tended to fall since the early 1960s (*See* Table 1.4). While in the case of Canada the figure increased from an average of 7.9% in the 1962−64 period, to 9.2% in the 1974−76 period, in the case of the US it fell from 12.0% to 7.1% and in the case of Japan from 28.2% to 13.5% over the period.

In the US over 400 trade bills were introduced in Congress between January and August, 1985, with the aim of protecting specific industries and as retaliation against specific countries.[13] Tariffs, of course, are a double-edged sword. They not only increase revenue, but raise prices for consumers who thus pay the price of inefficiency. High inflation rates in the US tend to spread to her trading partners, particularly those significantly dependent on her as a source of supply. High inflation rates also put the US at a cost disadvantage *vis-à-vis* her competitors. Protectionism, of course,

Table 1.4 Real rates of return on corporate capital, by country, 1962–1976

Period	Canada	France	Fed. Rep of Germany	Italy	Japan	UK	USA
Average							
1962–64	7.9	9.7	19.3	10.4	28.2	11.9	12.0
1965–69	9.6	10.0	19.5	11.4	27.9	10.6	12.2
1970–72	9.0	11.6	15.0	10.3	21.9	8.3	8.6
1974–76	9.2	8.0	11.4	n.a.	13.5	3.7	7.1

n.a. not available
Source: IBRD, World Development Report, 1984.

also entails certain efficiency or welfare losses. It has been estimated that with respect to the use of non-tariff barriers alone used by the US and the European Community against imports of clothing, automobiles and steel, the efficiency loss is well above a billion dollars in each case. For this loss the number of jobs saved in the protected industries was small, so that the cost per job saved exceeded the average labour compensation in each case. For each job saved in clothing for example, the US economy as a whole sacrificed about $169 600 to protect a worker earning about $12 600.[14]

There is no doubt that one major factor affecting trade policy in the first half of the 1980s was that of the relatively high levels of unemployment prevailing in some of the industrial countries. For instance, in Canada the unemployment rate increased from an average of 5.6% in the 1967–76 period to 11.9% in 1983 and has remained over 10% since. In the US the figure moved from an average of 5.4% in the 1967–76 period to 9.7% in 1982. While it has tended to decline since, the figure has generally been over 7%. In the UK the unemployment ratio increased from 6% in 1980 to 12.0% in 1985. Though unemployment has generally been low in Japan, the ratio for recent years has shown a slight increase reaching 2.6% in 1985 compared to 2.0% in 1980.

While in several of the industrial countries, as indicated, current rates of unemployment are high by historical standards, they are still low compared to that obtaining in developing countries where ratios of the order of over 20% are quite common. Traditionally, the unemployment problem in some developing countries has been alleviated by emigration to the developed countries. In this process, of course, they have lost a great number of their skilled people. One effect of the high unemployment rates in industrial countries is the institution of stricter immigration controls and this could exacerbate the unemployment problem in developing countries. Another effect is the resort to stronger barriers to trade. In trade wars between the industrial nations, the developing countries tend to suffer since little discrimination is made between them and other nations. The fact that some developing countries have developed a significant export capacity tends to encourage this posture, even while the benefits of the free market system are being exalted.

Given the importance of the US market in the world economy, the position taken by this country on trade matters exerts a significant influence on the trade policy of other countries. In this context, there has been considerable controversy over the causes of the increasing US trade gap which is being used by protectionists to bolster their case. While some blame the domestic budget deficit, high costs, inadequate domestic savings and the strength of the US dollar in some periods of the recent past, others cite the trade policies of other nations such as Japan, South Korea and Taiwan. There is considerable debate over whether the latter group of countries are in fact more protectionist than the US. Though it is recognised that the adoption of further trade restriction measures could disrupt world trade and growth, the political climate in the US could encourage further protectionism. Since such protectionism tends not to discriminate between countries, many of the debt-ridden nations could be affected. Based on a sample of sixteen indebted countries it was found that 70% of their exports were sold to industrial countries.[15] It is widely felt that one way in which debt-ridden countries could be helped is to encourage an atmosphere which could lead to expansion of their exports rather than a contraction of their imports. In the latter case, the financial crisis could worsen if the growth rate of output falls further through a lack of imports to expand and develop export industries.

Available data for the period since 1960 indicate that developing countries as a group have tended to grow at a faster rate than the industrial market economies. For instance, between 1965 and 1973, real GDP for the former group averaged 6.6% as compared to 4.7% for the latter. In the period 1973–80 the figure was 5.4% for the developing countries and 2.8% for the industrial market economies. Between 1981 and 1985 the pattern was generally the same except for 1983 (*See* Table 1.5). The relatively lower figures in the 1981–83

Table 1.5 Real growth of GDP, 1965–1985 (Annual percentage change)

Country group	1965–75 average	1973–80 average	1981	1982	1983	1984	1985
Developing countries	6.6	5.4	3.5	2.0	2.0	5.4	4.4
Low-income countries	5.6	4.7	5.0	5.3	7.8	9.4	7.8
Africa	3.9	2.7	1.7	0.7	0.2	0.7	2.1
Asia	5.9	5.0	5.4	5.8	8.6	10.2	8.3
China	7.8	5.4	4.9	7.7	9.6	14.0	10.6
India	4.0	4.1	5.8	2.9	7.6	4.5	4.0
Middle-income oil exporters	7.1	5.8	4.4	1.0	−1.9	2.5	2.5
Middle-income oil importers	7.0	5.5	2.1	0.8	0.8	4.1	3.0
Major exporters of manufactures	7.6	5.9	1.6	1.2	0.8	4.4	3.1
Brazil	9.6	6.8	−1.5	1.0	−3.2	4.5	7.0
Other middle-income oil importers	5.4	4.5	3.4	−0.6	0.8	3.1	2.8
High-income oil exporters	9.2	7.7	1.6	−1.7	−7.1	1.3	−5.0
Industrial market economies	4.7	2.8	1.9	−0.6	2.3	4.6	2.8

Note: Data for developing countries are based on a sample of ninety countries.
Source: IBRD, *World Development Report*, 1986.

period for both groups reflect the effects of the international recession which has affected both developed and developing countries. As is to be expected, the growth rate in output has varied from country to country. Generalisation can give a distorted picture of actual performance. Even before 1973 there were marked differences in the performance of mineral exporting countries and the other developing nations. The increase in oil prices between 1973 and 1974 strongly accentuated this distinction to the extent that international agencies thought it fit to separate the oil exporters from other poor countries in their statistical publications. Between 1965 and 1973 middle-income oil exporters grew at an average rate of 7.1% as compared to 3.9% for low-income Africa and 5.9% for low-income Asia. In the period 1973–80, the comparable figure for the first group was 5.8%, while that for low-income Asia was 5.0% and for low-income Africa 2.7%. Latin America and the Caribbean experienced a growth rate of over 5% between 1960 and 1980, but has also suffered from the international recession in recent years. Not only have the oil exporters such as Trinidad, Venezuela and Mexico suffered a sharp decline in income as a result of the drop in oil prices, but countries such as Brazil and Argentina have also experienced a decline in their respective growth rates. Brazil, for instance, whose GDP grew at an average rate of 6.7% between 1961 and 1982, could only muster a rate of 3.2% between 1983 and 1985. Similarly Venezuela's rate fell from 4.6% in the former period to an average rate of decline of -2.2% in the latter.

Though countries such as China, India and the export oriented economies have continued to experience high growth rates by international standards, growth in real GDP as indicated above, has declined in several countries in recent years. Lower oil prices and falling export volume have cut the growth rate experienced by middle-income oil exporters between 1973 and 1980 by more than half. Lower foreign exchange earnings, rising interest rates and declining private foreign investment have also affected heavily indebted countries. This development, coupled with persistent balance of payments and debt servicing problems, has intensified the focus on the need for structural transformation at the domestic level and for widening the scope of participation for developing countries in the international economy. The international trading framework in particular continues to be a major target for criticisms by developing nations who continue to complain about inadequate access to the markets of the industrial nations and the unsatisfactory functioning of commodity markets.

In examining the growth of output in any country, or for that matter in the world, an important variable that has to be kept in mind is the growth of population. The growth in the number of people can often offset any benefits stemming from increased production. Because of this, high population growth rates and their consequences for human welfare has long been a subject for study. The famous Malthusian model is, of course, well known. Thomas Malthus (1766—1834) has argued that because population tends to increase in geometrical progression while food production could be increased only in arithmetical progression, population growth unless checked would result in a falling standard of living.

Though the Malthusian trap has not materialised, the concerns raised by Malthus are never far away. The problems associated with rapid population expansion attract intense attention. The situation in many developing countries is that population growth rates still exceed 3% a year. Only in a few developing countries have population growth rates fallen below 2% a year in the past two decades. This situation reflects the result of both high fertility rates and a decline in mortality following improvements in medical science. Only in a few developing countries have fertility rates fallen.

If developing countries are looked at as a group, population growth rates are estimated to have risen from 2.0% in 1950 to 2.4% in 1965, largely as a result of falling death rates. Since then the population growth has slowed because of the tendency of birth rates to fall faster than death rates. This fall in the average growth is due almost entirely to the birth rate decline in China which alone accounts for a third of all the people in developing countries, and where the birth rate has fallen by over 50% since 1965. Other countries where birth rates have fallen include Hong Kong, Singapore, Korea and the middle-income countries of Latin America and the Caribbean (e.g. Brazil, Mexico, Jamaica). In many of the poorer countries birth rates are still more than 35 per 1000 and this has contributed to a growth rate in many cases of over 3%. The very countries that can least afford it are the very ones who find it difficult to break out of the population trap.[16]

In most low and middle-income developing countries population growth now ranges between 2 and 4% a year, as compared to 1% and less in most developed countries. An examination of Table 1.6 shows that despite this high population growth rate in developing countries over the past three decades, GNP has tended to grow faster than the population. As a result per capita GNP has generally increased. In the period 1970—80 this indicator grew at a faster rate (3.1%) for all developing countries as a group than in the industrial market economies taken as a group (2.4%).

Table 1.6 Growth of population, GNP, and GNP per capita, 1955–80 (Average annual percentage change)

Category group	Population 1955–70	Population 1970–80	GNP 1955–70	GNP 1970–80	GNP per capita 1955–70	GNP per capita 1970–80
All developing countries	2.2	2.2	5.4	5.3	3.1	3.1
Low-income	2.1	2.1	3.7	4.5	1.6	2.4
China	2.0	1.8	3.3	6.0	1.3	4.1
India	2.2	2.1	4.0	3.4	1.8	1.3
Other	2.4	2.7	4.4	2.7	2.0	0.0
Middle-income	2.4	2.4	6.0	5.6	3.5	3.1
Industrial market economies	1.1	0.8	4.7	3.2	3.6	2.4
Europe	0.7	0.2	4.8	2.6	4.1	2.4
Japan	1.0	1.1	10.3	5.4	9.2	4.2
United States	1.4	1.0	3.4	3.1	2.0	2.1
World[a]	1.9	1.9	5.1	3.8	3.1	1.9

[a] Includes high-income oil exporters and industrial non-market economies.
Source: IBRD, World Development Report, 1984.

Concluding observations

The 1980s are proving to be a challenging period for the world economy. A major objective in the early post-war years was to construct a more open world trading system in order to secure a more efficient allocation of resources at the global level. In pursuit of this goal, barriers to trade set up in the 1930s were progressively removed. In this context, multilateralism emerged as an important plank of the post-war world economy. The loss of momentum in the trade liberalisation process and the reversion to the settling of trade disputes on a bi-lateral basis in recent years have raised fears of a prolonged period of stagnation in the world economy. For developing countries the expansion of international trade and the growth of income in the developed nations are crucial to their development. In most of them trade accounts for a significant proportion of GNP. Their import capacity and debt servicing obligations depend critically on their ability to sell. While the need to institute export-oriented strategies is becoming increasingly recognised, the growing protectionism in the world economy has given rise to concern. Manufactured goods which developing countries are capable of producing are the ones that are most protected in the industrial nations. For the majority of poor countries agricultural products account for a large part of their production and exports. Yet the agricultural sector has traditionally been the most protected in the rich nations.

A major challenge facing the world community in the 1980s is the provision of greater trading opportunities for poor countries, many of whom find it difficult to raise loans in the context of their economic situation and debt position. There are some countries which need to do more to open up their markets in order to bring about a more balanced trading relationship in the international economy. The failure of economic integration schemes among developing countries points to the need for new approaches to trade liberalisation among poor countries themselves, and for the institution of policies which could make more effective use of resources. In the present world economy it is difficult, if not impossible, for countries, however small or large, to isolate themselves from developments taking place outside their national borders. Countries like China and the Soviet Union, which have traditionally operated closed systems, now find it necessary to increase their participation in the international economy. Where foreign exchange is scarce countries have resorted increasingly to trade by barter which is the exchange of goods taking place without the use of currency. There is also an increasing amount of counter-trade, a term used to describe two reciprocal trade transactions in which each party is paid in currency. It is estimated that barter trade may now account for 20–30% of world trade.[17]

Autarchic policies, particularly for small states with a skewed resource base, are difficult to entertain. Generally, states can only satisfy a part of their requirements from internal production. In pursuit of certain objectives (e.g. employment creation) some countries try to produce items which they can buy more cheaply from abroad. Protection is a disincentive to export, and countries that have not recognised this have found it difficult not only to increase non-traditional exports, but to make any serious dent on the unemployment problem as well.

Notes

1 In 1980 the US accounted for 21.8% of world output as compared to 40.3% in 1950. Over the same period Western Europe's share increased from 21.1% to 29.8%, Japan's from 1.6% to 8.8% and Developing Countries' from 12.7% to 17.9%. With respect to exports the US share fell from 16.7% to 11.0%, while Japan's increased from 1.4% to 6.5% and Western Europe's from 33.4% to 40.2%. See J. Bhagwati and D.A. Irwin, 'The Return of the Reciprocitarians: US Trade Policy Today,' *The World Economy*, June, 1987.
2 See OECD, *Competition and Trade Policy: Their Interaction*, Paris, 1984, p.10.
3 For a detailed background study on the New International Economic Order, see K.P. Sauvant and H. Hasenpflug (eds.), *The New International Economic Order: Confrontation or Co-operation Between North and South?*, Boulder, Colorado: Westview Press, 1978.
4 See J.K. Horsefield, *The International Monetary Fund 1945–1965*, Vol. I., Washington D.C.: IMF, 1964, *passim*.
5 J.E. Sanford, *US Foreign Policy and Multilateral Development Banks*, Boulder, Colorado: Westview Press, 1982, p.43.
6 See B. Gosovic, *UNCTAD: North-South Encounter*, International Conciliation, No. 568/May 1968, p.9.
7 See GATT, *International Trade, 1982/83*, p.4.
8 *Ibid*. p.3.
9 The World Bank, *World Development Report, 1984*, New York: Oxford University Press, 1984, p.13.
10 For a detailed analysis of recent developments in protectionism, see the IMF's, *The Rise in Protectionism*, Washington, D.C. 1978; see also The World Bank/IMF Development Committee's *Trade and Development*, Washington, D.C., 1978.
11 See The World Bank, *World Development Report 1986*, Washington, D.C., 1986, p.23.
12 See *ibid* pp. 13–17
13 See *Fortune* magazine, August 1985.
14 World Bank, *World Bank Development Report 1986*, *op. cit.* pp.22–23.

15 GATT, *International Trade 1982/83*, p.8
16 See The World Bank, *World Development Report, 1984*, op. cit. pp.63–65.
17 See B.S. Fisher and K.M. Harte, *Barter in the World Economy*, New York: Praeger, 1985, p.1.

CHAPTER 2
The economy of the Commonwealth Caribbean in transition

Commonwealth Caribbean countries attained their political independence with their economies strongly linked to the international economy on terms that were not satisfactory to them. The colonial experience had established a certain kind of relationship which was designed to serve the interests of the imperial power. In order to change the nature of this relationship it was recognised that there was a need to change the structure of domestic production. The framework for doing this, however, was not evident. The so-called Lewis Model[1] had started to influence policies in the Caribbean since the early 1950s. Lewis saw the need to expand the manufacturing sector without necessarily reducing the production of agricultural goods, as a means of solving the unemployment and food problems associated with high population growth rates. In Latin America, the centre-periphery analysis of the ECLA school made a direct link between the deteriorating terms of trade faced by developing countries and primary production.[2] The way to deal with this problem, it was concluded, was to move into the production and export of manufactured goods which were associated with a high income elasticity of demand.

To the extent that Caribbean policy-makers were influenced by this line of thinking, this would have served to strengthen the case for industrialisation. In an effort to develop a manufacturing sector (which traditionally was confined to a few light items and the processing of sugar and its by-products) greater incentives were offered in the post-independence period to attract foreign investors. With increasing incomes in the developed countries, falling air fares and the development of local tourist facilities, tourism also began to emerge as an activity in the 1960s to challenge the traditional foreign exchange earners. With the inflow of foreign investment in the mining and tourism sectors particularly, high growth rates were experienced in the 1950s and 1960s. The manufacturing sector also expanded its share of output in some territories. In fact in Jamaica by 1960 the sector's contribution to total product had exceeded that of agriculture.[3] With the decline of agriculture and the inability of the other sectors to provide the volume of jobs needed to match the growth of the labour force, unemployment has persisted at unsatisfactory levels, even in the face of rising wages and salaries. The 'demonstration effect' in these economies is strong and wage levels in the high productivity activities are easily transmitted to the lower productivity sectors, given the strong trade union movements in the region. In the light of the tendency for wages and salaries to exceed productivity, the Commonwealth Caribbean is generally regarded as a high cost area, though the situation in the OECS countries may be less so than in the other states. High costs, of course, may be a function of other factors as well such as poor management, outdated techniques, high mark-ups, etc. The persistence in some cases of unrealistic exchange rates for long periods of time has not helped the export effort. Public policies, too, have generally failed to focus sufficiently on efficiency and management.

Increasing levels of unemployment, falling nutritional standards, declining income, and balance of payments problems are forcing governments in the region to rethink the development strategy of the recent past. These economies have remained structurally weak with dependence of one kind being replaced by dependence of another kind. There are essential similarities between the plantation economy and the more recent assembly-type and tourist oriented economies in terms of the way they function.[4] The changing contribution of the various sectors to total output often hides these similarities. Whereas in the plantation economy the Caribbean served as the hinterland to the metropolis, providing raw materials and food in return for manufactured goods, in the 'modernised' economy, the essential characteristics operate through a large number of transnational corporations using a variety of strategies to satisfy national regulations and policies. Caribbean economies tend to be more closely integrated into the structures of these corporations than with each other.[5] The terms of this incorporation, however, are not generally in their favour given their weak bargaining position stemming from small size, lack of negotiating skills and precarious financial positions. Protection among themselves has contributed to Caribbean states' vulnerability in dealing with enterprises with massive technical, financial and other resources at their disposal.

In cases where foreign firms have sought to preserve or penetrate local markets through licensing and royalty agreements with local groups, these arrangements have often been poorly scrutinised with respect to the long term implications for the real transfer of technology and skills, or the development of exports. Short term pressures stemming from high unemployment rates can also force governments to abandon stated policy, or to succumb to demands from powerful economic groups in the society for permission to enter arrangements to preserve privileged positions, which may not be in the national interest. The pursuit of personal gain by key decision-makers is, on occasions, the only explanation for situations which make neither economic nor political sense. The bribing of politicians and officials in host countries is known to be a routine part of the *modus-operandi* of transnational corporations. Dependence as a dimension of underdevelopment is the result of the interaction of both internal and external factors. The significance of one set over the other would vary from case to case, depending on structural factors and the approach to development taken. We begin this chapter with a discussion of the main features of Caribbean economies and their recent performance. This is followed by an outline of structural changes in the economies since the 1950s and a critique of industrial strategy. In the final section we focus on some of the current issues and problems confronting Caribbean governments, which have emerged as a result of both internal policies and the crisis in the world economy.

Introduction to the economies of the Commonwealth Caribbean

With the exception of Belize which is part of the Central American isthmus, and Guyana which is located in South America, Commonwealth Caribbean countries are part of the chain of islands stretching from Florida in the north to the coast of South America. In other words, the bulk of them are island economies. Some of these (e.g. Barbados) consist of one island, while others (e.g. Trinidad and Tobago) consist of more than one island. The Bahamas is estimated to consist of over 700 islands and islets. Generally the islands are small both in terms of physical size, and population.

As can be seen from Table 2.1 Commonwealth Caribbean countries differ in terms of physical size, GNP, per capita GNP, and population. They also have different resource endowment. With respect to physical size, Guyana is the largest with a land area of about 215 000 km^2. Its estimated population of 806 000 in 1985, however, was less than that of Trinidad and Tobago (with an area of 2.4% of its size) and also less than that of Jamaica (with an area 5.3% of its size). The next largest in terms of physical size is Belize with an area of almost 23 000 km^2. Its estimated population of 159 000, however, was less than that of Barbados with less than 2% of its land area. The smallest of the group is Montserrat with an

28 The Commonwealth Caribbean

Table 2.1 Selected data on a select group of countries in the world economy

Countries	Area km²	Population[1] (1985) (000)	GNP (1985) US$mn	Per Capita[1] GNP (1985) US$	Real GNP 1973–85	Pop. 1973–85	Real Per Capita GNP % 1973–85	Life Expectancy at Birth (Years) 1970	1984
Commonwealth Caribbean									
Antigua & Barbuda	440	79	160	2030	4.0	1.2	2.9	n.a.	72
Bahamas	13 935	234	1670	7150	4.1	2.1	1.9	63	69
Barbados	431	252	1180	4680	1.8	0.3	1.5	68	72
Belize	22 965	159	180	1130	2.7	1.9	−0.1	60	66
Dominica	750	78	90	1160	2.3	0.7	2.8	n.a.	74
Grenada	344	96	90	970	2.5	1.8	n.a.	67	69
Guyana	214 970	806	460	570	−1.2	1.1	−2.3	63	66
Jamaica	10 991	2227	2090	940	−2.5	1.1	−3.5	67	73
Montserrat	102	12	31[a]	2583[a]	5.1	0.0	5.1	n.a.	63
St Christopher-Nevis	269	43	70	1520	3.3	0.0	3.3	n.a.	63
St Lucia	616	136	160	1210	5.0	2.1	2.9	n.a.	69
St Vincent	388	119	100	840	4.2	1.9	2.3	n.a.	70
Trinidad & Tobago	5128	1189	7140	6010	3.6	1.6	2.0	66	69
Selected Developing Countries									
Argentina	2 766 889	30 531	65 080	2130	−0.4	1.6	−2.0	67	70
Bangladesh	143 998	100 592	14 770	150	4.5	2.5	2.0	45	50
Brazil	8 511 965	135 539	222 010	1640	3.8	2.3	1.5	59	64
Comoros	2171	395	110	280	4.0	2.7	1.3	47	55
Costa Rica	50 700	2593	3340	1290	1.8	2.8	−1.0	67	73

Faeroe Islands	1 399	46	500	10 930	4.2	1.2	3.0	n.a.	n.a.
Fiji	18 272	702	1 190	1 700	3.0	2.0	1.0	61	65
Hong Kong	1 045	5 425	33 770	6 220	8.7	2.3	6.3	69	76
India	3 287 590	765 147	194 820	250	4.3	2.2	2.0	47	56
Korea, Rep. of	98 484	40 646	28 440	2 180	7.1	1.5	5.5	59	69
Kuwait	17 818	1 736	24 760	14 270	6.0	5.7	0.3	66	72
Mexico	1 972 547	78 820	163 790	2 080	4.2	2.8	1.3	61	66
Nigeria	923 768	99 669	75 940	760	0.3	2.8	−2.5	43	50
Saudi Arabia	2 149 690	11 521	102 120	8 860	6.6	4.8	1.7	52	62
Sao Tome & Principe	964	108	30	310	3.2	2.2	1.0	n.a.	63
Seychelles	308	65	n.a.	n.a.	n.a.	1.1	n.a.	66	70
Singapore	581	2 557	18 970	7 420	7.9	1.3	6.5	68	72
Tanzania	945 087	22 242	5 840	270	1.7	3.4	−1.6	45	52
Uganda	236 037	15 474	n.a.	n.a.	n.a.	3.2	n.a.	47	51
Vanuatu	14 763	134	n.a.	n.a.	n.a.	2.8	n.a.	n.a.	55
Venezuela	912 050	17 323	53 800	3 110	1.3	3.3	−1.9	66	69
Zambia	752 614	6 640	2 620	400	0.5	3.2	−2.6	46	51
Selected Developed Countries									
Canada	9 976 139	25 414	347 360	13 670	2.3	1.2	1.1	73	76
France	547 026	55 133	526 630	9 550	2.1	0.5	1.6	72	77
Germany, Fed. Rep	248 577	61 065	667 970	10 940	2.0	−0.1	2.1	70	75
Japan	372 313	120 579	1 366 040	11 330	4.3	0.9	3.4	72	77
United Kingdom	244 046	56 539	474 190	8 390	1.1	0.0	1.1	72	74
United States of America	9 372 614	238 780	3 915 350	16 400	2.5	1.0	1.4	71	76

[1] Preliminary estimates   n.a. not available

[a] 1984

Sources: The World Bank, *Atlas*, 1987; *The Europa Yearbook*, 1987; OECS *National Accounts Digest*, 1985.

area of 102 km² and a population of 12 000 (1985 estimate). When taken together, the total land area of Commonwealth Caribbean countries amounts to about 271 000 km². By comparison this would be less than 1% of the size of India, about 30% of the size of Venezuela, slightly larger than Uganda, larger than the UK and the Federal Republic of Germany respectively, almost three quarters the size of Japan, or almost 3% of the area of the US. When viewed as individual units, most Commonwealth Caribbean countries are small physically when compared to the industrialised nations, but some of them are larger than Singapore or Hong Kong which are ranked among the newly industrialising nations. The total population of Commonwealth Caribbean countries amounts to about 5.5 million which is small compared to that of the industrialised nations of North America and Europe, but is almost the same as that of Hong Kong and more than twice that of Singapore.

With respect to total GNP, the figure relating to Trinidad and Tobago in 1985 was US$7140 million (the largest for the group) as compared to US$2090 million for Jamaica (the next largest) and around US$31 million for Montserrat (the smallest). At least four other Commonwealth Caribbean countries had GNP of US$100 million or less in 1985. The Trinidad and Tobago total in 1985 was greater than that of the combined GNP of all the other Commonwealth Caribbean countries put together. In an international context, Trinidad and Tobago's GNP in 1985 was more than twice that of Costa Rica, a little less than half of Singapore's, almost a quarter that of Hong Kong, but it was larger than that of Tanzania, Uganda and Zambia respectively. The combined GNP of Commonwealth Caribbean countries of US$13.4 billion in 1985 was less than 0.4% of that of the US, 4% that of Canada, 2.8% that of the UK and 1.0% that of Japan.

At the global level, the distribution of GNP tends to be highly skewed. An examination of Table 2.2 will show on the basis of 1985 data that in the category 'less than $10 billion' there were 95 countries with a total GNP of US$227.2 billion. On the other hand, in the category 'more than $100 billion' there were only 16 countries with a total GNP of US$9248 billion. In Table 2.3 countries are grouped according to per capita GNP. In the category '$400 and less' there were 35 countries with a total GNP of US$639.1 billion and a total population of 2 318.2 million. At the upper end of the scale in the category '$4300 and more,' there were 48 countries with a total GNP of US$9025.9 billion, but with a total population of only 776 million people.

With respect to per capita GNP there is wide variation among

Table 2.2 Distribution of GNP by countries grouped according to size of aggregate GNP, 1985

GNP 1985	No. of countries	GNP US$ 1 000 000 1985	Population (000) 1985	GDP per capita US$ 1985
Less than $10 billion	95	227 230	437 756	520
$10 billion to less than $50 billion	25	636 840	547 738	1 160
$50 billion to less than $100 billion	15	1 045 120	531 264	1 970
$100 billion and more	16	9 248 340	2 722 002	3 400
No data	33	n.a.	549 961	n.a.

Source: World Bank, Atlas, 1987.   n.a. not available

Table 2.3 Distribution of GDP by countries grouped according to per capita, GNP 1985

GNP per capita 1985	No. of countries	GNP US$ 1 000 000 1985	Population (000) 1985	GNP per capita US$ 1985
$400 and less	35	639 210	2 318 153	280
$401 to $1635	47	524 960	672 211	780
$1636 to $4300	21	967 480	472 325	2 050
$4300 and more	48	9 025 880	776 071	11 630
No data	33	n.a.	549 961	n.a.

n.a. not available
Source: World Bank Atlas, 1987.

Commonwealth Caribbean countries. In terms of 1985 estimates, Guyana was at the bottom of the scale with US$570, while the Bahamas was at the top with US$7150, followed by Trinidad and Tobago with US$6010. In the early 1980s this latter country tended to rank fifth behind the US, Bermuda, Canada and the US Virgin Islands in the Western Hemisphere in terms of per capita GNP. With the decline of oil prices since 1982 per capita income has fallen, now placing this country behind the Bahamas whose economy is based on tourism and offshore financial activities. When viewed in an international context Commonwealth Caribbean countries are generally classified as middle-income countries, i.e. between the rich industrialised countries like the US (1985 per capita GNP US$16 400) and the very poor ones like Haiti (1985 per capita GNP US$320) and Ethiopia (1985 per capita GNP US$110). Countries like Trinidad and Tobago, the Bahamas and Barbados can easily fit into the upper middle-income group. The average income in the Caribbean is generally higher than that of African countries and some countries in Asia. An examination of Table 2.1 will show that per capita income of Commonwealth Caribbean countries tends to be greater than that of countries such as Bangladesh, India, Tanzania and Uganda. The average income in the OECS territories is estimated to be over US$900. At least five Commonwealth Caribbean countries have a per capita income higher than that of Brazil. Trinidad and Tobago's per capita GNP in 1985 was only 29% less than that of the UK.

Despite its common usage for comparative purposes the per capita income concept can be quite misleading as an index of development. India, for example, has a relatively low per capita income, but a fairly well-advanced industrial sector. High per capita income may be the result of the exploitation of a valuable mineral resource (as in the case of oil exporting countries), or the development of activities such as tourism which can generate a fairly high level of foreign exchange earnings. The concept overlooks the distribution of income. The computation of the statistics also encounters certain technical difficulties which call for a great deal of caution in making inter-country comparisons.

For most Commonwealth Caribbean countries, real GNP has tended to grow faster than population. With the exception of Guyana, Belize and Jamaica, all Commonwealth Caribbean countries experienced positive average rates of growth in real per capita GNP in the 1973−85 period. At least five countries had real per capita growth rates exceeding 2.5%. The comparable rate for the US in the period was 1.4%, for Japan 3.4%, for the UK 1.1%, for the Federal

Republic of Germany 2.1%, for Brazil 1.5%. for Singapore 6.5%, for South Korea 5.5% and for Saudi Arabia 1.7%. Despite this performance high rates of unemployment persist in the region, and in fact have been increasing in some states. This clearly indicates that output can grow faster than population without generating enough job opportunities to keep pace with the expanding labour force. Given the various sources which could inspire growth, a growth policy need not in itself be an employment creating policy.

A salient characteristic of Commonwealth Caribbean countries is the high degree of openness. One aspect of this openness is the heavy dependence on foreign trade. The significance of this can easily be seen in the well-known expenditure on GDP equation:

$$Y = C+I+G (X-M)$$

where
 Y = Gross Domestic Product
 C = Private consumption expenditure
 I = Private investment expenditure
 G = Government expenditure
 X = Exports
 M = Imports

Openness is often expressed as the proportion of GDP (or GNP) that is exported (i.e. X/Y), or the ratio of imports to GDP (M/Y) which shows residents' expenditure on imports. Alternatively, the position of imports often takes the form (M/M+Y) which shows the ratio of imports to total supplies or total availability of goods and services. A common approach is to add imports to exports (X+M) and express this as a proportion of GDP. When we speak of exports and imports we not only refer to goods, but to non-factor services such as tourism which is often termed an 'invisible' import or export giving rise to outflows and inflows of foreign exchange. In Table 2.4 the 'X' column shows the exports of goods and non-factor services expressed as a percentage of GDP (at current market prices), while the 'M' column shows the comparable import ratios. These figures are generally quite high. In the case of the Bahamas the average is around 90% for exports and imports respectively. For Trinidad and Tobago, it is around 40%. For large countries such as the US and Brazil exports and imports amount to 10% (or less) of GDP respectively. The UK is a more open economy. Here imports amount to around 25 to 30% of GDP respectively. In the case of Japan goods exports in 1984 amounted to 14% of GDP as compared to 10% for imports. The export oriented newly industrialising countries like Taiwan, Singapore, Republic of Korea and Hong Kong show ratios

Table 2.4 Exports of goods and non-factor services (X) and imports of goods and non-factor services (M) as a % of GDP at current market prices[1]

Countries	X	M
Antigua and Barbuda	66	100
Bahamas[2]	90	90
Barbados	65	71
Belize	57	77
Dominica	37	78
Grenada[3]	45	72
Guyana[4]	60	75
Jamaica	45	53
Montserrat	24	77
St Kitts-Nevis	55	83
St Lucia	62	101
St Vincent	70	97
Trinidad and Tobago[5]	41	38
USA	9	10

[1] Ratios generally represent average of the five year period 1978–83.
[2] Based on 1980–82 data.
[3] Based on 1978–82 data.
[4] Based on 1980–84 data.
[5] GDP figures used were at factor cost.
Source: Calculated from official publications and IMF, *Financial Statistics*, Various Issues.

above 30%. The share of service exports in the output of various countries has not only been growing, but varies widely from country to country. In 1984, for example, service exports amounted to 34.4% of the GDP of Belgium-Luxembourg, 51.6% of Singapore's and 20.4% of Switzerland's, but to only 3.9% of the US' and to 3.4% of Japan's. In Barbados the proportion is around 45% (tourism alone accounting for about 25%) as compared to less than 10% for Trinidad and Tobago.

A distinction is often made between openness and dependence. The UK's economy is said to be open, but not dependent in the sense in which Commonwealth Caribbean countries are said to be dependent. In the former case, the range of markets tends to be wider as are sources of supplies. The goods exported are also of a wide variety, and do not depend on any special marketing arrangements. The production structure is more resilient and more responsive to market developments. In the case of Commonwealth Caribbean countries, exports are concentrated in a few activities e.g. oil in Trinidad, bauxite and tourism in Jamaica, tourism in Antigua, Barbados, and the Bahamas, bananas in St Lucia and sugar in St Kitts. In most cases one or two activities account for the bulk of the foreign exchange earnings. The implications of this situation are that adverse developments in the markets affecting any one of the major activities are quickly reflected in the level of domestic activity through their impact on foreign earnings and government revenue. Another aspect of the export relationship is that as small producers in the world economy, Commonwealth Caribbean countries are in no position to influence world markets. They are price takers. Exports are also concentrated in a few markets.

On the import side, diversification of markets may be wider, but sources are still highly concentrated, with tradition and physical proximity being major influential factors. With respect to the range of imports, these cover luxury goods, essential raw materials and food, as well as consumer and capital goods. Almost all capital goods are imported. Food imports have also been growing. The manufacturing sector depends heavily on critical inputs from abroad. The implication here is that if foreign exchange is unavailable to pay for required imports, the level of domestic economic activity and social conditions are quickly affected. The typical Caribbean economy will grind to a halt without foreign exchange. Another implication of openness, of course, is that foreign price trends can easily be transmitted to the local economy.

Development experience

In recent years Commonwealth Caribbean economies have undergone certain structural changes which are worth noting. In most cases this experience has involved moving from dependence on one activity to dependence on another activity. Generally, manufacturing has increased its share of GDP in most economies, while tourism has emerged as an important sector. Because tourism affects a wide range of activities (e.g. restaurants, retail outlets, hotels, transport, handicraft) it is often difficult to say exactly what proportion of GDP is attributable to tourism. A notable feature of Caribbean economies has been the declining share of agriculture in GDP. A major factor here has been the shrinking of the traditional export sector, particularly sugar, cocoa, coffee and citrus. This has taken place despite a growing domestic agricultural sector in some cases. The share of government services in GDP has also increased in most cases. We begin this section of the chapter by outlining the structural changes which have taken place in individual economies.

Structural transformation in Caribbean economies

Antigua

In the early 1950s sugar was Antigua's staple product and main export. In 1958, sugar was the largest single contributor to GDP (at current factor cost) accounting for 28%. Cotton, other crops, livestock and fishing contributed another 17%. The share relating to manufacturing amounted to less than 1% as compared to 9% for construction and engineering, 11% for distribution and finance and 16% for government. By the early 1960s, agriculture's contribution to economic activity had shown a considerable decline, accounting in 1963 for less than 20% of GDP. Sugar's contribution dropped by more than 50%. By the early 1980s Antigua had been transformed into an economy almost totally dominated by tourism. The distributive trades, transport, hotels and restaurants emerged as major activities. Agriculture's share of the GDP dropped to less than 10%. The goods producing sectors account for less than 20% of the jobs available in Antigua.

Bahamas

Before the emergence of the tourist industry in the post-war period, the Bahamas was best known for its sponging and fishing activities. While offshore finance and tax haven facilities make a contribution to the economy, tourism is estimated to account for over 70% of the Gross National Product. In the 1970s it was employing about two-thirds of the labour force. In terms of foreign exchange earnings, tourism accounts for more than half of the country's foreign exchange earnings. Attempts to diversify the economy have met with little success. In recent years the growth rate has fallen considerably from that experienced in the booming 1960s as a result of the rapid growth of the tourism and construction sectors. From a fully employed economy in the 1960s, unemployment in the late 1970s had climbed to over 14% of the labour force. Unemployment continues to be a serious problem, while there is evidence of shortages of people with certain kinds of skills.

Barbados

In 1955, agriculture is estimated to have contributed 35% to Barbados' GDP. Of this, sugar cane alone accounted for 23%. The value-added resulting from the processing of sugar, rum and molasses amounted to 12%, as compared to 7% for the rest of the manufacturing sector which consisted largely of edible oil, soap, lard and margarine, clothes making, food, drink and tabacco, printing, brick, furniture manufacture and shell and leather work. Less than ten years later in 1963, agricultural activities continued to dominate the Barbadian economy, though agriculture's share had fallen to 30% with sugar again accounting for 24%. During the 1960s tourism emerged as one of the leading sectors in the Barbadian economy, and by 1980 it is estimated to have contributed about 12% of real GDP as compared to about 2% in 1956. Preliminary figures available for 1984 show that agriculture contributed about 7% to GDP. Sugar's contribution has fallen drastically as a result of both falling output and the expansion of other sectors. On the other hand the manufacturing sector has expanded significantly in recent years, contributing 9% and 13% to GDP in current values and real terms respectively in 1984. From an almost pure mono-crop economy in the 1940s and 1950s, some measure of diversification has been introduced into the Barbadian economy, thus reducing its economic vulnerability. The service sectors in the economy, however, still account for about 80% of domestic output.

Belize

Though a number of light industries have been established in recent years, the Belizean economy remains primarily an agricultural one with sugar, citrus and bananas being its main crops. In 1983 agriculture was estimated to have contributed 28% to real GDP, as compared to 14% for manufacturing and 17% for trade and industry. Sugar, citrus products, fish products, bananas and molasses taken together accounted for almost 80% of domestic exports in 1983. In recent years growth has fallen below the 4 to 5% experienced during the 1960s and part of the 1970s.

Dominica

Dominica remains more dependent on agriculture than perhaps any of the other islands. In 1984 value-added in this sector is estimated to have amounted to about 30% of GDP as compared to 35% twenty years earlier. The export component dominates the sector, the major products being bananas, citrus and copra. The manufacturing sector remains small accounting for about 7% of GDP. The main activities are the processing of lime and products from copra. The goods sector contributes an average of about 40% to domestic output as compared to less than 15% for Antigua and Montserrat respectively.

Grenada

Like most other members of the OECS, Grenada has an economy that is basically agricultural, but the contribution of this sector to total output has been falling. In the early 1960s, agriculture accounted for about 40% of GDP. By the mid-1980s this figure had dropped to around 20%. In recent years the output of traditional crops has not been encouraging. Value-added in the manufacturing sector has increased, but its contribution amounts to only about 5% of GDP. The future growth of this sector is being predicated on attempts being made to attract private foreign capital. Despite the efforts being made to diversify the economy, bananas, cocoa, nutmeg and fresh fruits account for over 80% of domestic exports. With the increase in the number of hotel rooms and the development of the new airport at Point Salines, tourism has emerged as a lead sector in the Grenadian economy. Earnings from tourism are now estimated to be around 40% of the export of goods and services.

Guyana

The Guyanese economy is significantly dependent on the products of four commodities, sugar, rice, bauxite and alumina. Though agriculture's share in GDP has declined since the 1950s and 1960s, it still accounts for over 20%. The contribution of bauxite and alumina has tended to decline as a result of internal problems and the state of the international bauxite market in recent years. In 1985, value-added in this sector amounted to 3.0% as compared to 13% in 1963 and 11% in 1953. Apart from the processing of sugar and its by-products, the manufacturing sector is very narrowly based. Particularly noticeable is the rapid increase in the government's share of GDP. Between 1960 and 1985, it more than doubled, the contribution moving from 9.7% to 21%. Since the early 1970s the government has become the main employer in the country following the nationalisation of major sectors of the economy. It also controls the bulk of the recorded import and export trade.

In recent years growth has been affected by declining production of major commodities, a weak bauxite market and falling sugar prices. The foreign exchange crisis has not only impacted on the ability to import, thus affecting consumption and investment, but has also encouraged the growth of an active underground economy of major dimensions. The emigration of skilled people has served to worsen the economic crisis, and is also likely to make the recovery effort more difficult.

Montserrat

In the 1950s Montserrat was a predominantly agricultural community growing cotton, sugar (mainly for the local market), limes and a wide range of crops. In 1953 primary products accounted for about half of the GDP. Apart from rum making, lime and oil production, manufacturing enterprise was virtually absent. In the 1960s there was a substantial decline in agriculture with this sector contributing only about 18% in 1969. Sugar and banana growing virtually disappeared, while cotton production continued its downward trend, particularly after the hurricane of 1967. With the emergence of tourism during the 1960s, investment in construction became a major factor in the economy. By its very nature, construction cannot remain at a perpetually high level, and its contribution can vary significantly from period to period. From a figure of about 20% in the mid-1960s, this sector's contribution fell to about 9% in 1983. During the 1960s manufacturing contributed less than 2% to GDP. During the 1970s a number of assembly-type operations were set up, and the products of these enterprises now dominate the export trade of Montserrat. In 1984 this sector is estimated to have contributed 7% to GDP.

St Kitts-Nevis

Data available for the 1950s indicate that sugar (including milling) amounted to between 40% and 50% of GDP. Other primary activities (including cotton growing) amounted to around 12% to 14%, while distribution and finance contributed around 12%. The share of the government sector increased from 8.8% in 1953 to 15% in 1957. By the early 1960s this had grown to between 15% and 20%. Manufacturing accounted for 1% to 2% of GDP in this period and while agricultural activities had declined, they still contributed around 40% to the domestic product. Export agriculture (mainly sugar) accounted for about 30%. Data available for the mid-1980s indicate that agriculture's share in GDP has fallen to about 12%. Sugar cane alone accounts for about 8%. The manufacturing sector contributes around 14%, while Government services amount to 18% to 20% of GDP.

St Vincent

During the 1960s agriculture accounted for between 30% and 40% of GDP. Export agriculture (bananas and to a lesser extent arrowroot, nutmegs and mace, coconuts and copra, sweet potatoes, cassava starch, ground nuts and cocoa) generally accounted for more than half of this. By the 1960s sea-island cotton, once the pride of St Vincent, had virtually disappeared as an export activity. During the 1960s manufacturing activities were confined largely to the processing of oil from copra, rum making, aerated beverages, bakeries, ice making, tailoring, dressmaking and cigarettes. In 1963 this sector contributed only 4% to GDP, but by 1984 this contribution had grown to 10%. This latter figure reflects the establishment of certain assembly type operations. Corresponding with the growth of manufacturing and tourism, agriculture has tended to decline, amounting to about 17% of GDP in 1984.

St Lucia

In 1964 agriculture was the largest single sector in the St Lucian economy, accounting for about 35% of GDP. Export agriculture (mainly bananas, copra, cocoa, nutmegs and mace) contributed 24% to this figure. Manufacturing, whose share amounted to about 5%, consisted largely of a few simple activities such as rum making and the processing of coconut products such as edible oil, soap, coconut meal or cake baking, tailoring, concrete blocks, aerated drinks and ice. As a result of the promotion of the garment industry and the setting up of a number of assembly type operations, the share of manufacturing in GDP is estimated to have reached about 12%. In 1984 agriculture's share (which is dominated by bananas) had dropped to 14%. Despite the decline of agriculture in GDP (which to some extent has been influenced by the growth of other sectors of the economy), the government's policy in recent years has been geared towards the promotion of a tri-sector economy based on agriculture, manufacturing and tourism. In recent times the latter has gained a significant position in the economy in terms of employment and foreign exchange earnings.

Trinidad and Tobago

In the early 1950s agriculture was estimated to account for about 17% to 18% of GDP (at current factor cost). By the early 1960s this had fallen to about 10%, and by the early 1980s to about 3%. In real terms there has been a noticeable decline in real value-added in this sector in recent years. At 1970 prices the contribution amounted to TT$100.6 million in 1975, but by 1984 the figure is estimated to have dropped to TT$78.7 million. In the early 1950s the petroleum sector contributed between 25% and 30% to GDP in current dollars. By the early 1970s this share had fallen to around 20%. As a result of oil price increases in the early 1970s the percentage contribution of this sector jumped from 20% in 1972 to 48% in 1975. The recent decline in oil prices has affected the performance of this sector, and in 1983 its contribution is estimated to have fallen to 24%. In real terms petroleum's share in 1986 amounted to about 16% as compared to about 10% in 1983. In recent years the contribution of the manufacturing sector to current GDP has averaged around 6% as compared to about 12% in the early 1950s. In real terms this sector's contribution has averaged about 10% in recent times. Since 1976 there has been an almost steady decline in real value-added in this sector.

Jamaica

The relative contribution of agriculture to Jamaica's GDP has declined significantly since the 1950s. In 1950 the value-added in 'agriculture, forestry and fishing' was larger than that of any other sector, amounting to 30% of GDP (at current factor cost). The contribution of the mining sector was negligible, while manufacturing's share amounted to around 11%. By the early 1980s agriculture's contribution had fallen dramatically to less than 10%, while manufacturing's share had increased to between 16% and 19%. One of the main features of the post-war Jamaican economy has been the emergence of the mining sector (particularly bauxite) and the growth of tourism. By the mid-1970s the contribution of the mining sector had increased to over 10%. Because of the difficulties facing the bauxite sector this share had declined to less than 5% by 1983. In real terms, mining's share in 1985 was estimated to be about 5% as compared to 9% for agriculture, 16% for manufacturing and 18% for government. Despite the growth of some non-traditional exports in recent years, three products, bauxite, alumina and sugar still accounted for 70% of the value of domestic exports in 1984.

In recent years the Jamaican economy has been facing serious economic problems. Between 1973 and 1980 the economy experienced a positive real rate of growth in only two years and in both cases this was less than 1%. In 1981 the real growth rate was 3.3%, in 1982 0.04%, in 1983 1.8% and 1984 0.5%, with −5.0% in 1985.

The emergence of the manufacturing sector

One of the main objectives of Caribbean governments in the post-independence period has been to diversify the structure of production, which traditionally has been oriented towards providing food and raw materials for the British market. If political independence were to have any meaning, it was widely felt that the colonial economies had to be transformed in a way that would reduce vulnerability to external developments. This meant reducing reliance on a few commodities (sugar, bananas, citrus, cocoa, etc.), as well as diversification of markets and sources of supply. For the Caribbean to develop, it was widely held that the growth of the manufacturing sector was crucial to the process. During the 1950s a number of light industries were set up in the Caribbean as a result of the shortages created by World War II and the promotional efforts of the local governments. During the 1960s and 1970s these efforts were intensified resulting in an expansion of manufacturing activities aimed mainly at the local and regional markets.

Many of the objectives aimed at in the industrialisation strategy have not materialised, and this has led to some re-thinking of the import substitution strategy which was generally embraced. Preoccupation with the establishment of an industrial base has led in many cases to a severe neglect of both domestic and export agriculture. Inadequate attention to agricultural credit, land tenure problems, access roads, marketing, remuneration to farmers and technical assistance has taken a heavy toll on agricultural production. The traditional dominant plantation system has raised from time to time the issue of land use in the context of agricultural reorganisation and the increasing costs of producing export crops. Even after the nationalisation of the foreign-owned plantations in the 1970s progress towards a more rational use of land resources has been slow, both at the national and regional levels. The increasing dependence by the region on imported food is not altogether the result of climatic conditions or factor availability, but the result of a lack of adequate policies to protect and advance agriculture. This has stemmed from a particular conceptualisation of development, which saw modernisation as essentially the production of industrial goods.

The structure of production in 1963 and 1984 is set out in Table 2.5. While agriculture is still an important sector in most Caribbean economies, there has been a steady decline over the years in its contribution to GDP, exports and employment. For instance, in 1954, agriculture, forestry and fishing accounted for 28% of Guyana's GDP as compared to 24% in 1983. For Barbados, the figure fell from 35% to 7% over the period, while for Trinidad it fell from 19% to 3%. In 1953, agriculture contributed 21% to Jamaica's output as compared to 7% in 1983, while for the smaller islands the percentage share declined from over 40% in the early 1950s to between 5% and 30% in the early 1980s. While part of this decline is attributable to the emergence of other activities, there is no doubt that the problems faced by such traditional export crops like sugar, cocoa, citrus, coffee, etc., have had an effect. The perception that agriculture was associated with backwardness and underdevelopment had a major influence on development policies which tended to put emphasis on other areas particularly manufacturing which was seen to be synonymous with development. In this context, the approach taken towards agriculture was ambivalent. The consequence was that not only did the export component decline, but the role of agriculture as a source of food and raw materials did not materialise in a significant way. Countries which are basically agricultural in nature now find themselves increasingly dependent on foreign sources to satisfy both the domestic food requirements and the needs of the tourist industry which has been expanding in all the countries of the region.

In Table 2.6 we show the growth of the manufacturing sector in four major Commonwealth Caribbean countries since 1970. In the case of Barbados, real value-added in the sector increased from B$55.5 million in 1971 to B$98.4 million in 1980. The subsequent figure reflects the stagnation which has set in since. As a percentage of GDP, the figure increased from about 9% in 1971 to almost 13% in 1978. There has been a slight drop in the contribution since. An examination of the figures relating to Jamaica will show that real value-added in the manufacturing sector has declined almost steadily since 1973. The 1985 figure was 26% below that of 1973. As a percentage of GDP, manufacturing's contribution amounted to almost 18% in 1973, but has averaged around 16% since 1978. In the case of Trinidad and Tobago real value-added in the sector doubled between 1970 and 1980, but since then the figure has fluctuated within a declining trend. Between the beginning and end of the 1970s decade the percentage contribution to total output increased from around 9% to 11%, but since then it has averaged around 10%. In the case of Guyana, real value-added in the manufacturing sector increased steadily between 1970 and 1981, but has tended to decline since, both in value terms and as a percentage of GDP.

With respect to the structure of the sector, data are not readily available. Generally, activities tend to centre around consumer goods, involving varying degrees of local value-added. Besides simple manufactures (food beverages, cigarettes, garments, bricks, furniture, etc.), some countries have now added assembly-type operations to the range of activities. These include not only consumer durable goods but also electrical components and equipment. In the case of Trinidad and Tobago, food, drink, tobacco and petro-chemicals accounted for 60% of real value-added in the manufacturing sector in 1985. The assembly industries (including motor vehicles) which have been declining since 1981 contributed 18%. With respect to Jamaica, food, beverages and tobacco products accounted for over half of the real output in manufacturing in 1983.

The process of industrialisation in the Caribbean has taken place within a framework of national import substitution strategies. The approach has been essentially an insular one, with little or no co-ordination taking place among the various states. This has inevitably resulted in a great deal of duplication and a wastage of scarce resources. Small operations often involve high per unit costs, and the survival of many industries, therefore, often depends on a certain level of protection.[6] Given the high costs and in some cases poor quality of the products, the majority of the firms have found it difficult to sell beyond the local or regional markets. The tendency in recent years for member states of CARICOM to protect national markets is one of the factors contributing to the poor performance of the sector. Given the heavy dependence on foreign inputs, the unavailability of foreign exchange has in some cases, also affected performance. Generally, the sector is a net user of foreign exchange. The way it has evolved raises a number of fundamental issues for future policy, and it is therefore necessary to go into the background of its growth.

Even before the trend towards political independence began in

Table 2.5 Commonwealth Caribbean: Sectoral contribution to GDP at current factor cost, 1963 and 1984 (Percentages)

Sectors	Antigua 1963	Antigua 1984	Bahamas 1970	Barbados 1963	Barbados 1984	Belize 1965	Belize 1984	Dominica 1963	Dominica 1984	Grenada 1963	Grenada 1980	Guyana 1963	Guyana 1984
Agriculture[1]	18.2	5.2	3.6	29.8	6.7	40.8	20.8	35.4	28.4	34.7	26.2	38.8	24.6
(export)	(13.6)	(n.a.)	(n.a.)	(24.4)	(2.8)	(16.1)	(n.a.)	(21.6)	(n.a.)	(20.6)	(n.a.)	(30.0)	(10.8)
Mining & quarrying	a	0.7	0.6	a	1.4	0.5	0.2	a	0.7	a	0.1	13.0	4.6
Manufacturing	2.7	4.9	9.0	8.9	13.3	12.7	14.6	5.9	7.0	4.7	2.4	5.8	13.0
(sugar & by-products)	(n.a)	(—)	(—)	(n.a.)	(n.a.)	(n.a.)	(n.a.)	(—)	(—)	(n.a.)	(n.a.)	(n.a.)	(2.6)
Construction	16.1	5.9	14.5	9.4	6.9	8.9	5.8	8.8	7.4	6.7	8.9	5.0	7.1
Utilities[2]	a	2.6	2.7	a	3.3	0.5	2.0	a	2.8	a	1.7	a	a
Wholesale and retail trade	15.6	11.1	7.2	22.2	19.9	5.6	17.5	5.8	7.4	13.3	13.7	13.3	8.9
Hotels & restaurants	9.1	15.2	19.4	a	10.0	a	b	a	1.1	a	2.5	a	a
Transport & communication	4.0	16.0	11.6	5.6	8.2	6.9	11.0	3.2	11.0	3.5	5.9	6.6	7.0
Banking & insurance	4.0	6.3	8.4	a	13.1	0.7	10.6	2.6	5.2	4.4	a	3.1	6.7
Real estate & housing	a	11.8	a	5.0	a	a	a	a	4.7	a	a	a	a
Government services	19.0	15.1	12.3	9.6	14.3	5.6	10.4	16.0	23.0	14.3	19.9	10.2	22.3
Other	11.3	5.4	10.7	9.5	2.9	19.1	5.8	22.3	1.3	18.4	18.7	4.2	5.8
Total	100.0	100.0	100.0	100.0	100.0	100.0	100.0	100.0	100.0	100.0	100.0	100.0	100.0

Sectors	Jamaica 1963	Jamaica 1984	Montserrat 1963	Montserrat 1984	St Kitts-Nevis 1963	St Kitts-Nevis 1984	St Lucia 1964	St Lucia 1984	St Vincent 1963	St Vincent 1984	Trinidad & Tobago 1962	Trinidad & Tobago 1984
Agriculture[1]	13.4	5.4	35.2	4.6	41.4	11.9	35.0	12.9	32.5	16.5	10.3	4.5
(export)	(6.8)	(1.1)	(4.3)	(n.a.)	(30.3)	(8.6)	(23.8)	(n.a.)	(19.3)	(n.a.)	(n.a.)	(0.1)
Mining & quarrying	8.9	8.5	a	1.0	a	0.2	a	1.0	a	0.3	29.4	25.8
Manufacturing	15.4	18.9	2.1	6.2	2.1	13.8	5.3	9.6	4.1	9.5	13.1	7.5
(sugar & by-products)	(3.3)	(0.4)	(n.a.)	(—)	(n.a.)	(5.2)	(n.a.)	(—)	(n.a.)	(n.a.)	(1.6)	(n.a.)
Construction	10.2	8.7	14.9	6.7	9.7	7.9	9.2	6.2	6.3	10.6	5.5	12.4
Utilities[2]	1.2	3.1	a	4.1	a	1.1	a	3.6	a	3.0	4.1	2.0
Wholesale and retail trade	15.1	19.8	10.8	17.0	11.2	12.9	17.8	14.3	14.5	11.2	13.4	6.8
Hotels & restaurants	2.0	1.8	a	4.4	6.5	3.3	1.5	6.6	1.2	2.0	a	0.4
Transport & communication	7.4	6.4	1.0	9.4	2.2	13.0	3.0	10.0	3.0	15.5	3.9	17.7
Banking & insurance	3.7	6.1	a	5.1	3.5	5.8	b	7.0	4.3	6.0	2.1	12.0
Real estate & housing	a	8.3	a	16.0	a	5.7	a	5.1	a	4.0	c	c
Government services	7.3	11.6	25.5	9.2	17.0	19.0	18.1	19.6	19.1	18.7	10.0	13.9
Other	15.4	1.4	10.5	16.3	6.4	5.4	10.1	4.1	15.0	2.7	8.2	3.0
Total	100.0	100.0	100.0	100.0	100.0	100.0	100.0	100.0	100.0	100.0	100.0	100.0

(—) nil
n.a. Not available
a. Included in 'other'.
b. Included in 'wholesale and retail trade'.
1. Includes forestry, fishing and livestock.
2. Essentially 'electricity and water'.
c. Included in 'banking and insurance'.

Source: Official Publications and Statistical Departments; Publications of the British Development Division in the Caribbean; ECLA, *Economic Activity In Caribbean Countries*, Various Issues; CARICOM Secretariat, *Statistics Digest*, 1970–81; OECS, *National Accounts Digest*, 1985.

Table 2.6 Contribution of manufacturing to GDP (factor cost) in real terms for selected countries, 1970–85

	Barbados		Jamaica		Trinidad & Tobago		Guyana	
Year	Real Value-added in manufacturing (1) B$mn	(1) as a % of GDP (2)	Real Value-added in manufacturing[1] (3) J$mn	(3) as a % of GDP (4)	Real Value-added in manufacturing (5) TT$mn	(5) as a % of GDP (6)	Real Value added in manufacturing (7) G$mn	(7) as a % in GDP (8)
1970	n.a.	n.a.	348.4	17.6	150.7	9.3	80	9.4
1971	55.5	8.8	356.5	17.4	157.2	9.3	94	10.6
1972	61.3	9.6	398.2	17.8	176.8	9.9	91	10.9
1973	65.7	10.0	400.7	17.9	174.3	9.0	86	9.9
1974	62.6	9.8	387.2	18.0	176.6	7.4	108	11.5
1975	69.3	11.0	396.0	18.5	188.5	9.3	119	11.5
1976	81.0	12.4	378.6	18.8	217.4	9.9	122	11.6
1977	83.6	12.3	350.5	17.9	244.0	9.9	123	12.0
1978	91.2	12.8	334.1	16.0	256.6	11.0	126	12.7
1979	92.8	12.1	317.8	16.4	280.0	11.3	131	13.4
1980	98.8	11.8	280.9	15.4	301.2	10.7	132	13.3
1981	91.4	11.6	282.7	15.0	294.1	10.5	140	14.1
1982	86.5	11.6	300.9	15.9	295.7	9.9	122	13.8
1983	88.7	11.8	306.7	15.9	290.6	10.5	102	12.7
1984[P]	90.4	11.6	294.4	15.2	252.6	10.4	96	11.7
1985[P]	n.a.	n.a.	296.4	16.1	216.5	9.2	93	11.2

[1] GDP at market prices   P Provisional   n.a. not available.
Sources: Official Publications

the early 1960s, the development of the manufacturing sector was seen as an integral part of the modernisation process. The most influential West Indian economist in the 1950s, Sir Arthur Lewis,[7] felt that agriculture as it was then organised could not provide jobs for a rapidly expanding population. In any event there were already too many people in the agricultural sector, and if productivity was to be increased in this sector, the excess labour had to be removed. Manufacturing held the key to the unemployment problem. Since Caribbean countries were short on capital and entrepreneurship, it was necessary to attract foreign investors. Reinvestment of profits would lead to an increasingly larger manufacturing sector which would provide jobs not only for the excess labour in agriculture, but for the natural increase in population. The supply of labour was assumed to be unlimited. Given the small size of the domestic market, Lewis advised that manufacturing should be promoted on a regional basis and production should be geared to export markets.

In order to attract foreign investors, Caribbean governments adopted several different measures. These included exemption from the payment of income taxes for a specified period, accelerated depreciation allowances, protection from foreign competition, exemption from the payment of duty on raw materials and capital equipment and the provision of industrial estates and other basic infrastructure. There was some controversy over the importance of the tax holiday incentives, since it was felt in some quarters that the income exempted in the host country was taxed when remitted back home. The exemption of capital equipment was counter productive since it encouraged the use of capital intensive techniques when a major objective was to provide jobs. The protection from foreign competition was rationalised on the infant industry argument, which holds that in its early years, an enterprise needs protection to survive. As the enterprise grows up, it is better able to withstand competition, and the protection could then be relaxed.

The Lewis model was flawed in several respects. One of the most important weaknesses was the investment behaviour assumed. This was contrary to the *modus operandi* of the transnational corporation which subsequently emerged as the most important vehicle of private foreign investment. Experience has shown that profits are more likely to be remitted back to head office rather than reinvested. Certainly investors were attracted, but they fell largely into two classes: those who saw an advantage in the relatively low labour costs and those who wanted to preserve their markets. Quite often the presence of the foreign investor was in the form of licensing arrangements with local business cliques. The inability of the governments to create employment opportunities to absorb a growing labour force has tended to result in increased importance being attached to those industries which generally enjoy monopoly positions in the respective local markets. Such a situation has served to encourage high prices and poor quality, both of which tend to militate against exports. It is well known, too, that arrangements with parent firms often forbid exports to neighbouring countries or specified markets where the parent might have a competing establishment. In an atmosphere of over-protection, the 'infants' have found it difficult to grow up. The continued heavy dependence on outside sources for capital goods and raw materials and the decline of traditional exports have contributed to the recent stagnation of the sector in some states. The competition for foreign exchange, of course, has intensified as a result of the failure of these countries to feed themselves so increasing their dependence on imported food.

Concluding observations

In the mid-1980s most Commonwealth Caribbean countries are being confronted with serious economic problems. In the 1950s and 1960s, the economy of Trinidad and Tobago grew at around 3% in real terms. Because of the significant increases in the price of oil in the 1974−81 period, growth was in the region of 6%. Between 1982 and 1986 real output fell by about 27%, representing an average annual rate of decline of about 8%. Since 1982 the overall balance of payments position has been consistently negative. As a result, the net foreign reserves of the country declined from US$3203 million at the end of 1981 to US$318 million at the end of 1986. Guyana's economy has been in economic difficulties since the mid-1970s. Between 1973 and 1985 real GNP is estimated to have declined by an average rate of 1.2%. At 1977 prices GDP in 1985 was 21% below the 1976 level. The foreign exchange crisis has been particularly acute in Guyana as a result of problems facing the bauxite sector (the country's major foreign exchange earner) and the servicing of a bourgeoning external debt. The net foreign assets of the country declined from plus US$72.8 million at the end of 1975 to minus US$588 million at the end of September 1986. In Jamaica real GDP grew by an average rate of over 5% per year in the 1950s and 1960s, largely as a result of the inflows of foreign capital in the bauxite and tourism sectors. Between 1954 and 1961 this growth rate averaged almost 8%. In the 1960s and early 1970s it had declined, but was still in the region of 5%. The first oil shock in 1974 and problems in the bauxite sector conspired with a number of other factors in the mid-1970s to send the economy into a tailspin from which it is yet to recover despite several programmes of IMF adjustment measures. Between 1974 and 1980, there were negative growth rates in six years. There have been some signs of recovery, but the 1984 real output was still 15% below the 1973 level. Between 1973 and 1985 total real GNP is estimated to have declined by an average rate of 2.5%, compared to 3.5% for per capita GNP. The net foreign assets of the country fell from US$107.5 million at the end of September 1976 to minus US$1 224.4 million at the end of September 1986.

Though Barbados depends on imported oil to satisfy half of its domestic requirements, the oil shocks of the 1970s did not have a particularly severe impact on the Barbadian economy. The expansion in output in the 1960s continued into the 1970s at a rate of 4% to 5%. Since 1981, however, the economy has tended to stagnate. Output fell in 1981 and 1982 and though there has been some recovery, real GDP in 1985 was still 5% below the 1980 level. Despite the effects of the high oil prices and the recession of the early 1980s, real GNP in a number of regional states (the Bahamas, Antigua, St Lucia, St Vincent) grew at an average rate of over 4%. Others, like Belize, Grenada, Dominica and St Kitts-Nevis, experienced rates of between 2% and 3%. In a growth sense, the less developed countries of the region seemed to have fared better than the more developed countries in recent years.

The economic crisis has manifestations other than in growth performance, and one therefore has to be careful in thinking that countries whose output has grown are not experiencing serious social, financial and developmental problems. Almost all the countries of the region are having difficulties raising enough revenues to finance current expenditure. With little or no savings in the current account, governments have had to place great reliance on borrowing (both internal and external) and grants to finance development programmes. With the growth of this debt, servicing requirements have absorbed not only an increasing share of revenue, but also of foreign exchange earnings. Even in cases where the debt-service ratio (i.e. repayment of interest and principal on foreign debt as a proportion of foreign exchange earnings) may appear small, debt-service payments may still be burdensome in terms of the share of government revenue they are absorbing. Because the ability to service debt affects credit-worthiness, debt payments are often given high priority in the allocation of expenditure. Despite this, at least two countries in the region have found themselves in the position where they are unable to meet debt obligations and have fallen in arrears.

Another problem that affects all the countries in the region (without exception) is that of unemployment. Whatever may be the difficulties in defining who is employed, or who is not, there is no question that the task of creating enough jobs to occupy the labour force in the various territories remains one of the most challenging. Reliable data on employment and unemployment in most territories do not exist. Estimates on the proportion of the labour force willing to work, but unable to find jobs, vary widely. In Jamaica the official ratio has ranged between 20% and 30% in recent years. In countries such as Antigua, Grenada and St Vincent estimates put the ratio at well over 20%. In most other cases the figures range between 10% and 20%. Certain countries such as Barbados and Trinidad and Tobago, which had made some progress in reducing the ratio during the 1970s, now find themselves in a position where the numbers of unemployed are growing faster than the labour force. With respect to Barbados the unemployment ratio increased from 11% in 1981 to around 18% in mid-1986. In the case of Trinidad and Tobago the figure moved from less than 10% in 1980 to about 17% in 1986. Though the growth rate of the population has fallen in recent years, to below 2% in most cases, the tightening of controls in traditional emigration outlets has exacerbated the unemployment problem. Increased female participation has also been an element in the growth of the labour force, which has attained dimensions of around 2% to 3% in most cases.

The crisis facing the Commonwealth Caribbean has both an internal and external dimension. There is no doubt that the significant increases in oil prices during the 1970s and the fall in commodity prices associated with the international recession in the early 1980s have had a tremendous adverse impact on several Commonwealth Caribbean countries. The decline in foreign exchange earnings in the context of larger payments for a given volume of oil imports and higher levels of debt-service payments have resulted in a situation where some countries have been unable to pay for imports essential for the functioning of their economies and for social well being. The sectors dependent on foreign exchange availability were immediately affected. In an effort to deal with their payments problems two of the most severely affected countries resorted to trade restrictions which did not exclude intra-regional trade. This policy in turn invited retaliatory measures by some other member states of CARICOM, and this has had the effect of further restricting intra-regional trade.

Trinidad and Tobago, as an oil producer and exporter, benefited immensely from the high oil prices during the 1970s. Between 1974 and 1982 the government collected US$8.8 billion from the oil sector. Its total revenue between 1974 and 1982 amounted to US$14.5 billion. The boom resulting from government expenditure gave rise, to a high level of imports from both CARICOM and non-CARICOM countries. This was facilitated by an open trade policy which encouraged the establishment of enterprises in other CARICOM states, with the Trinidad and Tobago market as the main target. The decline in oil prices in recent years has forced this country to adopt a number of trade measures which has affected production, exports and employment in other CARICOM states, thus reinforcing the adverse consequences stemming from the international recession.

The problems besetting the international economy has certainly served to expose structural weaknesses in Commonwealth Caribbean economies and the inadequacies of certain kinds of policies. Domestic political and economic management, however, has also contributed to the crisis by its failure to mobilise adequately the region's human and non-human resources and to articulate a framework which would allow the region to maximise its benefits from contact with the international economy. The early post-independence years witnessed a preoccupation with taking control of the 'commanding heights' of the economy and the promotion of manufacturing as the main pivot of the transformation of the colonial economy. Sugar, bauxite, the financial sectors and later oil attracted early attention for local control, though the extent of national participation in ownership and the pace of localisation have varied widely. In this situation, an ambivalence towards foreign investment lingered on. In this early phase the craving for greater control of the national economy stemmed more from the desire to reinforce political sovereignty than as part of a development strategy. This may explain why some governments acquired enterprises for no obvious economic reason, or having acquired an asset it saw as part of the 'commanding heights' of the economy proceeded to run it almost exactly as it operated before. Localisation policies in some areas were pursued without examining the implications of small markets on efficiency and cost of operation. A political objective was often to break the power of local cliques who had collaborated with foreign interests in controlling local economic activities, and to spread ownership over a broader segment of the population.

With no clear idea of where to head, having localised significant portions of their economies, governments entered a stage of indecisiveness which played a crucial part in the emergence of the present crisis. As a result of poor management, state-acquired enterprises found themselves unable to cover operating costs and became dependent on the finances of the central government. In some cases production capacity was lost through inadequate maintenance stemming partly from the lack of spare parts which could not be obtained as a result of foreign exchange shortages. The lack of certain kinds of skills also contributed. Land has remained strongly devoted to traditional uses, while mineral resources such as bauxite continue to be exported in raw or semi-refined forms. In a real sense diversification which was seen as a major objective in the 1960s has eluded the Commonwealth Caribbean governments, and this constitutes one of the major weaknesses in Commonwealth Caribbean economies.

Oil and related products account for about 80% of Trinidad and Tobago's exports. In his 1987 Budget Speech, the Prime Minister and Minister of Finance and the Economy admitted: 'We achieved political independence...with an economy dependent on one single resource, oil. Twenty-five years later, we are more than ever dependent on the vagaries of the international oil market. In twenty-five years... we have failed to develop an economy sufficiently diversified and sufficiently resilient to absorb or even cushion the shocks caused by periodic crises on the international oil market. Sectors such as agriculture, manufacturing, tourism and services of various kinds have remained relatively insignificant, their potential for development almost untapped.' The fact that this statement could come after government expenditure in the region of TT$61.4 billion (US$25.6 billion) between 1974 and 1985 points to the fact that the problem was not simply one of the lack of capital. There have been other booms in the history of this country (though not of this magnitude) and of the region generally of which full advantage has not been taken.

There is little question that the region has failed to use its resources (human, financial, and physical) effectively. The decision by regional states to seek political independence separately laid the foundation for the individualist approach to economic development. This has resulted in the competitive, rather than complementary development which now characterises the region, despite formal commitment to a process of integration. Since independence, development policy has been conceived on the basis of the problems, resources and limitations of individual countries. Insular political sovereignty, despite the political rhetoric of oneness among Caribbean peoples, has been guarded jealously. Any suggestion of implementing policies which could result in the loss of political sovereignty, or which seem to be in favour of a sister territory have been viewed with suspicion. Golden opportunities have been lost as a result of this attitude. Some projects which would not make economic sense for an individual country could do so in a regional setting. Commonwealth Caribbean governments have hesitated to deepen the integration process, even while seeing their economies succumb to the pressures of international developments, and also while being aware of the limitations of this highly individualistic approach to development in the region. The problems do not have their entire bases in the international economy.

Notes

1 This was articulated in two pieces: W. Arthur Lewis, *Industrial Development in the Caribbean,* Port-of-Spain: Caribbean Commission Central Secretariat, 1951; and 'Economic Development with Unlimited Supplies of Labour', *Manchester School,* 1954.
2 This thesis is well developed in Raul Prebisch, *The Economic Development of Latin America and its Principal Problems,* New York: U.N. 1950.
3 See Jamaica's *Five Year Independence Plan, 1963—1968,* p.14.
4 'In a plantation hinterland, the dominant unit of production is a subsidiary or affiliate of a metropolitan firm. Its purpose is to extract the staple. To this end, it is typically organized as a total institution in the fashion of a plantation. That is to say, in regard to the hinterland, it tends to be a self contained unit. Its primary links are external and almost exclusively with the parent firm in the metropole.' See K. Levitt and L. Best, 'Character of Caribbean Economy', in G.L. Beckford (ed.) *Caribbean Economy,* Kingston: ISER, 1975.
5 This observation is well argued by N. Girvan and O. Jefferson, 'Corporate versus Caribbean Integration', in *Readings in the Political Economy of the Caribbean,* Kingston: New World Group Ltd., 1972, edited by the same authors.
6 Writing with respect to the Jamaican experience, Mahmood Ali Ayub makes the following observation. 'The overall picture of the manufacturing sector that emerges confirms the generally held view of a highly protected domestic market with nominal protection on outputs amounting to about 35 per cent and effective protection of about 70 per cent'. See Mahmood Ali Ayub, *Made in Jamaica: The Development of the Manufacturing Sector,* Baltimore: The Johns Hopkins University Press, 1981, p. 80.
7 W. Arthur Lewis, *op. cit.*

CHAPTER 3

Major sectors of the Commonwealth Caribbean economy in a world context

While the export of manufactured goods from a few developing countries has grown over the last two decades, primary commodities continue to feature prominently in the export trade of poor countries. Commodity exports (including oil) in the 1970s accounted for almost 80% of the total export of goods earnings of the developing countries taken together.[1] As indicated several times earlier, Commonwealth Caribbean countries continue to be heavily dependent on a narrow range of activities for foreign exchange earnings. One consequence of this concentration is that a great deal of instability is experienced in foreign income as a result of variation in prices or production. To deal with this problem three complementary approaches have been followed in recent years. First, there is the long term solution which relates to the attempts being made by the countries themselves to diversify the range of their exports. At the global level efforts have been made (albeit with limited success) to stabilise commodity prices through international commodity agreements and the formation of producer organisations. The third approach has been the setting up of compensatory financing facilities designed to help countries experiencing export shortfalls.

Developing nations which are dependent on a narrow range of commodities for their foreign exchange earnings have long recognised the need to diversify their export base. As can be seen in Table 3.1, which shows the price trends for a few major commodities over the period 1950–85, prices can fluctuate widely over a very short space of time. Such fluctuations, of course, have a direct impact on foreign earnings and government revenue, and this can seriously affect a government's ability to plan its activities properly since import capacity is inevitably affected by foreign exchange availability. In periods of boom high prices often encourage governments to expand the scale of their operations as they try to foster new productive activities and increase the welfare of the population. Of course, when prices drop, the fall in real income which this may necessitate is often difficult to manage, since the population would have adjusted their lifestyles to the level of income attained in the boom years. The government itself may become saddled with a level of activity which its lower revenue base can no longer support. The experience of the 1970s oil boom has shown how easy it is for governments to lose sight of the need to diversify their export base in the absence of a foreign exchange problem. What it also proved is that the availability of foreign exchange by itself is not a sufficient condition for economic diversification and the generation of permanent job opportunities. For a variety of reasons, developing countries have found it difficult to diversify their economic structure at a pace they would like, and in a large number of cases they continue to be buffeted by the vagaries of commodity prices.[2]

In the early post-war years it was recognised that there was a need for agreement between producers and consumers in order to avoid excessive fluctuation in prices. The approach adopted was a case by case one which succeeded in producing fully-fledged international commodity agreements involving only about six commodities, namely wheat, sugar, tin, rubber, coffee and cocoa.[3] These agreements (which have been renegotiated from time to time) have contributed only to a limited extent in the stabilisation of their prices. UNCTAD feels that the problem of commodities ought to be treated in a more comrehensive and systematic way. In this connection it has suggested an Integrated Programme for Commodities, which was adopted at the Fourth Session of the UNCTAD in Nairobi in May, 1976. The Integrated Programme comprises five basic elements:

1. The establishment of internationally-owned stocks covering a wide range of commodities.
2. The establishment of a common financing fund, that will make resources available for the acquisition of stocks.
3. The institution, in circumstances which justify it, of a system of medium to long term commitments to purchase and sell commodities at agreed prices.
4. The institution of more adequate measures than are at present available to provide compensatory financing to producers to cover shortfalls in export earnings.
5. The initiation of an extensive programme of measures to further the processing of commodities by the producing countries themselves.

The programme proposed is intended to cover a range of commodities of interest to developing countries. A list of 17 commodities has been suggested. Included in the list are ten 'core' commodities which are not only regarded as storable products suitable for international stocking schemes, but are subject to excessive fluctuations in prices and export earnings. They are: coffee, cocoa, tea, sugar, cotton, rubber, jute, sisal, copper and tin. The other seven are:

58 The Commonwealth Caribbean

Table 3.1 Prices of selected commodities, 1950–1985

Year	World, raw sugar[1] US cents/kg Current $	1980 Constant $	Petroleum (Saudi Arabian market) Crude USA.barrel Current $	1980 Constant $	Aluminum[3] (New York market) US$/metric ton Current $	Constant $	Bauxite[4] US$/metric ton Current $	Constant $	Bananas[5] US cents/kg Current $	Constant $
1950	10.98	48.58	1.7	7.5	390	1726	7.50	33.19	16.1	71.2
1955	7.14	26.94	1.9	7.2	522	1970	7.50	28.30	16.5	62.3
1960	6.92	24.11	1.9	6.6	573	1997	7.50	26.13	14.3	49.8
1965	4.45	14.83	1.8	6.0	540	1800	7.50	25.00	15.9	53.0
1970	8.11	23.24	1.8	5.2	633	1814	12.00	34.38	16.6	47.6
1971	9.92	26.96	2.2	6.0	634	1736	12.00	32.61	14.0	38.0
1972	16.03	40.08	2.5	6.3	582	1455	12.00	30.00	16.2	40.5
1973	20.83	44.89	3.3	7.1	551	1188	12.50	26.94	16.5	35.6
1974	65.39	115.73	9.6	17.0	752	1331	23.20	41.06	18.4	32.6
1975	44.91	71.50	10.5	16.7	877	1397	25.34	40.29	24.7	39.3
1976	25.49	40.02	11.5	18.1	978	1535	27.20	42.70	25.7	40.4
1977	17.90	25.37	12.4	17.7	1132	1617	30.80	44.00	27.5	34.3
1978	17.20	21.37	12.7	15.8	1170	1453	34.30	42.61	28.7	35.7
1979	21.30	23.36	17.3	19.0	1310	1436	36.60	40.13	32.6	35.8

Table 3.1 (Cont'd)

Year	World, raw sugar[1] US cents/kg Current $	1980 Constant $	Petroleum (Saudi Arabian market) Crude USA.barrel Current $	1980 Constant $	Aluminum[3] (New York market) US$/metric ton Current $	Constant $	Bauxite[4] US$/metric ton Current $	Constant $	Bananas[5] US cents/kg Current $	Constant $
1980	63.20	63.20	29.4	29.4	1534	1534	41.20	41.20	37.9	37.9
1981	37.40	37.21	33.2	33.0	1676	1668	40.00	39.80	40.1	39.9
1982	18.56	19.02	34.0	34.8	1712	1717	36.00	36.89	37.4	38.3
1983	18.67	19.37	29.5	30.6	1712	1776	34.70	36.00	42.9	44.5
1984	11.47	12.11	29.0	30.6	1786	1886	33.20	35.06	37.0	39.1
1985[2]	8.36	—	28.1	—	1786	—	31.50	—	39.8	—

[1] From 1950 to 1960 quotations refer to New York World Contract No. 4, f.a.s. Cuba; beginning 1961 International Sugar Council 'World' daily price, f.o.a., and stowed Caribbean ports.

[2] January-October.

[3] For 1950–59 primary pig; 1960 onwards unalloyed ingot, 99.5%, producer list price.

[4] US import reference price based on imports from Jamaica.

[5] From 1950 to November 1961, Central American importer to jobber f.o.b. port of entry, 1001b series. From December 1961, first class green stems from Central America and Ecuador, importer to jobber or processor, f.o.b. port of entry; 1001b series up to 1962; from 1963, 401b boxes.

Source: World Bank, *Commodity Trade and Price Trends*, 1986 edition.

wheat, rice, bananas, beef and veal, wool, bauxite and iron ore. While the UNCTAD commodities form only about 5% ('core' commodities) or about 10% (all commodities) of the imports of the developed countries (excluding the Centrally Planned Economies) they constitute a much higher proportion of poor countries' exports.[4]

The Integrated Programme has been extremely slow in implementation and developing countries have had to rely on other mechanisms to deal with the problem of fluctuations in export earnings. One of the most important of these is the compensatory financing facility, two of the best examples of which are operated by the IMF and the European Community (EC) respectively. The IMF's compensatory financing facility was established in 1963 with the aim of providing additional assistance to member countries experiencing balance of payments difficulties stemming from export shortfalls that are viewed as temporary and largely attributed to circumstances beyond the member's control.

Inclusion of arrangements for the stabilisation of export earnings of African, Caribbean and Pacific countries (ACP) in the first Lomé Convention, concluded in 1975, was regarded as a very innovative feature of the EC's association policy. Prior to this, arrangements largely centred around trade co-operation, financial aid and technical assistance. One of the distinct features of the stabilisation of export earnings scheme (STABEX) operated by the EC is that it is limited to a certain list of goods. When the first Lomé Convention was signed the list included twelve products, but seven more were added in 1977. The products are largely agricultural commodities. Attempts to include mineral products have been resisted by the EC on the grounds that the scheme would be too expensive to administer. The STABEX arrangements made in the present Lomé Convention (Lomé III was signed on 8 December 1984) include some 48 products. An amount of 925 million ECU has been allocated to the system for the duration of the Convention, or almost 11% of the total financial resources provided under Lomé III.

To qualify for assistance on the basis of any of the approved products, earnings from the export of that product to all destinations (re-exports excluded) in the year preceding the year of application are required to represent 6% of the country's earnings from exports of goods. The percentage for sisal is 4.5%. In the case of the least developed, landlocked and island ACP states, the percentage is 1.5%. This is often referred to as the 'dependence threshold'. The second criterion that has to be met before a transfer is effected is a 'fluctuation threshold' and this requires that earnings from the export of the product to the Community be at least 6% below the reference level (1.5% for the least developed, landlocked or island countries). The reference level is taken as the average export earnings in the four years (three years in certain cases) preceding the year of calculation.

One of the major purposes of commodity agreements is to bring both producers and consumers together with the aim of achieving some degree of stability in the particular market. As indicated earlier, this has not been possible for a large number of commodities. A different approach used by producers, particularly since the early 1970s is to take unilateral action by forming producer organisations[5] in the hope that through consultation, exchange of information and co-ordination of policies they would be able to avoid excessive price fluctuations — something they could not do individually. The Charter of Economic Rights and Duties adopted by the UN in 1974 recognises the rights of states to exercise sovereignty over their natural resources and to form producer organisations. The best known of such organisations is the Organisation of Petroleum Exporting Countries (OPEC) which was formed by Iraq, Kuwait, Saudi Arabia, Iran and Venezuela[6] as far back as 1960, largely as a consultative body in response to a declining price trend. The original main purpose was 'to study and formulate a system to ensure the stabilisation of prices...', but OPEC was not able to exert any significant influence on prices until the 1970s following the Arab-Israeli conflict of 1973. The OPEC approach inspired producers of other raw materials who saw in it a strategy to advance mutual interests. The Intergovernmental Council of Copper Exporting Countries (CIPEC)[7] was formed in 1967 (by Chile, Peru, Zaïre and Zambia) for among other things to foster, through the expansion of the industry, dynamic and continuous growth of real earnings from copper exports...'. In a similar vein the International Bauxite Association (IBA)[8] was formed in 1974 by the world's major bauxite producers with the purpose of 'promoting the rational and orderly development of the bauxite industry and to guarantee member countries that the exploitation, transformation, and marketing of bauxite will assure them a "just and reasonable" real income' (Nairobi Resolution, 93IV).[9] Producers of other mineral resources such as iron ore, phosphates and mercury also tend to undertake a fair measure of collaboration.[10] OPEC-type producer organisations are not limited to minerals. In 1974 seven Latin American countries[11] joined to form the Union de Paises Exportadores del Banano (Union of Banana Exporting Countries) in the hope that such co-operation could halt the continued slide in real prices. 'Some banana exporting countries had to grant subsidies to growers in order to cope with rising costs and sustain their exports.'[12] The Association of Natural Rubber Producing Countries was also formed in the 1970s in response to the same kinds of concerns shared by other commodity producers.

While there was a broad range of considerations motivating the formation of such organisations by primary producers, there is no doubt that the major concern was the desire to get better prices for their raw material exports. Some countries also saw the need for greater local processing in order to diversify domestic production and generate employment and revenue. There are several aspects to the price question. Some economists have long argued that there is a chronic tendency for the terms of trade to move against primary producers as a result of the low-income elasticity of demand for food products, the substitution of natural materials by synthetics and technological break-throughs which permit more economic use of raw materials in the developed countries.[13] On the other hand because of their dependence on the rich countries to supply manufactured goods, they have had no choice but to pay the higher prices associated with these imports – prices which have increased at a faster rate than those of their primary exports.[14] The advantages of technological developments in rich countries, it is argued, are not generally shared by poor states in the form of lower prices.[15] There is another factor complicating the price question. In developing countries exploitation of domestic resources has traditionally been carried on by vertically integrated transnational corporations (TNCs) operating in more than one country. Such companies are involved not only in the mining (or growing) end, but in smelting (or processing), transport, manufacturing, and marketing. Because of the intra-firm nature of the transactions, taxing such companies is not an easy matter since prices used are deliberately aimed at minimising tax payments. Given that it is their overall financial situation that matters, transnationals often respond to tax measures by shifting production from one part of their global operations to another, and this flexibility serves to weaken the bargaining position of host states.

With respect to the ability to influence prices, other producer organisations have not been as effective as OPEC. The latter's basic strength has been derived from the absence of competitive substitutes for petroleum as a source of energy, at least in the short term. The fact that OPEC is responsible for a substantial proportion of world production[16] with exports contributing to this strength, is as important as the fact that all member states are developing countries with certain common interests.[17] The latter point has generally served to overcome differences arising from political outlook or geographical location. With the formation of producer organisations, certain industrial states saw in such a strategy a threat to their security since the traditional easy access to a wide range of critical raw materials appeared to be in jeopardy.[18] Fear of retaliation in the form of aid reduction and market loss has no doubt affected the stance of the more vulnerable members of other producer clubs on the question of price adjustments. Some (like the IBA) do not control production levels or are weakened by not having major producers of the commodity within the fold. Organisations involving products with economically close substitutes or where members are divided with respect to strategy, have found their effectiveness considerably hampered. The transnationals themselves have reacted in some cases by shifting production to more favourable locations,[19] and the co-operation within certain producer organisations appears not to be enough to discourage this practice. There is evidence of pressure being brought to bear on individual member states by companies not to adhere to the rules of their organisations.[20]

In the following section we discuss some of the problems facing major sectors of the Caribbean economy against the background of developments in the world economy. The discussion focuses not only on commodities, but on tourism which accounts for a significant part of the economic activity in most Caribbean countries.

Sugar

Sugar can be obtained from a number of different plants. The world's two main commercial sources, however, are the sugar cane and sugar beet. The former is grown in tropical climates while the latter is cultivated in temperate countries. Some countries, whose location and size give rise to variety in climatic conditions (e.g. the US), grow both sugar cane and sugar beet. Sugar is one of the most widely produced agricultural commodities in the world, being found in both developed and developing countries. At the turn of the century beet sugar accounted for one-half of world centrifugal sugar production. Cane sugar, however, gradually increased its share until it accounted for some 70% in the 1945–46 period. With the encouragement given to beet sugar production after the war, cane sugar's share fell to less than 60% of the world total by 1960. In the drive for greater self-sufficiency, sugar production has increased in both beet and sugar producing countries. New producers have also entered the market. As a result of research and the application of improved methods of production, yields in beet producing countries have increased tremendously in recent years. Europe has gone from a net importer of sugar to a net exporter with 20% of the world market. Despite these developments, however, sugar production from cane has remained at about 60% of world total sugar production in recent years.

Only a part of world sugar production is traded on the open market. It is estimated that over half of current net world sugar exports are taken by a few preferential markets. The bulk of the sugar going into the free market is of cane origin. Traditionally, the major part of the sugar exported by Commonwealth Caribbean countries has gone to the UK market where these countries enjoy protection and the advantage of a negotiated price which generally has been above the world free market price. The latter fluctuates widely in response to supply and demand factors.

While the US produces sugar, it does not produce enough to meet its domestic requirements. Until recently, the distribution between domestic and foreign supply quotas was determined by the 1948 Sugar Act and its subsequent amendments. This Act was abandoned some years ago and annual quotas are now determined by the US Department of Agriculture. These quotas, which are highly influenced by US domestic farm policy, lobbying by domestic interests and by US foreign policy, are basically aimed at protecting high cost local sugar producers. The attractiveness of the US as a market is that it pays a premium price (several times the world price) in order to maintain parity with production costs for US sugar producers. The costs are passed on to consumers and, therefore, do not represent a call on the Treasury. One of the implications, of course, of keeping the price of sugar artificially high is that it encourages the production of substitute sweeteners.

In recent years US sugar import quotas have tended to fall. In 1974 sugar imports accounted for 51% of domestic sugar requirements, but this has now fallen to less than 40%. The total dropped from nearly 5 million short tons in 1980–81 to about 2.3 million short tons in 1984–85. Per capita consumption of sugar peaked at 102.3 lb in 1972 but this declined to 79.4 lb in 1981 and 67.5 lb in 1984. The combined US sugar quota for the six CARICOM countries that export sugar dropped from 162516 short tons in 1983–84 to 53440 short tons in 1987 or by 67.2%. Because of lack of access to lower cost sugar from outside a number of refineries in the US are reportedly threatened with closure since they cannot compete with the artificial sweeteners. What are the factors behind this increasingly protective stance of a country that is said to be committed to free trade and has legislated a programme in the form of the Caribbean Basin Initiative to encourage exports from certain Caribbean and

Latin American states to the US? While sugar is an important commodity in the export trade of some Caribbean and Latin American countries, sugar crops (beet and cane) play a minor role in the US economy. These crops are produced in less than 1% of the nation's 2 370 000 farms. Less than 1% of the country's acreage is devoted to sugar cane. The lobby for protection has not only come from this group, but from the makers of high fructose corn syrups (HFCS). Since 1978 HFCS have replaced 30−40% of refined sugar usage in the US. Major beverage producers like Pepsi and Coca Cola are now using HFCS for all their sweetening.

In raw sugar terms Europe is now producing over 30% of world sugar production which is now in the region of 100 million tonnes. The EC alone is responsible for about 12%. The latter's sugar regime, which is based on a system of production quotas supported by guaranteed prices, import levies and export subsidies, not only encourages production, but enables surpluses to be exported at prices well below the cost of production. Before Britain entered the EC in 1973 Commonwealth Caribbean countries enjoyed a guaranteed market for a high proportion of their sugar production in this country. The prices received for about 70% of their exports were negotiated periodically to take account of costs of production, movements of prices in the world market, etc. With the accession of Britain to the Rome Treaty, Commonwealth Caribbean countries have continued to enjoy a protected market for part of their production with the arrangements formalised as a Protocol in the Lomé Convention. The two main markets for Commonwealth Caribbean sugar continue to be the UK and the US. With fluctuating production, some states often find it difficult to meet the EC quotas. Between 1982 and 1984, an average of 87% of Jamaica's sugar exports went to the UK and the rest to the US. The inability of Trinidad and Tobago, however, to meet its quota resulted in a reduction of that quota in 1985 from 69 000 tonnes to 47 300 tonnes. In the 1985−86 marketing year this has been further reduced to 43 500 tonnes. The quotas for the other countries in the same period were: Guyana (158 935 tonnes), Jamaica (118 300 tonnes), Barbados (50 048 tonnes), Belize (40 104 tonnes) and St Kitts-Nevis (15 394 tonnes).

Sugar production in the Commonwealth Caribbean

Sugar production in the Commonwealth Caribbean is a legacy of the colonial era during which these countries were developed as suppliers of food and raw materials to Britain. Although there is some evidence of sugar cane being grown in certain of the Commonwealth Caribbean countries in the sixteenth century, commercial production did not begin on a significant scale until the second half of the seventeenth century. Sugar became the dominant activity in almost all these territories. While production has now ceased in some of them and declined in others, Tables 3.2 and 3.3 show that up until the 1950s sugar production was still a major activity in a number of them. In 1958 sugar cane occupied 71% of Antigua's cropland acreage, 70% of Barbados', 60% of St Kitts' and over 20% of Trinidad and Tobago's, Guyana's and Jamaica's respectively. Data for 1957 indicate that in that year sugar and its by-products still accounted for about 90% of Antigua's, St Kitts' and Barbados' respective domestic exports, over half of Guyana's and 51% of

Table 3.2 Proportion of total acreage under sugar cultivation in sugar exporting countries, 1958

Country (1)	Estimated total acreage in sugar			Estimated total acreage crop land* (5)	% of total in sugar (6)
	Peasant (2)	Estate (3)	Total (4)		
Antigua	3 834	8 586	12 450	17 556	70.9
Barbados	10 000	37 241	47 241	67 847	69.6
Guyana	2 144	84 547	86 988	304 314**	28.6
Jamaica	86 538	66 585	153 123	662 052	23.1
St Christopher	1 347	13 007	14 354	21 682	60.0
St Lucia	1 500	2 267	3 767	46 830	8.0
Trinidad & Tobago	42 200	48 257	90 257	320 711	28.1
Total	147 363	260 490	408 180 327 967 (1950)	1 440 992	28.3

* Cropland is land under tree crops and medium and short-term crops; land in process of preparation for crops or normally cropped but fallow.
** Sugar, rice and coconuts.
Source: Federal Ministry of Trade and Industry, *Sugar Statistics*, 1962.

Table 3.3 Sugar and by-products as a % of total domestic exports

Sugar exporting countries	1957	1984
Antigua	90.0	–
Barbados	92.0	12.4
Guyana	55.8	36.0
Jamaica	51.1[a]	27.0[a]
	29.0[b]	9.0[b]
St Kitts-Nevis	93.0	60.0[e]
St Lucia	32.0	–
Trinidad and Tobago	49.0[c]	8.6[c]
	8.0[d]	1.5[d]

[a] excluding alumina and bauxite from total domestic exports.
[b] including alumina and bauxite in total exports.
[c] excluding petroleum products from total exports.
[d] including petroleum products in total exports.
[e] 1983.
Sources: Official trade reports.

Jamaica's non-bauxite exports and 49% of Trinidad and Tobago's non-petroleum exports.

Since the 1950s, sugar has played an increasingly smaller role in Caribbean economies. In some countries production has ceased altogether. In only six of the Commonwealth Caribbean countries is it still produced for export (see Table 3.3). Generally production has been declining. The figure for 1985 for all the exporting territories was 766 000 tonnes which was 14% below the 1950 figure. Sugar as a proportion of total exports has fallen dramatically over the last decade. In the case of Barbados the proportion was about 10% in 1985 as compared to over 90% in the 1950s.

The decline in Caribbean sugar production can be attributed to several factors – some internal, some external. Sugar cane has traditionally occupied and still occupies some of the best agricultural land in the region. Sugar has been important, not only for its contribution to foreign exchange earnings, but for the livelihood provided to a large proportion of the labour force. As part of the 'commanding heights' of the respective economies, the industry became an easy target for nationalisation. The desire to take control from the expatriate owners, however, was not simply aimed at satisfying a psychological or nationalistic craving, but was also intended to halt the decline in a situation where the industry still had high social significance. It was also evident that in the light of developments in the international sugar industry, the local operations could not survive without rationalisation. Local costs have been increasing at a faster pace than the price being received. For instance in Barbados it cost B$1220 to produce a tonne of sugar in 1982, but the average export price received was only B$776.30. In Trinidad and Tobago the difference is even larger. This situation implies a net transfer of resources to foreign countries. In an era of national control, wages not unexpectedly, have increased rapidly. To improve productivity, some degree of mechanisation has been undertaken, marginal lands abandoned and inefficient factories closed. Despite these efforts, however, production and productivity continue to be affected by inept management, poor management-labour relations, the use of obsolete equipment and machinery and a lack of adequate research relating to both field and factory operations. The continued poor state of management-labour relations in an era of national control reflects the inability to fashion a framework that could minimise conflict and provide the basis for a more vibrant industry.

In the 1970s a number of studies were undertaken with the aim of rationalising the industry.[21] Some of the recommendations made called for the diversion of part of the sugar lands to other food crop production and the setting up of industries based on the raw materials generated by sugar production. The argument was that with rationalisation along these lines, competitiveness could be increased while keeping the level of employment high. By producing a greater amount of food for local consumption foreign exchange could also be saved. Rationalisation, however, has been slow in coming, as the industry continues to decline in the absence of serious initiatives. In Jamaica the government has signed a ten-year contract with British refineries, Tate and Lyle, to manage three of the government-owned factories. Tropicana International has expressed its intention to build a 4 million-gallon per year fermentation plant in Jamaica (in addition to one planned for the Dominican Republic). The hydrous ethanol from both plants will be upgraded to anhydrous alcohol at Tropicana's installation in Jamaica, and then exported to the US where it will enter duty free under the US' CBI.

Given the shrinking world market, the increasing cost of domestic production, the competition from artificial sweeteners and beet sugar production, and the trade policy of the US, it is difficult for the industry to survive in its present form. Sugar production for

Table 3.4 Sugar production, 1950–1985 in '000 Tonnes (figures rounded to nearest tonne)

Year	Barbados	Belize	Guyana	Jamaica	St Christopher-Nevis	Trinidad & Tobago	Antigua	St Lucia	St Vincent	Grenada
1950	161	—	199	276	42	149	32	11	3	2
1960	156	17[a]	340	431	51	221	20	6	4	—
1970	157	68	311	364	27	220	4	—	—	—
1971	137	66	369	373	25	217	11	—	—	—
1972	117	n.a.	315	367	27	235	—	—	—	—
1973	118	69	266	321	24	184	—	—	—	—
1974	110	88	341	361	23	186	—	—	—	—
1975	98	82	300	349	25	163	—	—	—	—
1976	104	61	333	362	35	204	—	—	—	—
1977	124	90	242	295	41	176	—	—	—	—
1978	104	112	325	283	38	147	—	—	—	—
1979	119	97	298	284	40	143	—	—	—	—
1980	137	102	270	230	35	112	—	—	—	—
1981	98	96	301	200	32	93	—	—	—	—
1982	89	104	288	199	36	80	—	—	—	—
1983	86	113	252	208	28	77	—	—	—	—
1984	100	102	242	197	30	70	—	—	—	—
1985	100	102	247	209	27	81	—	—	—	—

n.a. not available
— indicates nil or negligible
[a] 1954

Source: Official statistical publications.

export has become increasingly unviable and has only been maintained because of the employment generated by the industry and the foreign exchange earned.

It is argued in some quarters, not without some justification, that the subsidy given to the sugar industry in the interests of providing employment is no different from the protection afforded the manufacturing sector. In the latter case, the consumer bears the cost; in the former, the public treasury. Given the state of the public revenue, there is an urgent need for measures to reduce costs. As indicated before, there are other considerations involved in rationalisation. With the growing labour force new industries have to be encouraged to provide additional jobs. In this connection sugar cane has to be seen not only as a source of sugar, but as an important raw material for a range of spin-off industries which technological developments have made possible.

An important issue that has to be resolved is the size of the industry to be maintained, should cost per tonne of sugar continue to be higher than revenue. The foreign exchange earnings aspect of the industry is by no means insignificant in a situation where there are few foreign currency earners. Assuming, however, that governments in the region are unable or unwilling to continue to subsidise the industry, what are the courses open? Should the industry be closed down completely thus worsening the unemployment situation, and placing reliance on imported sugar which would add to the competition for foreign exchange? Or should it be reduced to a scale sufficient to satisfy only the local market? In the latter case would it be economical from a scale point of view, even if some employment is provided? These are questions to which little attention has so far been directed, since there is a tendency to assume perpetuity in the marketing arrangements offered by the EC.

Bananas

Bananas are a tropical fruit produced almost exclusively by developing countries. In 1983 world production was estimated to be 41 million metric tons. Of this, developing countries accounted for 39.7 million metric tons or 97%. Contributing to this figure of 39.7 million metric tons were Latin America and the Caribbean (excluding Martinique and Guadeloupe) 18.4 million metric tons (46.3%), Africa (11.3%), Asia and Oceania 16.6 million metric tons (41.8%). The largest producers are not necessarily the most significant exporters. Brazil, for example, is one of the largest producers in the world, but tends to export less than 5% of production. In 1983 Ecuador exported less than half of its production as compared to over 90% by Costa Rica, 80% by the Windward Islands and Cameroon respectively. By world standards the Commonwealth Caribbean (Jamaica, Belize and the Windward Islands) is a fairly small producer, accounting in 1983 for less than 1% of world production.

Though production varies from year to year, bananas are an important commodity in the economy and foreign trade of a number of Commonwealth Caribbean countries. Table 3.5 shows that banana exports from Dominica increased from 15 800 long tons in 1954 to 57 600 long tons in 1969. Since then production and exports have tended to decline. The figure of 7500 long tons in 1980 reflects the effects of the hurricane in the previous year. In St Lucia, St Vincent and Grenada production and exports also increased significantly from the early 1950s to the late 1960s. In these countries a declining trend during the 1970s is also noticeable. The Windward Islands generally were severely affected by the adverse weather conditions in 1979, and this is clearly visible in the 1980 figures. Besides the weather factor which can have a devastating effect on production, the industry has been plagued by pests, diseases and poor farming techniques. Despite the experience of recent years, the major producing countries in the Caribbean are committed to increasing production and exports. There has been a remarkable recovery since 1980 in Dominica, St Lucia and St Vincent. In Grenada, however, production appears to be stagnant. In Jamaica there has been a significant drop in banana production and exports since the 1950s. Between 1954 and 1960 the country exported an average of 140 000 tonnes per year. By 1983, however, this had fallen to 23 000 tonnes and in 1984 to 10 000 tonnes. Like Jamaica, Belize has found it extremely difficult to increase banana production in recent years. At present exports contribute less than 5% to foreign exchange earnings from the goods sector. The industry which is largely government owned is a high cost one because of low productivity resulting from poor soil conditions, transport, management and organisational problems.

Bananas are not only an attractive cash crop, but they are also a major source of foreign exchange and employment in the Caribbean. A major part of the attractiveness of banana growing (as opposed to some other crops) lies in the fact that it yields farmers a year round income. It is estimated for instance that in the case of St Lucia the industry injects almost US$400 000 into the economy every week. In 1978 banana exports from Dominica accounted for 57% of domestic exports. In the following few years production dropped drastically

Table 3.5 Banana exports from the Windward Islands, 1954–1985 (in Tons)

Year	Dominica	St Lucia	St Vincent	Grenada	Total-Tons
1954	15 834.0	3 539.3	362.0	1 422.7	21 158.0
1955	15 027.0	5 169.0	1 306.0	1 103.1	22 605.1
1956	22 357.0	10 439.6	4 798.0	981.8	38 576.4
1957	17 325.0	12 092.7	15 810.0	7 816.9	53 044.6
1958	20 315.1	13 069.5	17 368.0	11 712.0	62 464.6
1959	27 878.7	30 499.4	25 233.3	13 833.5	97 444.9
1960	28 574.7	28 439.4	22 495.8	12 211.5	91 521.4
1961	28 755.7	40 450.2	21 432.0	11 581.8	102 219.7
1962	28 238.6	49 468.0	21 678.2	12 580.5	111 965.3
1963	30 738.1	53 311.3	25 623.9	14 539.3	124 212.6
1964	42 230.5	60 925.5	25 948.6	14 572.8	143 677.4
1965	49 755.1	80 532.9	30 070.5	21 055.5	181 414.0
1966	43 477.9	83 744.1	29 726.1	20 684.6	177 602.7
1967	46 795.8	69 107.3	26 800.6	26 145.6	168 849.3
1968	54 910.8	71 467.1	30 507.3	26 757.9	183 643.1
1969	57 587.2	84 761.6	33 796.7	22 577.4	198 722.9
1970	44 419.3	50 120.7	28 229.1	18 782.5	141 641.6
1971	38 253.5	45 020.4	28 857.3	14 082.6	126 213.8
1972	35 760.8	46 799.4	24 898.5	12 512.2	119 970.9
1973	27 928.4	35 156.5	20 086.5	10 989.6	94 161.0

1974	30 938.7	21 442.9	9 740.3	105 251.4
1975	27 002.6	18 331.9	13 438.8	90 390.3
1976	32 300.8	29 468.9	15 447.9	120 593.2
1977	30 446.6	26 782.5	14 206.4	111 141.8
1978	36 576.3	30 416.6	13 908.1	130 934.7
1979	14 295.8	22 685.7	13 798.1	97 558.3
1980	7 485.5	18 602.5	11 815.6	66 899.3
1981	26 470.0	29 421.0	11 201.3	110 680.0
1982	26 682.9	26 284.1	9 835.45	104 665.3
1983	28 221.4—	27 139.4	8 597.7	117 437.7
1984[a]	31 400.0	30 100.0	8 500.0	135 100.0
1985[a]	33 300.0	40 100.0	8 000.0	162 100.0

Note: 0.984 ton = 1 tonne (metric)
[a] The figures for 1984 and 1985 refer to total production. Domestic consumption, however is insignificant.
Source: WINBAN; Statistical Offices.

as a result of the devastation of the 1979 hurricanes, as indicated earlier. By 1983, however, bananas were again accounting for over 40% of the value of domestic exports. In St Lucia bananas contributed more than half of the earnings derived from visible exports in 1984. In Grenada (14% in 1985) and St Vincent (25% in 1985) the contribution to total exports may be less in percentage terms, but banana production is an imporant sector of these economies. Precise data on the number of people employed in the banana sector of each economy are not available. The indications are, however, that a significant number of people, particularly in the Windward Islands, are dependent on the industry for survival. In St Lucia, for instance, it is estimated that more than half of the population are directly dependent on it.

It is estimated that more than 80% of world production of bananas is consumed or wasted in the countries of production, and these are, as indicated earlier, almost exclusively developing countries. Exports to the industrial countries amount to only 15% of world production. The pattern of banana trade is determined by several factors. Perishability of the fruit and transportation costs are important influences. Historical relationships, however, appear to be a major factor in explaining the present pattern of banana trade. In some cases existing trade is simply a continuation of the old colonial commercial ties and has a protective element built into it. The needs of the US (the world's biggest consumer), West Germany and Canada are met almost exclusively by Latin American production. Latin America is also a supplier to a number of other industrial countries, but in most cases they act as a residual supplier, meeting the difference between requirements and the amount bought from preferred producing nations. Jamaica, the Windward Islands and Belize enjoy a preferred position in the UK market (where almost all their exports go) as do Martinique and Guadeloupe in the French market. The Philippines' biggest market is Japan, and this may be explained by proximity of the two countries. The UK's annual consumption has stabilised at around 300–320 000 tonnes, of which the Commonwealth Caribbean supplies about 40% to 50%.

As indicated earlier, bananas are a very vulnerable crop. Recent experience has shown that bad weather conditions can lead to a significant loss in foreign exchange earnings. Besides the natural factors which affect the industry, the experience of the early 1980s has shown that earnings can also be affected by movements in the exchange rate. The point can be illustrated with respect to the Windward Islands, which were severely affected because of their particularly heavy dependence on banana exports. Since the local currency (the Eastern Caribbean dollar) is pegged to the US dollar and the export price of bananas is quoted in sterling, it means that any appreciation of the US dollar against sterling results in less foreign earnings for these countries and decreased income for farmers. In these circumstances to maintain a given level of income farmers would have to produce more. One can, of course, envisage a situation where increasing production is being accompanied by falling income as a result of movements in currency rates over which the countries have no control. To counter the disincentive effect of such movements, Caribbean governments had suggested in the early 1980s the creation of a 'banana pound', but this evoked no response.

While income has tended to fluctuate in recent years, costs have been rising steadily. Labour costs tend to account for more than half of total banana farm production cost. Adequate shipping capacity and freight costs can also affect net income. The fact that prices received for bananas tend to be determined more by demand conditions in the UK market than by costs of production puts constant pressure on farmers to increase productivity in order to offset costs that are outside their control. As a result of research into pests and diseases, more effective use of fertilisers, and better farming techniques both production and productivity have tended to increase. Despite this, however, costs of production continue to be higher than in neighbouring Martinique and Guadeloupe and in Latin American countries.

Farmers, particularly in the Windward Islands, feel confident that with the right incentives they can satisfy a greater share of the UK banana market. An important part of current development strategy in the islands involves increasing the production of traditional crops, while pursuing policies aimed at economic diversification. Part of the high costs mentioned earlier is explained by soil conditions, the small size of farms, cropping practices and in some cases low labour productivity. Programmes aimed at increasing productivity need to be accelerated.

In the context of the integration movement in the Caribbean and the need to reduce costs, it was suggested some years ago that there was some scope for rationalisation of the industry in the region and for a greater measure of collaboration.[22] Recognising that a large part of the higher costs associated with Caribbean bananas stemmed from the growing of the fruit in unsuitable areas from the point of view of both transport and yield, the argument was made that Caribbean countries could increase their overall exports if they agreed to guide their production levels in a framework of comparative advantage, allowing the more efficient countries to increase their exports to the world market in return for granting market access to the manufactured goods of less efficient Caribbean competitors. These suggestions have not been actively pursued by policy-makers, and as a result the regional rationalisation of land resources has not materialised. However, collaboration is undertaken on a limited scale. The members of WINBAN, i.e. Dominica, St Lucia, Grenada and St Vincent, co-operate in terms of purchase of fertilisers and pesticides, research and marketing. Bananas provide an example where lack of a wider regional initiative may have contributed to the failure to develop a stronger export capability in the context of a framework aimed at the optimum use of the region's resources.

Bauxite

Because of its strength and lightness, aluminium has become one of the world's most important and widely used metals after steel. Aluminium, of course, is derived from bauxite ore which at the moment is mined only in Guyana and Jamaica among the Commonwealth Caribbean countries.[23] While bauxite continues to play an important part in the economies of both these countries, their position in world bauxite production has declined dramatically since the 1960s.

Though bauxite deposits in Guyana were noticed by government geologists as far back as 1868, it was not until 1906 that the mineral was clearly defined.[24] For a few years the find seemed to have aroused little interest. War conditions, however, and the increasing use of aluminium soon aroused the interest of at least two companies. Among them was the Aluminium Company of America (ALCOA) which incorporated a local subsidiary, Demerara Bauxite Company (DEMBA) in 1916 to hold and work the concessions acquired over the previous three years. With the incorporation of Aluminium Limited in Canada (ALCAN) in 1928 by ALCOA, most of the latter's foreign properties, including DEMBA, were transferred to this company. 'From 1928 through 1950 Guyana's bauxite was the raw material foundation for burgeoning power and position of ALCAN as an aluminium company.'[25] While DEMBA remained the major bauxite producing company in Guyana until it was nationalised by the government in 1972 another smaller company (Reynold Metal Company) was also involved. The latter was nationalised in 1975.

Though Jamaica was long suspected of possessing bauxite, it

was not until the 1940s that its potential was recognised and steps were taken to develop it.[26] It took some years to ascertain the extent of the deposits and to resolve the technical problems that arose from treatment of the ore and to establish the most suitable economic processing method. In October 1943, Aluminium Limited set up Jamaica Bauxite Limited (renamed Alumina Jamaica Limited in 1952) as a fully-owned subsidiary. Reynolds Metals Company entered the scene in 1944 and was followed by Permanente Metals Corporation (later to become Kaiser Aluminum and Chemical Corporation in 1947). A local subsidiary, Kaiser Bauxite Company, was founded in 1952. In 1951 the British Aluminium Company had also begun prospecting in areas not occupied by the other three companies. Following the find in Jamaica, bauxite was also discovered in Haiti in 1943 and a short time later in the Dominican Republic. The first shipment of bauxite left Jamaica in 1952 and in 1954 the export of alumina began. The combined bauxite production of Alumina Jamaica Ltd. (later to be renamed ALCAN Jamaica Ltd.), Reynolds and Kaiser amounted to less than one million tonnes in 1953.

In 1952 when bauxite production began in Jamaica this sector contributed less than 2% to GDP. By the time of independence in 1962 the contribution had risen to almost 9%. Bauxite and alumina production increased steadily from the 1950s to 1974 when bauxite production totalled 15 167 thousand tonnes and alumina 2 781 thousand tonnes. In this year the bauxite sector contributed about 9% to GDP. Since then production has fluctuated within a declining trend. The mining sector as a whole contributed only about 6% to GDP in 1984. Real value-added in this year was some 42% below the 1974 level.

In Guyana production of bauxite and alumina peaked in 1970, with bauxite production totalling 3030 thousand tonnes and alumina 317 thousand tonnes. Though Guyana is an older producer, these figures are considerably lower than those for Jamaica. Since 1970 production has declined almost steadily. In 1952 the mining sector as a whole contributed 9% to Guyana's GDP. By 1960 this had grown to about 14% and in 1970 to 20%. The estimated figure in 1984 is 9.0%. In 1985 real value-added in the mining sector was calculated to be 60% below the 1975 level.

As a result of their own declining production and the increased mining activities in other bauxite producing countries, the position of Guyana and Jamaica in the world bauxite industry has changed since the 1950s and 1960s. Operations in Haiti and the Dominican Republic have now virtually ceased. On the other hand production has increased significantly in such countries as Australia, Guinea, Surinam and Brazil. In 1953 Jamaica produced 8.5% of world bauxite production, as compared to 41.5% for Guyana and Surinam taken together. By 1954 the latter's share had dropped to 22.3% while the former had increased to 22.6%. Though Australia has been the world's leading producer since 1972, large scale production did not commence until 1963.[27] In 1965 Australia was responsible for only 3.2% of world bauxite output. Five years later this proportion had increased to 15.5%. In 1953 Surinam supplied 68.5% of the US imports of crude and dried bauxite, as compared to 2.3% for Guyana and 26% for Jamaica. By 1959 Surinam's share had declined to 37.8%, while Jamaica's share had increased to 51.8%. Guyana's share remained small, about 2%. By the mid-1960s Jamaica had emerged as the largest producer in the world accounting for almost half of the Western Hemisphere's production and 24% of the world total. Figures available for 1984 indicate that Jamaica contributed 9.8% to world bauxite production, as compared to 18.1% ten years earlier. She now ranks third behind Australia and Guinea as a producer.

Several factors have contributed to the decline of the bauxite industry in the Caribbean.[28] The significant reduction in alumina and aluminium production rates in the USA and the reduced growth in demand for aluminium globally are major ones. In the case of Jamaica, the decline as world producers of Kaiser and Reynold's (two of Jamaica's major purchasers of bauxite and alumina) and the heavy dependence of the industry on oil have also contributed, as has higher taxation compared to other major producers. The latter factor has to be seen in historical perspective.

Following independence the need for revenue and the desire for natural resources to make a greater contribution to national development forced the Jamaican and Guyanese governments to review their relationship with the transnational corporations that were engaged in their respective industries. It was long felt that these companies were not making a sufficient contribution to national development. For instance, in the case of Guyana it was estimated that of the industry's total exports of G$1200 million in the period 1917–69 the government's revenue from royalties and export duties amounted to G$21.1 million, or 1.6%. Even when income tax was added, the government's total revenue from the company in the 1963–68 period amounted to only 3.4% of the value of exports.[29] In November of 1970 the Guyanese government announced its intention to acquire majority control of DEMBA's operations. Failure to arrive at a satisfactory arrangement with DEMBA's parent, ALCAN, led to its complete nationalisation in 1971. A state company was then formed to run the operations.

In Jamaica, where there were six companies operating in early 1974, the government opted to impose a levy and to seek participation rather than go for complete nationalisation. The production levy was imposed unilaterally in June 1974 on all bauxite companies after discussions with the companies for better taxation arrangements failed to yield satisfactory results. Prior to this date Jamaica was reported to be earning the lowest revenues from a tonne of bauxite in the Caribbean area.[30] The levy was originally set at 7.5% of the realised price on shipments of primary aluminium to the major North American companies. Between 1974 and 1983 the levy earned in net terms was US$1691 million on a production of 111.1 million tonnes of ore. In the previous ten years (1964–1974) only some US$269.8 million were earned in the form of income tax and royalties from a production of 114.3 million tonnes.[31] Because of the vertically integrated nature of the companies and the transfer price system governing intra-company transactions, these companies are difficult to tax.[32] The price given for tax purposes is often significantly lower than the real value of the transaction.

There are some (including the companies) who have argued that the imposition of the levy adversely affected the competitive position of Jamaican bauxite, and this was the major factor behind the decline. It is worth pointing out, however, that despite two revisions of the levy arrangements (in 1979 and 1983) in favour of the companies the slide has continued. One observer has explained Jamaica's decline more in terms of the development of facilities elsewhere in the context of the strategic planning decisions of the companies.[33] In the case of Guyana, the decline in production since nationalisation is explained not only by market conditions, but by poor management and inadequate plant maintenance.

With the closure of certain companies the Jamaican government has become increasingly involved in mining and processing operations. Both Guyana and Jamaica have been trying to find new markets for their bauxite and alumina. In early 1983 the Jamaican government signed a contract to sell annually to the USSR one million tons of bauxite starting in 1984. Jamaica will receive machinery and other merchandise as partial payment for the bauxite. Given the depressed state of the primary aluminium market which has resulted in the closing or reduction in capacity of a number of refineries, markets have not been easy to find. The US government assisted by signing an agreement in March, 1983 to buy one million tons of metal grade bauxite for its National Defence Stockpile. A second agreement signed in November of the same year increased the quantity to two million tons. The first million tons were sold for cash. The second payment was to be for dairy products.

One of the problems facing production of alumina in Jamaica is the large amount of oil used to produce a tonne of alumina. The present average for the industry is 2.8 to 3.0 barrels. The conversion rate from bauxite to alumina is also high. In Jamaica it takes about 2.45 tonnes of bauxite to make a tonne of alumina, as compared to 1.95 tonnes for Guinea and 2.2 tonnes for Brazil.

Bauxite is a non-renewable asset, and there is some concern that the pressures for foreign exchange could push both the Jamaican and Guyanese governments to dispose of their resources without getting an adequate return. It has long been recognised that the economy derives greater benefits when bauxite is processed or refined locally. Over the years the companies have tended to export (to their refineries) the bulk of the ore in raw and semi-refined form thus depriving the local economy of income and employment. Recent attempts to expand alumina capacity significantly and to set up smelter installation to produce aluminium and other downstream industries have not met with success. Smelting needs a great deal of power, and therefore one proposal put forward within the integration framework was to set up a smelter (jointly-owned by Trinidad, Guyana and Jamaica) in Trinidad to use this country's abundant energy resources. The project failed to materialise largely because of political squabbling.

Oil

Though possessing very little oil of its own, the Caribbean has been an important refining and transhipment centre since the early part of the century.[34] Its location between major oil-producing areas and main consuming centres has been a critical factor in this development. The good natural harbours, the incentives offered by local governments and the lack of regulatory controls also helped. The refinery set up by the Royal Dutch Shell group in Curaçao (Netherlands Antilles) in 1917 was one of the earliest established to refine foreign crude. This was followed by Exxon's in Aruba (Netherlands Antilles) in 1929. Both these islands are about 90 miles from the Venezuelan oilfields. In the post World War II period both these refineries were expanded and modernised to become the world's largest and most efficient. New ones also entered the scene to meet the growing demand for oil in Europe in the wake of the reconstruction efforts, and in the US which became a net importer of oil in 1948. Texaco, induced by government incentives, local crude, and the location of Trinidad near the Venezuelan oilfields, came to Trinidad in 1956 and set up a refinery that was to become the largest in the British Commonwealth. Just previous to this (1955) the Commonwealth Oil Refinery Company (CORCO) in which Tesoro had an interest set up facilities at Pennelas in Puerto Rico. Another was to be set up in the same country (at Yabucoa) in 1968 by the Sun Oil Company. Amerada Hess entered St Croix in the US Virgin Islands in 1967, and later also established a storage facility in St Lucia. Refining and bunkering facilities to accommodate supertankers were established jointly in 1970 by the New England Petroleum Corporation (65%) and Standard Oil of California (35%) in Grand Bahama in the Bahamas, which is about 50 miles off the US coast.

Developments in the international oil markets in recent years have reduced the importance of the Caribbean refining facilities to the transnationals, and they have either drastically reduced their operations, or pulled out completely. While denying it was allowing its installation at Pointe-à-Pierre in Trinidad to run down, Texaco gradually reduced its average daily throughput from 266 742 b/d in 1976 to 59 952 b/d in 1984. With dwindling revenues and increasing unemployment the Government was virtually forced to act, and it eventually purchased most of Texaco's assets in 1986. In Curaçao the government too was led to take control of the subsidiary companies and property of Shell, which it then leased to Petroleos de Venezuela, S.A., in order to mitigate the effects that closure would have had on the economy. Almost 2000 people were employed. Aruba has not been so fortunate with the Exxon refinery located there. Efforts to work out a deal with Venezuela to save the installation from being dismantled had met with no success by mid-1986.

During most of the post-war period the companies found it easier and more profitable to supply the US market with foreign fuel rather than use domestic supplies. With the decline of Venezuelan production in the 1960s they turned to Middle Eastern and North African sources. In Europe the gap between demand and refining capacity narrowed, reducing the need for refined products. At the time of the first oil shock, the US was dependent on foreign supplies for over 30% of its requirements. With increasing prices during the 1970s a number of measures were set in train to reduce dependence on foreign energy supplies. Among other things, local legislation was reviewed with a view to providing companies with greater incentives to increase local crude oil production. The higher oil prices themselves were instrumental in bringing many marginal fields into production.

Commonwealth Caribbean producers

Among Commonwealth Caribbean countries the two main producers of oil are Barbados and Trinidad and Tobago. Barbados is a relative new-comer in the field of oil production, with commercial production beginning about 1973. Production has increased gradually from 13.4 thousand barrels in 1973 to 635 thousand barrels in 1984. The latter figure represents about half the country's requirements.

Trinidad and Tobago is one of the oldest oil producing countries in the world. The search for oil in Trinidad and Tobago began as far back as 1857.[35] The first deposits, however, were not found until 1866, at Aripero, by the Paria Oil Company, formed by Walter Darwent, an American engineer. Oil, however, was not discovered in commercial quantities until 1907. The first export cargo of crude was shipped in 1910. In 1913 Shell International and Trinidad Leaseholds entered the local oil scene, each setting up both producing and refining operations. By 1914 Trinidad and Tobago was producing one million barrels of oil per year and by 1919 refining capacity had increased to the extent that about two-thirds of the two million barrels of crude being produced were refined locally. The depression of the 1930s took a heavy toll on the local industry, leading to the folding of a number of small companies. This situation was brought about to some extent by the huge discoveries in Texas and Oklahoma, which depressed world prices. Despite this, however, local crude oil production had increased to ten million barrels by 1930-31. With the outbreak of World War II production was affected by the lack of finance and equipment. Once the War was over, production soon picked up as a result of the new technology and equipment being employed. By 1946 over 20 million barrels of oil were produced and refined in Trinidad and Tobago.

In the pre-war period refining was geared towards the processing of domestic crude oil. In the post-war period the main British companies moved increasingly towards processing as their major activity — a trend that was strengthened by the entry of Texaco in 1956, with the purchase of the Trinidad Oil Company (formerly Trinidad Leaseholds Ltd). By 1962 Texaco's refinery had become the largest in the British Commonwealth. British Petroleum entered in the late 1950s followed by Amoco in 1961. That year the Trinidad and Tobago government bought up the assets of Shell and BP, and formed a jointly-owned company (Trinidad Government 50.1%) with Tesoro Petroleum Company of Texas to own and manage BP's former assets. With the purchase of Texaco's refinery at Pointe-à-Pierre, domestic refining operations are now under full national control.

By world standards Trinidad and Tobago is a small oil producer. Total production of crude reached a peak of 83.8 million barrels in 1978. This was followed by five years of decline. Production in 1984 and 1985 were 62.0 and 64.2 million barrels respectively. In 1984 export of crude amounted to 32.5 million barrels as compared to 54.0 million barrels in 1978. Refining activities have declined significantly in recent years. Exports of refined products fell from 132.4 million barrels in 1973 to 28.8 million barrels in 1984. In the latter year Texaco utilised only 25.5% of installed refinery capacity as compared to 18.9% for Trintoc.

There are six companies actively engaged in oil production. The largest producer is the Amoco Trinidad Oil Company whose production in 1984 averaged 90 136 barrels per day. The average daily production for the country was 169 515 barrels. In 1977 OPEC production reached a peak of 31 million barrels per day. By 1983 average production had fallen to 17 million barrels per day. Even if we take the latter figure, Trinidad's production in 1983 would have amounted to less than 1% of OPEC's.[36]

As indicated earlier, oil and oil products account for over 80% of domestic exports in Trinidad and Tobago. Between 1980 and 1985 petroleum's contribution to GDP has averaged 11.8%. The contribution of the sector to public revenue is substantial. In the late 1970s/early 1980s over half of government's current revenue came directly from oil activities. Because of the decline in oil prices in recent years, the contribution has fallen both in absolute terms and as a proportion of the total. Oil, however, still accounts for about 40% of current revenue. Despite the downturn, the petroleum industries in mid-1986 were still providing some 18 000 jobs (4.5% of the employed labour force).

The effects of falling oil prices

The international oil market has changed significantly since the early 1970s. With increasing prices OPEC production fell both absolutely and as a proportion of world total production. In 1973 OPEC's share amounted to more than 50%, but by 1983 this had fallen to about 31%. Correspondingly, the non-OPEC share increased from

46% to 69% between 1973 and 1983. While some new oil producers have contributed to this trend, the major factor has been the significant expansion in production by traditional producers outside the OPEC framework.

International oil prices increased steadily from less than US$5 per barrel in 1973 to over US$30 per barrel in the early 1980s. A short period of stabilisation was followed by a rapid decline in prices with the figure plummetting from more than US$30 per barrel in late November 1985 to under US$10 a few months later. During the period of increasing prices, many high cost producers were encouraged to increase production. Fields that were unprofitable during the period of low prices were brought into production. The process was helped by the desire to become less dependent on imported fuels. Between 1973 and 1983 UK production (largely in the North Sea area) increased from less than 100 thousand metric tons to over 110 000 thousand metric tons. In the same period, Norway's production increased almost twenty times. Even in traditional oil producing countries like Mexico, USSR and the USA, there were significant increases in production. The greatly increased production in the face of a falling demand resulting from the energy-saving measures adopted by oil importing nations, and the recession that hit the industrial countries in the early 1980s were no doubt major factors affecting the fall in oil prices. Another and perhaps more important was the development of energy alternatives. It has been estimated that oil consumption per unit of economic output in the Western industrial countries fell by 36% between 1973 and 1984. Two-thirds of this is explained by improved energy efficiency and one-third by the substitution of other energy sources.[37]

It has become increasingly recognised that the sharp decline in oil prices will have both costs and benefits. The major beneficiaries will be the oil importing nations who will now have more foreign exchange to spend on other things including the servicing of their debts. Lower energy costs should also result in lower domestic prices, thus giving a boost to exports. Lower fuel costs should also stimulate international travel, thus benefiting tourist oriented economies. Overall, there should be an improvement in their balance of payments. With the removal of subsidies where these existed, the budget position should also improve.

On the other, hand smaller earnings from oil will reduce the import capacity of the oil exporting nations, not only affecting their own development but the economies of countries from which they buy. Oil exporting nations are also among the most heavily indebted countries in the world. This means that debt servicing in the face of falling prices will become increasingly difficult, notwithstanding the expected drop in interest rates. It has been estimated that if oil prices averaged US$18.50 in 1986, there would be a transfer of US$70 billion income from oil exporting to oil importing countries.[38] About 80% of this gain would go to the industrialised nations, and the rest to oil importing developing nations. Oil exporters like Mexico, Venezuela, Nigeria, Indonesia, Egypt and Algeria are expected to experience a severe drop in the standard of living. In the case of Mexico it has been estimated that every $1 fall in the price of oil will result in a loss of US$550 million in export earnings.[39]

The artificially low prices for oil in the 1950s and 1960s encouraged consumption and wastage and discouraged oil exploration and development of alternative energy sources. The higher prices orchestrated by OPEC during the 1970s had the opposite effect. They not only provided an incentive for greater output (from both OPEC and non-OPEC sources), but encouraged the adoption of energy saving measures and the search for cheaper sources of energy. The industrial countries found themselves compelled to put into place policies aimed at reducing their dependence on imported fuel as a source of energy. In this situation the transnational oil companies also changed their strategy, resulting in the abandonment of their offshore refineries and transhipment centres in the Caribbean.

A number of factors (including poor marketing strategies)[40] by OPEC conspired to bring oil prices crashing in 1986. With greater control over quotas, prices have risen in 1987, but they are still below those of the early 1980s. In Trinidad and Tobago, the major oil companies are making a greater production of crude contingent upon a downward revision of the tax structure. Deteriorating economic conditions in the country weakens the bargaining position of the government in this situation. Even though the government has increased its ownership stake in the petroleum industry in recent years, it is clear that vital decisions are still outside its control. Developments in the local oil sector are critically influenced by trends and forces in the international industry.

Tourism

Between 1970 and 1981 international trade grew by 18.5% per year. In the same period international tourism receipts experienced a growth rate of 16.5%. In 1960 international tourism receipts were estimated to be around US$38.6 thousand million, but by 1970 this had grown to $100.0 thousand million and by 1982 to over $550 thousand million. In the early 1980s international tourism receipts amounted to about 5% of world exports. These figures point to the fact that tourism is an important activity in the world economy.

Tourism, it should be recognised, has both a domestic and international component. Domestic tourism arises from the visits of residents of a country to other parts of the same country, while international tourism refers to an activity concerned with the visits of residents of one country to another country. In the latter case visits by non-residents generate foreign exchange for the receiving country in the same way that the export of goods does. In the case of tourism the export is a service, and as such cannot be seen — hence the reason why it is commonly referred to as an 'invisible' export. This service or 'tourism product' is centred around a range of assets and activities, such as sun, beaches, hotels, restaurants, historical sites, scenery, sporting facilities, cultural interests, entertainment, etc. The enjoyment of this product requires the physical presence of the visitor in the host state and this is the major difference with an international transaction involving the export of a goods item. Tourism, therefore, raises issues which goods export does not. The presence of a large number of visitors in a country, for example, often gives rise to concerns about the social and cultural impact on the local community, but these concerns are generally pushed into the background in the context of the need for foreign exchange and poor performance of the export (goods) sector.

Although in recent years, tourism has emerged as an important activity in almost all Commonwealth Caribbean countries, the latter receive only a small proportion of world tourists. In 1982 the Caribbean region as a whole (including Venezuela and Surinam) is estimated to have received about 7 million visitors out of a world total of 33.6 million. Gross tourism receipts were estimated to be around $4 billion as compared to the world total of $118 billion in that year. If we were to take the Commonwealth Caribbean by itself, stay-over tourist arrivals in 1982 numbered 2.4 million. The Bahamas alone accounted for 44% of the total number of stay-over visitors, while Barbados, Jamaica, Belize, Trinidad and Tobago accounted for 43%, and the OECS countries received 13%. Though Commonwealth Caribbean countries have been trying to diversify their markets, the US remains the most important single source for tourists to the Caribbean (*See* Table 3.6). For example, in 1984, over 75% of stay-over visitors to the Bahamas and Jamaica respectively came from the US, as compared to 40% for Barbados, and 53% for Antigua. For most other Commonwealth Caribbean countries the proportion is lower. The Caribbean, however, receives only a

Table 3.6 Stop-over visitors by country of residence, 1984 (%)

Countries	UK	USA	Canada	Other European	Other	Total
Barbados	12.6	40.3	18.3	a	28.8	100.0
Jamaica	3.3	77.5	13.1	2.0	4.1	100.0
Trinidad	8.5	27.7	12.4	3.2	48.2	100.0
Bahamas[b]	1.5	84.8	7.0	2.1	4.6	100.0
OECS						
Antigua	11.0	52.9	9.9	6.7	19.5	100.0
Dominica	8.3	17.7	5.3	14.9	53.8	100.0
Grenada	6.0	21.3	3.6	a	69.1	100.0
Montserrat[b]	8.7	49.1	9.3	2.9	30.0	100.0
St Kitts-Nevis	7.7	36.6	6.2	1.1	48.4	100.0
St Lucia	20.7	24.6	14.4	13.1	27.2	100.0
St Vincent	n.a.	n.a.	n.a.	n.a.	n.a.	100.0

[a] Included in 'Other'.
[b] 1983 data.
n.a. Not available.
Sources: OECS, *Annual Digest of Statistics, 1984*; Official Publications.

small part of American tourists, and this could be deduced from the Caribbean's share of total travel payments of US travellers in foreign countries. In 1984 out of an estimated total travel payment of US$16 008 million, the Caribbean and Central America as a whole received US$1929 million or 12%. The Commonwealth Caribbean (including the Bahamas) is estimated to have received US$1034 million or 6.5%.

With the decline of traditional primary exports, such as sugar, cocoa and citrus fruits, as indicated, tourism has emerged as an important source of foreign exchange for most of the territories in the region. In some states (e.g. Bahamas, Antigua, and Barbados) tourism is now the dominant activity. In the case of the Bahamas gross tourism expenditures in 1984 were estimated to be about US$800 million as compared to export earnings of US$262 million. Tourism receipts accounted for about 60% of total earnings. In Antigua net tourism expenditures in the period 1979–83 averaged almost four times the earnings from domestic exports. In Jamaica gross tourist expenditure of US$498 million in 1984 was equivalent to more than half of the earnings from domestic exports. In Grenada and St Lucia too gross tourism expenditure in recent years has been estimated to be almost as large as earnings from exports.

The growth of tourism in the Caribbean, and for that matter in the rest of the world, is the result of several factors. The increase in income both in the industrialised countries and in the developing world is a major factor, as have been developments in the transport industry. It has also been the result of efforts made by individual countries in terms of promotion, the development of their physical infrastructure and the adoption of postures more favourably disposed towards the encouragement of the visitor industry. Even countries which initially may have been sceptical of the benefits to be derived from tourism, or who were concerned about its social effects, have been forced by economic circumstances (and more particularly by the failure to develop vibrant new exports) to change their position to one of active encouragement.

Tourism tends to be seen as an easy foreign exchange earner, particularly in the context of the protectionist measures facing goods exports and the failure to effect significant transformation in the traditional economy. While Boards or Ministries of Tourism have been established to promote the industry, in many cases they are badly under-staffed or under-financed. Promotion is significantly below desired levels. The Caribbean territories find themselves not only competing with other resorts, but among themselves. The idea of joint promotion or marketing, though often mentioned, has never been fully explored. Individual territories, therefore, not only find themselves putting out more resources on marketing than they might have in a co-operative arrangement, but also have been unable to exploit the diversity of the territories by promoting the Commonwealth Caribbean as a single destination.

Tourism not only brings benefits in the form of employment or foreign exchange generated by payments for transport, accommodation, meals, etc. but it is also associated with costs, some tangible, some not so tangible. The need to build and maintain infrastructure puts a certain amount of pressure on any governments' fiscal position. The intangible costs derive from the cultural impact and economic and social consequences that flow from this. It is often contended, for instance, that the conspicuous spending habits of visitors tend to adversely affect local attitudes towards savings. It is also felt that the holiday atmosphere associated with tourism encourages idleness and promotes a lifestyle not in keeping with development.

Caribbean tourism has grown up very haphazardly. In most

territories there has been an absence of planning in terms of the use of resources and the relationship of this activity to other economic activities. Scarce land resources, for example, have often not been put to their best use in the absence of proper zoning policies. The size of hotels and forward planning with respect to accommodation requirements have tended to receive scant attention. Training aimed at providing an adequate number of trained personnel to service the various aspects of the industry has tended to lag. The result of this has been a low level of professionalism in certain areas, and an inadequate amount of maintenance of certain critical equipment.

Given the limited resources of Caribbean countries and the high level of unemployment, one would have expected that greater attention would have been placed on policies aimed at obtaining the highest possible returns from the available stock of land, labour and capital which too frequently are allowed to gravitate to uses which do not bring optimum returns. Failure to develop stronger inter-sectoral linkages within Caribbean countries has resulted in a great deal of the benefits from tourism being lost. A high proportion of the tourist dollars earned tend to flow back out again in various forms such as profits, payments for imports (including food) and other services. It is estimated that in a number of cases more than half of the tourist dollar earned is lost. This means that gross tourism expenditure, or the number of visitors is not a fair indication of the benefits derived from the industry. There can be situations where the number of visitors may be growing but the financial benefits to the host countries may be declining. This could arise, for example, where visitors are spending less. It could also arise as a result of some of the novel arrangements which have come to be associated with the industry. One of these is the packaged tour concept. In this arrangement the visitor settles most of his financial obligations with the tour organiser even before he leaves his home country. Certainly some part of these payments have to be remitted to the tourist destination to cover local expenses. It is strongly suspected, however, that in packaged tours, a greater proportion of tourist expenditure remains abroad than is ordinarily the case.

International tourism is a highly competitive business. New resorts are constantly emerging. Besides the cultural and sporting attractions and the natural assets of sun, sea and sand, some destinations offer additional facilities such as casino gambling and tax and offshore banking attractions. Imitations among resorts is a common feature of the industry. Given the similarity in attractions among many destinations, the price factor can be an important issue. Changes in the price of fuel, or in the value of major currencies can have a significant impact on the industry. A destination that is favoured today easily loses its attraction at some future time.

Some of the elements in the cost of a vacation, of course, are outside the control of host countries. There are areas, however, where a certain amount of influence can be exerted. An increase in productivity or efficiency, for instance, can lower domestic costs. A more economic use of power and more proficient management can also favourably affect the cost of operation. In the Caribbean there are fears that some resorts may be pricing themselves out of the market. Despite the growth in tourist numbers in recent years and the high occupancy rates in some resorts, a large number of hotels in the region are reported to be experiencing financial difficulties. In certain resorts there may have been some over-expansion in accommodation facilities. Generally, however, the inability to maintain a year-round satisfactory occupancy rate has been a factor. This itself is related to the failure to resort to more imaginative marketing and development of new markets. Increasing labour costs coupled with poor management in some cases have also contributed to the problems of the industry. A major factor has no doubt been the failure of Caribbean territories to develop the tourism product in order to increase their competitiveness. Generally, shopping facilities are absent or highly inadequate. Quality restaurants are also lacking, particularly in the smaller islands. Access to historical sites remains highly undeveloped, while the marketing of local handicrafts is in need of greater organisation. In certain cases greater control needs to be exercised over domestic transportation which is excessively priced. With respect to some of these shortcomings, the limited resources of the state can be held responsible. There are others, however, which can be resolved with some organisational effort and initiative by both the state and private sector.

Given the limited resources of Commonwealth Caribbean countries, the decline of major traditional exports and the problems the region has experienced in developing new exports, the attraction of tourism as an aid to development is not difficult to understand. The lack of a systematic approach to the industry and failure to incorporate it in the overall planning process is partly the result of the early ambivalence to the industry stemming from both an inability to harness its potential and to deal with the perceived socio-cultural impact. In most territories major issues are yet to be resolved. The size of the industry desired in the context of national concerns and planning objectives has received little attention. There exists a notable preoccupation with simply trying to attract greater and greater numbers of visitors rather than trying to maximise benefits. The type of tourism the various states wish to encourage remains a controversial issue. In order to differentiate their product, some territories offer casino gambling facilities. Certain states which feel that benefits have declined while numbers have grown are giving consideration to what they call quality tourism. The idea here is to attract the 'big spenders' desiring high quality accommodation, transport and food. Exactly how this is to be done, however, remains a problem, since providing only high cost hotel rooms could also result in less tourists being attracted. There is need for a greater amount of research to be undertaken if policy formulation is to be properly informed. Small countries with limited resources have to be more systematic in their approach in a highly competitive field.

There is concern in some quarters that a growing dependence on tourism is likely to increase the vulnerability of Caribbean countries, given the fickleness of tourists, the intense competition in the industry and the quick impact which adverse publicity can have on the volume of visitors. Too heavy a dependence on the industry, it is argued, would tend to influence domestic political posturings and weaken the ability to bargain, even in areas outside of tourism. This point, of course, could be made with respect to other activities, dependent on particular markets. In some senses tourism does have features in common with primary exports. The question is, do Caribbean countries have much of a choice, given the need for foreign exchange to meet existing commitments and to restructure the economy? One way to deal with the issue of dependence, of course, is to adopt a strategy aimed not only at market diversification, but one which could assist in the growth of other sectors of the economy. In this connection the encouragement of intra-Caribbean tourism needs to be pushed more strongly, in the same way that trade is being promoted.

Notes

1 See F. Gerard Adams and J.R. Behrman, *Commodity Exports and Economic Development*, Lexington: D.C. Heath and Company, 1982, p.3.
2 Not surprisingly, the world economic recession of recent years has had several consequences for developing countries. During the period 1981−86 the loss in commodity export earnings of developing countries, measured against the average of 1979−80 was US$7 billion per year. This has taken a heavy toll on growth rates and the level of investment. The terms of trade and the purchasing power of the commodity exports

of poor countries have also been affected. During 1981−85 the cumulative losses in their net barter terms of trade and export purchasing power amounted to US$93 billion and US$13 billion, respectively. Another consequence is the falling share of primary commodities in world trade and the declining importance of developing countries in world commodity exports. See *UNCTAD Bulletin*, No. 231, April 1987.

3   For a good background discussion to these Agreements see C. Nappi, *Commodity Market Controls*, Lexington, Mass.: D.C. Heath and Co. 1979.

4   See P. Ady, 'Developed Countries' Attitudes to the Integrated Programme of Commodities and the Common Fund', in A. Sengupta (ed.) *Commodities, Finance and Trade: Issues in North-South Negotiation*, London: Frances Pinter (Publishers) Ltd., 1980.

5   Sometimes the word 'cartel' is used; but since this tends to have a sinister ring of exploitation of consumers through price manipulation, we shall use the term 'producer organisation' which encompasses a broader range of objectives, besides trying to get a fair or just return to its members from exploitation of their resources.

6   The complete list of OPEC member states at present is as follows: Algeria, Ecuador, Gabon, Indonesia, Iran, Iraq, Kuwait, Libya, Nigeria, Qatar, Saudi Arabia, United Arab Emirates and Venezuela.

7   This is the acronym for *Conseil Intergouvernemental des Pays Exportateurs de Cuivre*.

8   The members are Australia, Guinea, Guyana, Jamaica, Sierra Leone, Surinam, Yugoslavia, Indonesia, Ghana, Haiti, and Dominican Republic. The first two countries have the world's largest bauxite reserves. In 1974 IBA members produced 63% of the world's bauxite.

9   The general functions of the IBA are: (1) to facilitate the exchange of information in connection with all aspects of exploration, processing, marketing, and use of bauxite; (2) to assist in harmonising the policies and decisions of member countries; (3) to help secure maximum national ownership and control of the industry; (4) to help to offset the power of multinational corporations in relation to individual member countries; and (5) to conduct joint research. See M. Manley, *Up the Down Escalator*, London: Andre Deutsch Ltd., 1987, p.46.

10 See Z. Mikdashi, *The International Politics of Natural Resources*, Ithaca: Cornell University Press, 1976.

11 Colombia, Costa Rica, Ecuador, Guatemala, Honduras, Nicaragua, and Panama.

12 Mikdashi, *op. cit.* p.12.

13 This thesis has been particularly associated with the name of Raul Prebisch. See 'The Economic Development of Latin America and Its Principal Problems', in *Economic Bulletin for Latin America*, Vol. 7 (1962), pp.1−22. Also, by the same author, 'Commercial Policies in Underdeveloped Countries', *American Economic Review*, Vol. 49, pp.251−73. See also Hans Singer, 'The Distribution of Gains between Investing and Borrowing Countries', *American Economic Review*, Vol. 40, (May), pp.473−85.

14 As a result of this trend developing countries since the early 1960s have

been arguing that the prices received for their primary exports should be linked to those of manufactured goods imported from the rich countries. This is sometimes referred to as the indexation issue.
15 See Prebisch, 'The Economic Development of Latin America and its Principal Problems', *op. cit.*
16 OPEC crude oil production as a percentage of total non-Communist world production increased from an average of 46% in the 1960−62 period to an average of 67% in 1973−75. By the early 1980s it had declined to around 50%. OPEC countries supply a significant proportion of the oil imports of the industrial countries.
17 The collapse of oil prices in the mid-1980s is to a large extent the result of poor marketing strategies. Low production accompanied by inappropriate price levels induced too much conservation, development of alternative sources of energy and exploration and production of oil outside of OPEC. See Abdullah El-Kuwaiz, 'OPEC and the International Oil Market: The Age of Realism', in *OPEC Review*, Winter, 1986.
18 See C. Fred Bergsten, 'The Threat from the Third World', in R.N. Cooper (ed.), *A Re-ordered World: Emerging International Economic Problems*, Washington, D.C. Potomac Associates, 1973.
19 See M. Manley, *Up the Down Escalator*, London: Andre Deutsch Ltd., 1987, pp.57−58.
20 See Mikdashi, *op. cit.* pp.115−116.
21 See for example, *The Report of the Committee to Consider the Rationalisation of the Sugar Industry in Trinidad and Tobago*, December, 1978.
22 See G. Beckford, *The West Indian Banana Industry*, Mona: I.S.E.R. 1967. See also A. McIntyre, 'Decolonization and Trade Policy in the West Indies', in *The Caribbean in Transition*, Proceedings of the Second Caribbean Scholars Conference, (eds.) Fuat Andic and Thomas Matthews, Institute of Caribbean Studies, University of Puerto Rico, 1965.
23 The other major producer in the region is Surinam where bauxite and alumina output in 1985 amounted to 3699 and 1242 metric tons respectively.
24 For a history of the early exploration efforts in Guyana see reports compiled by D.W. Bishopp (revised by E.R. Pollard), *The Bauxite Resources of British Guyana and their Development*, Georgetown: The Daily Chronicle, 1955.
25 Norman Girvan, *Corporate Imperialism: Conflict and Expropriation*, New York: M.E. Sharpe, Inc., 1976, p.162.
26 For a good discussion on the early history of bauxite in Jamaica see V.A. Zans, *Bauxite Resources of Jamaica and their Development*, London: HMSO, 1954. See also Michael Manley, *op. cit.* Chap. 1.
27 See the Rt. Hon. J.D. Anthony, 'Australia in the World Bauxite/Alumina/Aluminium Industry', *JBI Journal*, Summer, 1983.
28 See Carlton E. Davis, 'The Aluminium Industry in Crisis: Some Reflections and Prescriptions', The *JBI Journal*, Vol. 3, No. 2 1985.
29 See N. Girvan, *op. cit.* p.164.
30 N. Girvan, 'The Jamaican Production Levy − A View of the Past, A Vision of the Future', in *The JBI Journal*, Vol. 3, No. 1, 1984.

31 Wesley Hughes, 'Mineral Taxation and Economic Development: The Use of Jamaica's Production Levy Earnings 1974–83', *JBI Journal*, Vol. 3, No. 1, 1984.
32 See A.A. Francis, *Taxing the Transnational in the Struggle Over Bauxite*, Kingston: Institute of Social Studies in Association with Heinemann Educational Books, Caribbean Ltd., 1981.
33 N. Girvan, 'The Jamaican Production Levy...', *op. cit.*
34 For an interesting and compact report on the saga of oil in the Caribbean see NACLA, *Latin America and Empire Report*, Vol. X, No. 8, October 1976. Much of the information in this section is derived from this study.
35 See Ministry of Energy and Natural Resources, *Information on the Petroleum Industry of Trinidad and Tobago*, June, 1984. See Also T. Bhoopsingh, 'Trinidad and Tobago's Petroleum Industry: The Next Decade', in the *JBI Journal*, Vol. 1, No. 2.
36 Trinidad and Tobago is not a member of OPEC. There are unconfirmed reports that an application for membership some years ago was turned down. OPEC statutes limit membership to countries with a substantial net export of crude petroleum. This criterion is not precisely defined. Applicants must be accepted by a three-quarters majority of full members, subject to a veto power by any of the founding members. New applicants should have 'fundamentally similar interests to those of member countries'.
37 See extract from Christopher Flavin's paper 'Energy Efficiency and New Energy Sources', in *OPEC Bulletin*, February, 1986, p.18.
38 Energy Survey Section in *OPEC Bulletin*, May 1986, p.63.
39 *Ibid*.
40 See Abdullah El-Kuwaiz, *op. cit.*

CHAPTER 4

Offshore finance — The Caribbean connection

In order to deal with problems relating to foreign exchange, development finance, employment and government revenue a number of countries in the Caribbean have turned to a range of activities which are often summarily described as 'offshore'. Offshore banking, offshore medical schools, offshore casinos, offshore ship registration centres and offshore insurance companies are now popular (if often misunderstood) terms in the West Indian vocabulary. The resort to offshore activities has its roots in several factors. To some extent it stems from a dissatisfaction over the performance of some of the more traditional activities (and strategies) in resolving urgent economic problems or effecting the kind of transformation initially envisaged. It is also based on a perception that such activities have contributed significantly to the prosperity of certain other states, and therefore, by extension they should have the same effect in the imitating states. The widespread duplication of almost identical facilities bears ample testimony to the strength of this perception among the political directorate in the region, often searching for miraculous cures or instant solutions to deep-seated social and economic problems. In their eagerness to adopt what they see as a relatively easy path to development, critical considerations relating to the nature of the activity or its social and economic consequences in the context of long term objectives tend to be easily ignored by policy makers, some of whom tend to see the issues in terms of their own personal well-being rather than in a development perspective.

In this chapter it is not our intention to concentrate on the whole range of offshore activities which are proving to be increasingly attractive to West Indian governments, or on the issues pertaining to the broader question of tax haven status.[1] Instead, we shall focus our attention on certain selected aspects of offshore finance in a changing regional and international environment. The chapter is divided into four sections. In the first part we discuss the concept of an offshore financial centre. The second provides some details on the Bahamian model which is often a source of inspiration to other aspiring countries. The third section is taken up with problems of regulations and the experience of some of the newer centres in the

Caribbean. Finally, we make some concluding observations on the problems arising from, and the prospects facing the operation of offshore financial centres.

What is an 'Offshore Financial Centre'?

The term 'offshore' is used loosely to describe a wide variety of situations, though the basic connotation is one of location. A common usage nowadays is with respect to oil exploration activities taking place off the coast of some island or land mass, in describing which the term 'offshore mining' or 'offshore exploration' is used to distinguish them from 'onshore' operations. The Americans have traditionally referred to the string of so-called Caribbean Basin islands stretching from Florida to the South American coast as 'offshore'. It was one step from here to describe many of the activities hosted by these islands as 'offshore,' regardless of their geographical orientation or direction. The islands themselves have been a little more discriminating. Generally, the term 'offshore' is reserved for activities which though located within their boundaries, are almost wholly or exclusively oriented to a foreign (offshore) market or clientele. Thus, we speak of 'offshore' casinos which are intended to provide a service mainly to foreigners. We also have the phenomenon of 'offshore' medical schools located in places like Grenada,[2] St Vincent and Montserrat, which cater mainly for foreign students who have been unable to gain places in University schools abroad. 'Offshore' banking is, of course, well known. Here borrowing and lending activities are largely with a clientele outside the country where the banks are registered or located.

In recent years countries like Barbados, Antigua, St Vincent, Anguilla, Montserrat and the Turks and Caicos Islands have instituted measures with the aim of becoming offshore banking centres like Panama, the Cayman Islands and the Bahamas. Some of these centres (old and new) have also taken steps to expand the range of facilities offered such as providing for offshore insurance (for which Bermuda has become internationally famous) and ship registration (for which Liberia and Panama are well known). In order to enhance their tax haven status, the secret or numbered account facility for which Switzerland is famous is becoming increasingly attractive. As far as offshore banking is concerned, the Bahamas, as the oldest offshore banking centre in this hemisphere, has not only been the inspiration to the surge of other centres in the Caribbean, but has served as a model to emulate. In some quarters the Bahamas is seen as a country which has solved all its economic problems, including that of capital needs, by hosting offshore banks. Since it appears that little indepth thought has been given to the structure of the Bahamian model, to its uniqueness or to the spatial and time factors that shaped it, we shall look at the Bahamas' experience in the following section in some detail.

Before we do so, however, it is useful to draw reference to the distinction Thomas Kelen has made between an 'offshore financial centre' and a 'tax haven'.[3] The latter, he defines as a territory where assets can be held and profits can be accumulated and transferred without any local tax consequence, or at least, where such transactions precipitate a substantially smaller tax liability than they would have done elsewhere. An 'offshore financial centre' on the other hand is seen as a place where international financial business can be carried on in a fiscally neutral way. The most distinguishing feature in the latter case is the separation of the domestic and international markets by the intelligent use of foreign exchange control and taxation. A location, of course, can be both a tax haven and an offshore financial centre, and this is often the case because the regulations, laws and general conditions that define each tend to be related to some extent.

With respect to tax havens themselves, these can differ widely in terms of the scope and level of taxation, and the particular facilities and conditions offered. For example, in traditional havens like the Bahamas, Bermuda and the Cayman Islands, income, profits, corporation, withholding and capital gains taxes tend to be absent. There are some havens (e.g. the British Virgin Islands) which impose taxes, but at relatively low rates. Others like Hong Kong, Liberia and Panama, tax income from domestic sources but exempt all income from foreign sources. Yet a fourth category includes countries (e.g. Luxembourg) which are not generally considered to be tax havens, but are suitable as such for limited purposes only.

Finally, the distinction should be made between an 'offshore', financial centre which is largely a 'conduit' (or 'window') and the traditional onshore centres like New York, London or Zurich, which perform a genuine international intermediary function between lenders and borrowers of all nationalities. A number of factors combine to give the latter this distinctive feature. One is the high level of domestic savings. Another is the status of their respective national currencies and the underlying economic and financial policies affecting their role in international transactions. A third is a highly developed money and capital market which is important not only in terms of encouraging local savings, but in attracting foreign funds. A fourth relates to the conscious decision not only to allow foreigners to invest or place funds in the local market, but to be able to borrow there as well. While offshore centres tend largely to be recording or book-keeping centres, some (e.g. Singapore) are more functional than others in terms of actual deposit taking and final lending taking place by financial entities.

The Bahamian model

The Bahamas was well known as a tax haven and tourist resort long before it attained a reputation as an offshore banking or financial centre during the 1960s and 1970s. At the end of the 1950s, there were only a dozen or so commercial banks doing business in the Bahamas. At the end of 1967, there were 187 institutions (90% held public licences) licensed to carry on business of a banking or trust nature in or from within the Bahamas. As Diagram I shows, by the end of September 1986, the number had grown to 375, despite the competition from new centres. Of this number, 272 were licensed to do banking and/or trust business with the public, while 95 had a restricted licence (i.e., they could do business only with the people or institutions stipulated in the licence). The other eight were of a non-active or nominee nature. Of the 272 institutions with public licences, 19 were authorised dealers and agents, 133 were Euro-currency branches of foreign banks (largely American) while 120 were Bahamian incorporated. An authorised dealer is a bank authorised by the authorities to deal both in Bahamian dollars and foreign exchange. An authorised agent is permitted to deal in Bahamian and foreign currency securities and to act as depositaries for certificates of title to these securities. At the end of September 1986, there were seven authorised dealers, ten authorised agents (all trust companies) and two institutions authorised to be both a dealer and an agent. Altogether, therefore, there were nine institutions authorised to deal both in Bahamian dollars and foreign exchange. The 133 Euro-currency branches of foreign banks would be deemed non-resident for exchange control purposes i.e. they operate only in foreign currency without reference to the Central Bank whose powers to impose reserve ratios or control interest rates tend to be confined to the authorised dealers. It should be pointed out here that the authorised dealers also engage in Euro-currency operations, but the latter aspect is also exempt from the Central Bank's powers. Of the 120 Bahamian incorporated financial institutions, 89 were subsidiaries of banks and trusts based outside the Bahamas, while 33 were based in the Bahamas which they apparently use as their head office. Most of these 108 financial institutions (which are made up of merchant and investment banks, finance houses, etc.) are also non-resident for exchange control purposes. Many of them are also deeply involved in the foreign currency business.

Of the 375 financial institutions registered in the Bahamas, only about two dozen or so may have a physical presence. Among them are the nine authorised dealers who are engaged in both Bahamian dollar and foreign currency business. Some of these have branches scattered in certain strategic areas. The 'shell banks' which comprise the bulk of the institutions have their registered office in the form of a brass plate located in the premises of a trust company, or in an accountant's or lawyer's office. The functions of the managers or managing enterprise are quite routine, and this enables them to manage a large number of companies or banks. One of their functions is to help the foreign entities comply with local regulations in return for which they are paid a fee. Their role is largely a passive one.

The term 'offshore banking' can cover a very broad field of financial activities which are not always clear to people approaching the subject for the first time. Citizens of foreign countries often find it necessary to set up their own private banks with the aim of managing the finances of a family or estate. In the Bahamas such institutions will operate on the basis of a restricted licence. That is to say, as we have indicated before, the persons from whom the bank can accept funds or those to whom it can loan money are specified in the licence by the local authorities at the time of issue. There is another group of banks which is formed (or purchased) by one or more individuals (or institutions) with the aim of soliciting business on an international scale, though not participating in the Euro-currency (inter-bank or wholesale markets). As we saw earlier, the major part of the institutions holding a public licence are the branches of foreign banks (most of them based in the US) which were set up during the 1960s to permit the parent banks to engage in the Euro-currency market. These are also part of the so-called 'shell' or 'paper' group of banks, and it is important to understand their *raison d'etre*.

With the growth of the Euro-currency market[4] (and particularly the dollar component of this market) during the 1960s and 1970s, and with the emergence of London as the centre of the system, the large American banks felt the need to have a more functional presence in the British capital than a correspondent relationship. Since

100 The Commonwealth Caribbean

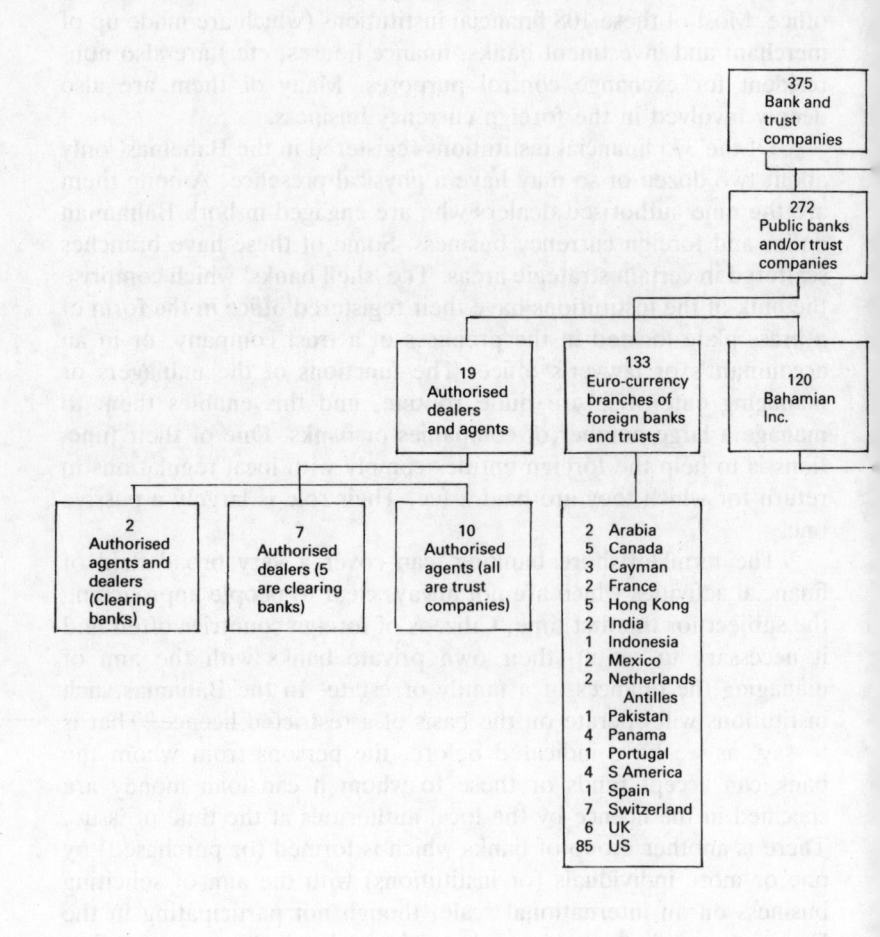

```
                        ┌─────────────┐
                        │    375      │
                        │  Bank and   │
                        │    trust    │
                        │  companies  │
                        └──────┬──────┘
                               │
                        ┌──────┴──────┐
                        │    272      │
                        │ Public banks│
                        │  and/or trust│
                        │  companies  │
                        └──────┬──────┘
        ┌──────────────────────┼──────────────────────┐
   ┌────┴────┐          ┌──────┴──────┐         ┌─────┴─────┐
   │   19    │          │     133     │         │    120    │
   │Authorised│         │Euro-currency│         │ Bahamian  │
   │ dealers │          │branches of  │         │   Inc.    │
   │and agents│         │foreign banks│         │           │
   │         │          │ and trusts  │         │           │
   └────┬────┘          └─────────────┘         └───────────┘
        │
   ┌────┼────────────────┐
┌──┴──┐ ┌──┴──┐    ┌─────┴─────┐
│  2  │ │  7  │    │    10     │
│Authorised│ │Authorised│ │Authorised│
│agents and│ │dealers (5│ │agents (all│
│ dealers │ │are clearing│ │are trust │
│(Clearing│ │  banks)  │ │companies) │
│ banks)  │ │          │ │           │
└─────────┘ └──────────┘ └───────────┘
```

2	Arabia
5	Canada
3	Cayman
2	France
5	Hong Kong
2	India
1	Indonesia
2	Mexico
2	Netherlands Antilles
1	Pakistan
4	Panama
1	Portugal
4	S America
1	Spain
7	Switzerland
6	UK
85	US

Diagram 1 Banks and trust companies in the Bahamas as at September 30, 1986
Source: Central Bank of the Bahamas, *Quarterly Review*, Sept. 1986

Offshore finance

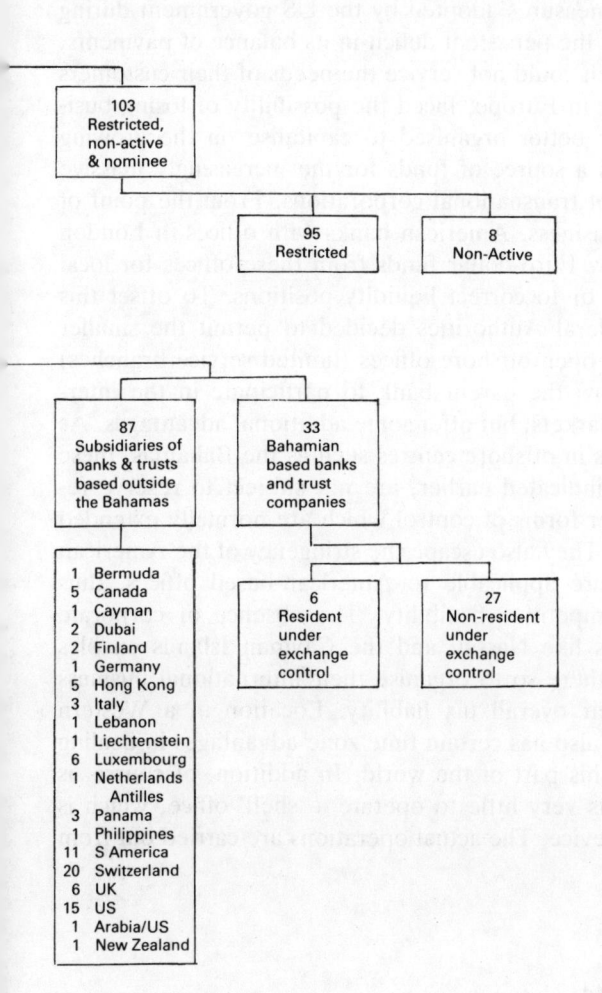

```
┌─────────────────┐
│      103        │
│   Restricted,   │
│   non-active    │
│   & nominee     │
└────────┬────────┘
         │
    ┌────┴────┐
    │         │
┌───┴───┐ ┌───┴───┐
│  95   │ │   8   │
│Restric│ │Non-   │
│ted    │ │Active │
└───────┘ └───────┘

┌─────────────────┐   ┌─────────────────┐
│       87        │   │       33        │
│  Subsidiaries of│   │    Bahamian     │
│ banks & trusts  │   │   based banks   │
│   based outside │   │  and trust      │
│   the Bahamas   │   │   companies     │
├─────────────────┤   └────────┬────────┘
│  1  Bermuda     │            │
│  5  Canada      │       ┌────┴────┐
│  1  Cayman      │       │         │
│  2  Dubai       │   ┌───┴───┐ ┌───┴────┐
│  2  Finland     │   │   6   │ │   27   │
│  1  Germany     │   │Resident│ │Non-    │
│  5  Hong Kong   │   │ under  │ │resident│
│  3  Italy       │   │exchange│ │ under  │
│  1  Lebanon     │   │control │ │exchange│
│  1  Liechtenstein│  │        │ │control │
│  6  Luxembourg  │   └────────┘ └────────┘
│  1  Netherlands │
│     Antilles    │
│  3  Panama      │
│  1  Philippines │
│ 11  S America   │
│ 20  Switzerland │
│  6  UK          │
│ 15  US          │
│  1  Arabia/US   │
│  1  New Zealand │
└─────────────────┘
```

the London authorities insist on a physical presence, being represented there is an expensive proposition. The medium and smaller American banks who could not afford to open an office in London were placed at a severe disadvantage not only in terms of international competition, but with respect to their domestic operations.

One effect of measures adopted by the US government during the 1960s to correct the persistent deficit in its balance of payments, was that banks which could not service the needs of their customers abroad, particularly in Europe, faced the possibility of losing business to competitors better organised to capitalise on the growing Euro-dollar pool as a source of funds for the increasingly massive financial demands of transnational corporations. From the point of view of domestic business, American banks with offices in London were able to borrow Euro-dollar funds from these offices for local lending in the US, or to correct liquidity positions. To offset this advantage, the Federal Authorities decided to permit the smaller American banks to open offshore offices (limited service branches) which not only allow the parent bank to participate in the international currency markets, but offer some additional advantages. As 'non-resident' banks in offshore centres such as the Bahamas, these institutions, as we indicated earlier, are not subject to reserve requirements, or other forms of control which are normally extended to 'resident' banks. They also escape the stringency of the American regulations which are applicable to American-based offices, thus increasing their competitive flexibility. The absence of corporate taxes in tax havens like Nassau and the Cayman Islands enables banks with offices there so to organise their international business as to minimise their overall tax liability. Location in a Western Hemisphere centre also has certain time zone advantages in dealing with customers in this part of the world. In addition, of course, is the fact that it costs very little to operate a 'shell' office, which is largely a booking device. The actual operations are carried out from head office.

Costs and benefits

With respect to the benefits and costs associated with operating an offshore banking office, there tends to be a great deal of controversy. One reason for this is the difficulty of quantifying costs and benefits and separating these out from those of other activities. Published data often refer to the entire financial (domestic and offshore) operation, and this often leads to a highly exaggerated level of importance to offshore activities in the domestic economy. With respect to benefits, these can be divided into contribution to government revenue, contribution to domestic expenditure (salaries, wages utility payments, etc.) and employment.[5] With respect to the first, the contribution generally tends to take the form of licence fees, company fees and work permit charges. Even in jurisdictions with a broad range of taxes the practice is to exempt income from offshore operations from the major forms of taxation. This applies both to the 'record keeping' or 'paper' centres and to some of the more functional centres like Hong Kong. Though this latter country taxes personal incomes and profits, the rates are relatively low and are confined to local source income or assets only. It should be pointed out, however, that in recent times the Hong Kong authorities (pressed for more revenue) have tended to tax profits (at standard rates) arising from certain forms of offshore financial activities. This is no doubt possible because of the high functional value of location in Hong Kong. Generally, offshore financial centres are not encouraged with the aim of boosting government revenue, even though for a country with a small revenue base, the licence fees collected may look quite impressive. A major part of their attraction lies in the largely tax free (and regulations free) environment which they offer.

As far as the Bahamas is concerned, the licence fees collected from banks and trust companies in 1980 amounted to about US$2 million as compared to a total revenue of US$244 million in that year. Generally, revenue from this source has accounted for less than 1% of total revenue. A survey done by the Central Bank of the Bahamas[6] and covering some 220 financial institutions in the Bahamas showed an employment figure of 1916 (274 non-Bahamian) in 1973 as compared to 2184 persons (255 non-Bahamian) in 1977. This latter figure represented about 2% to 3% of the estimated labour force in that year. Contrary to common misconceptions, it is tourism and related activities which provide the bulk of the employment opportunities in the Bahamas. (Tourism has been estimated to contribute over 70% to GNP, while it provides jobs for over half of the labour force).[7]

Companies and work permit fees paid by the surveyed institutions increased from US$579 000 in 1973 to about US$2.2 million (1.6% to total revenue) in 1977. The salaries figure increased from US$18.2 million in 1973 to US$26.6 million in 1977, while administrative and miscellaneous expenses increased from US$12 million to US$23.2 million over the same period. The institutions with a physical presence also undertake certain expenditures related to the upkeep of premises. In the absence of the respective contributions of 'resident' and 'non-resident' institutions, one has to be careful in parading these figures as an indication of the benefits of offshore business. From what we have said before, it is clear that the contribution by the offshore entities could hardly be significant. The 'shell' operations tend to be handled by a small number of trust companies, lawyers and accountants who would need to employ only a few more clerks and typists than they normally require. As pointed out earlier, there are some institutions with completely offshore operations which may find it necessary to have a physical presence in the offshore centre. Very often the latter may serve as the regional or international head office for the entity. These would require people with a certain amount of skill who may be secured either locally or abroad. The major providers of employment in the financial sector are the institutions engaged in onshore business, which, as mentioned earlier, may also be engaged in some offshore operations. The same staff servicing the domestic business are generally used in the offshore business as well.

With respect to benefits, a commonly held belief is that the setting up of an offshore banking centre will bring capital for development. This can be exaggerated out of all proportion. We have already discussed the nature of the 'shell' banks whose business is carried out from head office, and whose operations largely involve a foreign clientele. They have virtually no significance for domestic finance. In the Bahamas, it is largely the few authorised dealers (who, as we indicated earlier, also participate in the Euro-currency market) who from time to time put funds at the disposal of the local government. Because of the country's good balance of payments performance and repayment record, the government has had little difficulty raising funds. This is not a guaranteed position, however. The situation could change as the revenue position tightens and questions begin to arise about its ability to repay.[8]

The private sectors of the economy tend not to be as fortunate as the government sector. This is particularly so with respect to high risk borrowers such as agriculturists, fishermen, small business, etc. Nor are the banks necessarily concerned with social development, particularly with a sector such as housing. There is no automatic or ready made solution to the capital problem in the development process. There is another point worth making here about the view that there is a huge amount of funds waiting for some lucky country to tap. Because of both political and currency risks, banks pursue certain policies of their own. Uncertainty in exchange rates lead them to balance their assets (in terms of currency) in relation to the structure of their liabilities. The extent of conversion that takes place depends on the rate of return, the perception of the exchange risks, and so on. Local investment also depends on the range of available instruments. Because of the growing nationalism, in developing countries particularly, banks are wary of having too large a concentration of their assets in any one place. Even when domestic interest rates are higher than international rates, the volume of local lending (whether through conversion or in foreign currency) would tend to be dictated by house rules of the banks themselves.

Besides the direct benefits, it is often claimed that there are other indirect benefits attached to the operation of an offshore banking centre. For one, it would provide a boost to the local tourist industry as a result of the movement of bankers (the holding of board meetings, etc.) and the desire by clients to visit the place where their money is banked. Given the nature of offshore banking, this benefit might be overstated. It is also sometimes argued that offshore banking centres 'may gain improved access to international capital markets', or that 'the domestic financial system may become more efficient, both through increased competition and through exposure to the practices of the offshore banks', or that a 'cadre of local staff may be trained which will contribute to a faster growth of the domestic economy'. As McCarthy correctly points out, this group of benefits could hardly materialise in 'recording centres', specialising in 'shell' operations.[9] Another benefit which is of an intangible nature is that there is prestige in being an 'international banking centre'. Experience has shown that this prestige can easily turn into notoriety.

So far as costs are concerned, it is often argued by ardent proponents of offshore banking centres that even if the benefits are minimal, there are little or no costs to be incurred. Any jurisdiction serious about preventing its facilities from being abused certainly has to invest in a competent licensing and regulatory administrative machinery. The infiltration of entities intent on engaging in fraudulent activities will not only affect the reputation of the centre, but would also drive away the genuine financial concerns who help to make the name of a financial centre, whether it is a 'paper' or a 'functional' one. The more 'functional' a centre (i.e. one where actual borrowing and lending takes place) the greater the benefits are likely to be. But the costs are also likely to increase correspondingly. Developing and maintaining a sound infrastructure (telecommunications, airports, etc.) is a necessary requirement, particularly in a competitive situation. The increased demand for land, office space, and housing is also bound to exert pressure on domestic prices.

The newcomers

As indicated earlier, Barbados,[10] Antigua and St Vincent have recently adopted legislation with the aim of becoming offshore banking centres. In fact the latter two (like Anguilla and Montserrat) appeared to have gone into the business even before proper legislation was in place, and a legal framework was prompted only after certain difficulties arose, some of which were widely reported in the regional and international press. An examination of the statements made by politicians and officials would seem to indicate that the aim was to attract institutions operating in the growing Euro-currency market. It was felt that offshore banking activities would not only boost government revenue and local employment, but that there would be an increased availability of capital funds to the domestic economy. The tourism industry would also receive a fillip. We do not have data on the number of offshore financial institutions which have registered in Anguilla, Antigua, Barbados, Montserrat and St Vincent, or on the size of their assets. In fact this information itself appears to be highly secretive. Newspaper reports, however, indicate that there is a fairly large number of banks registered in Anguilla, Montserrat and St Vincent. What is not clear is the proportion that might be termed genuine wholesale Euro-currency banks and the proportion registered for other purposes.

The problem of regulation

For small countries with limited expertise, the problem of regulation is an extremely grave one. Even for the older centres like the Bahamas and the Cayman Islands which have been able to tailor their regulatory framework on the basis of experience, the lack of adequate resources and skilled personnel make it impossible to carry out the kinds of checks required to maintain a 'clean' industry. On paper, the newly adopted legislation (some of which was drafted with foreign help) looks impeccable. Implementing or enforcing legal requirements, however, could be quite a different thing.

The reputable banks which open offices in the context of their Euro-currency business create little problem for regulation, since they themselves have their reputation to protect. The problem is with the other types of 'shell' banks which may be set up (with very little capital) to take advantage of gullible people, or to help people evade tax laws in their own country, or simply to engage in some form of illicit activity. It has been found 'that offshore havens are no longer used exclusively by criminals. Instead they are increasingly being used by otherwise law-abiding Americans to avoid paying taxes and to shield assets from creditors'.[11] This situation has led to a great demand for banks which are now marketed like some commodity by individuals and companies (brokers) claiming to be experts in the setting up of offshore banks. These individuals and companies (who familiarise themselves with the laws and regulations in particular jurisdictions)[12] provide a service by obtaining charters and then reselling them for a profit to people who want to own a bank. Some claim they are very careful about whom they sell a charter to, while others would sell a charter to anyone with the cash.[13] (Obviously if the paid-in capital were substantial as in say Panama, this would not be as easy to do). The fact is, a bank licence offers limitless possibilities to the person owning it. 'An offshore bank licence enables an individual to exploit the investigative difficulties and complexities encountered with criminal activities which extend beyond the sovereign limits of a single nation. These problems are exacerbated when secrecy laws prevent co-operation with the offshore governments'.[14]

Generally, offshore banks are not allowed to do business with residents of the jurisdiction where they are located, and in this way protection is afforded to citizens. They are also not required to have any actual office or local place of business. 'There is no actual staff, fixed assets, or other accoutrements of actual banks'.[15] In most instances a lawyer or solicitor is the mail drop and the answering service. Where capitalisation is required, funds are generally not required to be held locally. Capitalisation itself could be fabricated to satisfy local requirements through a network of paper transactions (between related companies) which the licensing authorities may be incapable of verifying.[16] Since the offshore centres may perceive their importance to be measured by the number of banks registered within their respective jurisdictions, the temptation not to operate within regulations, or where the latter exist, not to enforce them strictly, can be great. There is evidence to indicate that jurisdictions which were initially attractive because of the absence of laws, soon lost their attractiveness when legislation was passed. The footloose nature of 'shell' banks means that they can easily shift their location from one centre to another. The easy availability of banks means that when a particular name is under suspicion or investigation, its owner or owner(s) may simply drop that one and purchase another. In places like Anguilla, a bank can apparently be purchased for cash with no questions asked.[17] The middlemen who obtain bank charters for purposes of re-selling to final owners may claim they make a special check on the people to whom they sell banks, but there is no guarantee that a bank would not be put to illegal uses once it is acquired.[18]

The facility of secrecy which all the centres offer is a double-edged sword. The stronger the secrecy provisions offered by the various legislations, the more attractive the centre may be to certain types of banks, particularly those wishing to engage in illegal trade. This very secrecy, however, may work against the jurisdiction in that it may encourage the authorities to be very lax in investigative requirements, and thus allow questionable entities to slip through, which become known only after some embarrassing episode.

Implications for the Caribbean

It is possible to divide the offshore banking centres in the Caribbean into two groups: (a) the older centres such as the Bahamas and the Cayman Islands, and (b) the newer banking sanctuaries like St Vincent, Turks and Caicos Islands, Anguilla, Montserrat and Barbados. The former group have managed to develop a certain amount of expertise in regulation, though the procedures they follow are by no means entirely foolproof. When one examines the recent experience of the latter group and scrutinise the statements of the politicians, it would appear that this group is not quite certain about the nature of the animal they are dealing with. The glossy pictures painted about what offshore banking can do and the riches envisaged are yet to materialise. Caribbean islands have unknowingly and unconsciously played hosts to criminals who have used 'briefcase banks' to issue millions of dollars of worthless paper, which have caused serious problems in US banking circles. A common technique used is to employ names (e.g. Chase Overseas or Midland Overseas) similar to the large well known international banks in an obvious attempt to mislead.[19] The US comptroller of currency has identified as many as 125 banks that may have been engaged in fraudulent operations.[20]

What of the future? Countries like Anguilla, Antigua, Barbados, Montserrat, and St Vincent are small countries in both land space and population. None of them have mineral resources of any significance. Tourism is fast replacing whatever traditional economic activities may have sustained the islands. The increase in oil prices during the 1970s served to increase the pressures on these countries which were already having problems with their foreign payments. While in the OECS foreign debt service payments in relation to exports are generally below 15%, these payments take a relatively higher proportion of current revenues which have tended to grow at a slower rate than current expenditures. All these countries run deficits on current account of the balance of payments. In certain cases (e.g. St Lucia) the inflow of foreign direct investment has helped in bridging the foreign exchange gap, but in most cases grants have played a crucial role. Any serious decline in inflows of concessional finance would increase the economic pressures on these countries since servicing hard loans, even if they could be obtained, entails higher servicing burdens.

In this situation one could understand the pressing need to find new sources of revenue and employment. The revenue derived from licensing fees may not be large in absolute terms, but given the plight of these countries and the small revenue base, any income is welcome. The economic conditions described create a vulnerable situation which, as we saw, can have dangerous consequences. Unwittingly, some of these islands can (to some extent they already have) become the playground for crooks who show little concern for the integrity of the monetary, financial and fiscal systems of other countries. The retaliatory measures which this behaviour invite is bound to affect even the reputable and legitimate institutions, as well as the region as a whole.

Some final observations

The desire to operate offshore banking or financial centres is based on the belief that the associated activities can contribute significantly to economic development. This belief is to a certain extent sustained by the perception that some of the older centres have derived immeasurable benefits from hosting offshore financial activities, and therefore the experience can easily be duplicated. In some instances, the perception has not only failed to appreciate the environmental and historical factors which contrived to create the older centres, but has been erroneous in assessing the role and place of offshore financial activity in the economic landscape. For example, in an interview carried in the *Advocate News* of 7 May, 1980, the former Prime Minister of Barbados, Mr Tom Adams is reported to have said that 'presently more Bahamians were employed in offshore banking than tourism'. As we saw earlier, the opposite is the case.[21] Another 'expert' writing in the *Sunday Digest (Trinidad) Express* of 9 November, 1980 made the following observation: 'Bermuda is the best example of a good tourist "plant", and caters for a healthy mix of tourism and offshore banking'. The fact is Bermuda is not an offshore banking centre. The country has only about four banks.[22] This country is perhaps the world's leading centre for offshore insurance companies which are a different matter altogether.

The emergence of several centres in the Caribbean region means increased competition.[23] In an effort to attract business away from the others, some may be tempted to offer greater incentives (reminiscent of the 'industrialisation by invitation' strategy). In this situation the tendency would be to become lax in one's regulatory approach. Even when laws exist (e.g. those pertaining to capital requirements, liquidity, etc.), the temptation may be to relinquish enforcement, if this can attract business away from competitors. The unavailability of competent personnel to vet applications for registration or to carry out the necessary investigations and periodic examination may serve only to encourage this attitude. In this kind of atmosphere, the consequences can be disastrous. Already, as we have seen, jurisdictions like the Bahamas, Anguilla, Montserrat and St Vincent are especially being singled out by US government agencies as sanctuaries from which criminal activities are being conducted. Once a centre becomes tainted, the reputable institutions tend to flee. Even worse, the very character of the people and government become associated with fraud and dishonesty. The region as a whole can suffer, since it is often difficult for the outside world to distinguish between the different units.

It is not unusual to find that many of the reputable banks registered in the Bahamas also have offices in the Cayman Islands and Panama. The banks tend to follow each other around, so as not to find themselves in a disadvantageous position in relation to each other. Despite the emergence of the relatively newer centres, the older ones like the Bahamas, the Cayman Islands and Panama have retained their attractiveness. My feeling is that the offshore business may well have reached a kind of saturation point, with countries vying for a given level of business. Even in Singapore there is concern that there are now more banks than business.[24]

It also needs to be pointed out that besides the tax free arrangements, a major element in the attractiveness of the offshore centres lies in the secrecy facilities which they offer. Of the 29 countries with which the US had tax treaties at the end of 1981, there were seven in force with tax havens in the Caribbean – most by extension of the US tax treaty with the UK. Those covered by this extension include Antigua, Barbados, Belize, British Virgin Islands, Grenada and St Vincent.[25] Also to be included are Anguilla, Montserrat and the Turks and Caicos Islands. There is also a treaty with the

Netherlands Antilles, which is being renegotiated. The British treaties are aimed largely at eliminating double taxation of the citizens of the states involved, and do not cater for the exchange of banking or corporate information.

Havens like the Bahamas, the Cayman Islands and Panama have no tax or mutual assistance treaties with the US whose agencies have found it extremely difficult to obtain information from these jurisdictions. There are indications that the US government will increasingly use its foreign aid programmes (such as the Caribbean Basin Initiative) to pressure offshore governments into co-operating more fully with the US Internal Revenue Service. The latter is convinced that offshore centres are used by US citizens in a large way to escape paying taxes at home. The US authorities also associate these centres with criminal activity. The drug problem in the US and the conviction by US officials that the islands are not only important transhipment points for drugs entering their country but that offshore banks are being used to hide the ill-gotten gains, have resulted in a more intense effort by US authorities to obtain exchange of information treaties with Caribbean governments. In the case of the Bahamas, undercover activities by US agents without local authorisation and the pressure for greater co-operation from the Bahamian government, have strained relations between the two countries in recent years. Designation of the Bahamas as a beneficiary under the CBI was delayed until 1985. Even though the Bahamas is more dependent on tourism than Jamaica, the former does not benefit from tax provisions relating to the holding of conventions.

Finally, we need to say something on what has been one of the more important developments in recent times, and one which may have tremendous significance for the future of offshore banking. We refer here to the establishment of international banking facilities (IBFs) in the US since 1981.[26] This has come about as a result of legislative and regulatory changes both at the federal and the state level. In 1981, the Federal Reserve Board not only changed its regulations to permit the establishment of IBFs, but also enacted legislation to exempt IBFs from the insurance coverage and assessments imposed by the FDIC. In addition, of course, several states have granted special tax status to the operating profits from IBFs, or modified existing restrictions affecting the growth of IBFs, in an effort to promote themselves as international financial centres. The effect of these legislative and regulatory changes is that IBFs may transact business with non-residents of the US on more or less the same terms as banks located offshore. They cannot, however, deal with US residents at all, apart from their parent institution or other

IBFs. IBFs are not subject to reserve requirements, interest rate ceilings and deposit insurance assessment that apply to domestic banking. In order to separate the operations of IBFs from the domestic money markets, a number of restrictions exist with respect to the maturity of deposits with non-bank customers, the issuing of negotiable instruments, etc. It should be pointed out that the establishment of IBFs do not necessarily represent the coming into being of new institutions or new physical facilities, but they are essentially a separate set of books within existing banking organisations.

The establishment of IBFs has encouraged US banks with foreign branches to shift a large part of their business from places like the Bahamas and Cayman Islands to onshore offices. As far as business with US residents is concerned, however, the Caribbean branches may still have some relevance. The relevance may further diminish with any relaxation of interest regulation on domestic US banks.

With respect to actual numbers, recent data indicate an increase in offshore institutions in some centres. For instance in the case of the Bahamas the number of banks and trusts registered there increased from 338 at the end of March 1982 to 375 at the end of September 1986. The number of US Euro-currency branch banks declined only slightly over this period, from 88 to 85, or by less than 4%.

Concluding comments

Tax havens and offshore financial centres function on a very tenuous basis. Changes in the laws and regulations of the developed countries easily affect the level of business. Over time an erosion of certain forms of tax haven activities has been taking place, and this is finally taking a toll in certain centres, some of which are being forced to take a new look at their fiscal arrangements. For the very small resourceless islands of the Caribbean one can understand the urge to capitalise on anything which appears to contribute to the sustenance of life. In these countries even small benefits assume significant proportions, and this, of course, makes them easy prey to speculators and crooks who have little difficulty in gaining access to politicians and policy makers. The political indifference to the genuine concerns expressed over the establishment of casinos and offshore medical schools in the region reflects the depth of insensitivity that can exist.

There is increasing evidence that offshore banks play a major role in 'laundering' money derived from the drug trade. An important element in the souring of relations between President Noreiga of

Panama and the US is the freedom with which drug dealers use the banking facilities of Panama. The fact that the US dollar is also the currency of Panama put the latter in an even more vulnerable position than other jurisdictions, and the US did not hesitate in using this arrangement to 'turn the screws' on Noreiga, even though the entire economy has suffered.

Notes

1. For a discussion on this subject, see R. Ramsaran, *The Monetary and Financial System of the Bahamas-Growth Structure and Operation*, I.S.E.R., Mona 1983. See also R. Ramsaran, 'Issues and Problems in Offshore Finance', in *ASSET*, Vol. 5, No. 1 (1986)
2. The Grenadian School was temporarily located in Barbados following the US invasion in 1983.
3. See Thomas Kelen, 'The World of Offshore Finance', in *The Banker*, April, 1977.
4. In net terms the market is estimated to have grown from US$160 billion at the end of 1973 to US$590 billion at the end of March 1983.
5. See I. McCarthy, 'Offshore Banking Centres: Benefits and Costs', *Finance and Development*, December, 1979.
6. See Central Bank of the Bahamas, *Quarterly Review*, March, 1979.
7. In the early 1970s it was estimated that the entire sector 'Finance, Insurance, Real Estate and Business Services' contributed about 12% to GDP and accounted for about 9% to 10% of the employed labour force.
8. The public debt of the Bahamas has shown a strong tendency to grow in recent years. The direct debt increased from US$108.2 million (of which US$67.9 million represented foreign currency loans) at the end of 1974 to US$478.2 million (US$146.7 million foreign currency loans) at the end of 1985. As a percentage of GNP, the 1985 figure amounted to about 29%.
9. See I. McCarthy, *op. cit.*
10. Barbados' approach has been different from that of the other islands. By signing an exchange of information agreement with the US it clearly indicated that it was prepared to forgo hardline bank secrecy laws, and instead to sell itself on price, treaty connections, and natural attributes. See Colin Brewer *et al.* 'Barbados: Offshore Financial Centre', in *Caribbean Finance and Management*, Summer, 1986. It is instructive to note that by the end of 1987, only about four or five offshore banks were attracted.
11. See *Crime and Secrecy: The Use of Offshore Banks and Companies*, Hearings before the Permanent Sub Committee on Investigations of the Committee on Government Affairs, US Senate, 98th Congress, First Session, p.2.
12. In some cases they have helped in shaping the laws and regulations.
13. US Senate Hearings, *Crime and Secrecy, op. cit.* p.182.
14. *Ibid.* p.148.

15 *Ibid.* p.148.
16 *Ibid.* pp.175–76.
17 *Ibid.* pp.200–201.
18 The myriad illegal uses to which offshore banks can be put are well documented. These include tax evasion in home countries, the laundering of money derived from illegal transactions, the creation of bogus instruments to establish credit, the creation of bogus letters of credit that can be used to establish banks or companies elsewhere, including certification of non-existent assets for such purposes, to verify non-existent credit and assets in insurance swindles, etc. See R.H. Blum, *Offshore Haven Banks, Trusts and Companies*, New York: Praeger, 1984.
19 See US Senate Hearings, *Crime and Secrecy, op. cit.*, p.155.
20 *Ibid.* p.147.
21 In the same interview, Mr Adams also claimed that offshore banking would result in the creation of three to four thousand new jobs.
22 By law, at least 60% of a Bermuda bank's ownership and control must be in the hands of Bermudians.
23 They all claim more or less the same kind of advantages, e.g. stable political climate, the English system of laws, excellent transport and communication facilities, high quality professional services, etc.
24 See Quek Peck Lim, 'Nothing Ventured, Nothing Gained', in *Euromoney*, September, 1984.
25 Staff study of the Permanent Sub Committee on Investigations of the US Senate, *Crime and Secrecy: The Use of Offshore Banks and Companies*, February, 1983, pp.12–13.
26 For a good background discussion on the establishment of IBFs in the US, see S.K. Key, 'International Banking Facilities', *Federal Reserve Bulletin*, October, 1982.

CHAPTER 5 | Trade and economic relations

The issues of foreign trade are closely intertwined with the larger question of economic development. For developing countries generally, it is difficult to separate the two areas. Development is facilitated not only by increasing the volume of trade, but by policies which have the effect of changing the composition of trade. Transforming the structure of trade is often an objective in itself, and in this case domestic economic strategy is as important as international trade policy. Aid in this context means not only the transfer of financial resources or technical assistance, but access to foreign markets and technology, as well as the freedom to choose the most appropriate goods in terms of price and quality among the widest possible range of sources. Aid, of course, often loses some of its effect because recipient countries are required to purchase from specified sources which may not be in a position to provide the most appropriate goods or the best prices. Inadequate foreign exchange can also force a country to change its trade patterns, or the way it conducts its trade in the same way that lack of knowledge can contribute to the persistence of certain trade practices. In this chapter we shall discuss the recent evolution of Commonwealth Caribbean trade and some related economic issues as they affect relations with major trading partners. We shall reserve the question of trade policy and capital flows for later chapters.

The growth, structure and direction of Commonwealth Caribbean trade

As indicated in chapter 2, the Commonwealth Caribbean countries are heavily dependent on foreign trade. This applies to both goods and services. The growth in income has led to increasing demand for both consumer and investment goods. Caribbean societies are very open and are in close touch with foreign trends through books, magazines, newspapers and films. The wide-spread presence of television has made cultural penetration even easier. This constant exposure to foreign tastes and consumption habits has a deep influence on local consumption patterns and trends. Improvement in the standard of living implies higher levels of consumption. The narrow production bases in these territories, however, means that a significant part of local consumption has to be satisfied by imports. The small markets also do not encourage the setting up of capital goods industries, and the result has been almost total dependence on foreign sources for such goods. With the exception of Trinidad and Tobago and to a lesser extent Barbados, the other countries of the area are dependent on imported oil to supply most of their energy requirements. In this situation the availability of foreign exchange is crucial to the standard of living and the level of economic activity. Insufficient foreign exchange easily degenerates into social and economic crises of major dimensions. In recent years falling production levels of traditional exports and depressed commodity prices in the context of a rapidly rising import bill has been a major factor in the economic difficulties facing Caribbean states. Tourism, remittances, gifts and public and private capital inflows have helped in sustaining a high level of imports. In the face of deteriorating balance of payments positions, protectionism and trade restrictions have emerged as an important issue in Caribbean trade relations.

Given the situation outlined above, it is not difficult to see why the state of Caribbean economies is easily influenced by trends in the international economy. Growth in the developed countries for instance often results in increasing demand for exports from other countries. In the same way a restrictive trade policy responding to recessionary conditions can lead to a curtailment of imports. Fluctuations in commodity prices and production levels also easily affect the wellbeing of states critically dependent on the commodities in question. The volume of production, of course, can be affected by internal factors that are in some cases completely outside the control of the governments. Pests, diseases, and weather conditions can take a heavy toll on agricultural crops. Natural disasters like hurricanes can bring about destruction which can take years to repair. A good harvest in one year could be followed by several years of lean production. Depression in a commodity market (as is the case with bauxite at the moment) can also have severe economic and social repercussions. On the other side, heavy dependence on imports implies a strong influence of foreign prices on the local economy.

In order to understand the nature of the link between the Commonwealth Caribbean economies and the world economy, we need some insight into the structure and direction of the region's trade.

In most countries of the region imports have tended to grow faster than exports. Trade deficits are the norm rather than the exception. For the region as a whole imports grew on average by 8.6% per year in current values between 1955 and 1984. The value of exports grew by about 8.3% annually. As can be seen in Table 5.1, the trade growth rates have varied widely among regional states. The reason for this can be found in differences in population and income growth rates, the pace of development, development strategy, size, etc. There are indications that foreign trade has grown faster than national income leading to an increase in the trade/income ratio for some countries. For instance in the case of Jamaica, imports of goods and services expressed as a proportion of GDP increased from an average of 41% in the 1974−78 period to an average of over 50% in the 1980−84 period.

The structure of Commonwealth Caribbean trade

Domestic exports

As indicated earlier, the commodity exports of Commonwealth Caribbean trade continue to be heavily concentrated on a narrow range of products. Some of the major traditional exports have declined in terms of the volume of production, but continue to be important in terms of employment and even foreign exchange. In some of the islands the export of services related especially to tourism and finance has grown increasingly important, overtaking or replacing traditional exports as providers of employment and generators of foreign exchange. In Antigua, for instance, sugar production has ceased and tourism has emerged as the dominant activity. In countries such as Barbados, Antigua, and Montserrat, manufactured goods now account for a significant proportion of domestic exports. It should be noted, however, that these are largely assembly-type operations heavily dependent on imported inputs. The Bahamas is one of the countries where the exports of tourism and financial services account for the bulk of the foreign exchange earned. In Belize sugar and citrus account for over 60% of the value of domestic exports. In Dominica, bananas and soap accounted for almost 70% in 1983. In Grenada, the dominant export items are bananas, cocoa, nutmeg, and fresh fruits, while in Guyana, it is sugar, alumina, bauxite and rice which together contributed 88% to export earnings in 1984. Jamaica's position is not much different. Bauxite, alumina and sugar accounted for 75% of the value of domestic exports in

Table 5.1 Growth of Commonwealth Caribbean trade, 1955–1984 (US$ million)

Countries	Imports (c.i.f.) 1955	1983	1984ᵖ	Annual percentage growth rate 1955–84	Domestic exports (f.o.b.) 1955	1983	1984ᵖ	Average percentage growth rate 1955–84
MDCs								
Barbados	32.2	561.0	662.3	17.2	20.9	255.1	291.8	9.5
Guyana	55.1	248.3	214.3	4.4	51.9	186.5	212.4	5.0
Jamaica	127.9	1 281.1	1 181.6	7.9	90.8	673.1	724.1	7.4
Trinidad & Tobago	171.7	2 577.0	1 919.2	8.7	162.7	2 263.2	2 101.8	9.2
1. Sub-Total	386.9	4 667.4	3 977.4	8.4	326.3	3 377.9	3 330.1	8.3
OECS								
Antigua	6.0	101.1	135.4	11.3	2.9	14.4	8.6	3.8
Dominica	3.5	47.1	58.0	10.2	2.9	27.1	25.0	7.7
Grenada	6.0	57.2	75.5	9.1	5.1	18.3	17.7	4.4
Montserrat	0.7	20.1	17.5	9.0	0.2	1.6	1.5	22.0
St Kitts-Nevis	5.4	51.0	51.9	8.1	5.2	17.0	19.5	4.7
St Lucia	3.6	106.8	119.0	12.8	2.2	41.8	45.8	11.0
St Vincent	3.7	71.4	103.4	12.2	2.1	39.8	52.7	11.7

Trade and economic relations 119

2. **Sub-Total**	28.7	454.7	560.7	10.8	20.6	160.0	170.8	7.6
3. Belize[a]	10.0	112.9	129.0	9.2	4.9	65.0	n.a.	9.3[b]
Total = 1+2+3	425.8	5 235.0	4 667.1	8.6	351.8	3 602.0	n.a.	8.3[b]

p Provisional
[a] Import figures for 1983 and 1984 exclude un-recorded trade with Mexico
[b] 1955–1983
n.a. Not available
Sources: Official Trade Reports

1984. Sugar continues to be the dominant export item in the foreign trade of St Kitts-Nevis, while in Trinidad and Tobago, petroleum and petroleum products still account for over 80% of foreign exchange earnings. (*See* Table 5.2) It is clear that after several years of independence (Jamaica and Trinidad and Tobago have been independent for 25 years) the Commonwealth Caribbean continues to be dependent on a narrow range of products or activities for foreign exchange.

Aware of the vulnerability that stems from heavy dependence on a narrow range of products (particularly when some of these also depend on protected markets), economic diversification has long been an objective of Commonwealth Caribbean states. Success in this area, as indicated earlier, has been limited. As a net earner of foreign exchange the manufacturing sector has been disappointing, given its high import content and orientation towards the domestic market. In certain cases, however, a few new products have entered the export trade of these countries, even though their share in the overall total may not be extremely significant. In Dominica, for instance, two non-traditional items (soap and galvanised sheets) accounted for 31.2% of total exports in 1984. In St Lucia, paper, paperboard and clothing contributed 25% in the same year. In Jamaica the value of non-traditional exports (e.g. vegetables and wearing apparel) has also been increasing reaching 20% of total domestic exports in 1984. In Trinidad and Tobago the value of non-oil exports (a significant part of chemical origin) increased from US$192.5 million (7.5% of domestic exports) in 1979 to US$388 million (18.4% of domestic exports) in 1985.

The structure of imports

In a fundamental sense the composition of imports tends to reflect the kind of development taking place at the domestic level. This, of course, may not be the case where (as has happened in Guyana and Jamaica in recent years) severe foreign exchange shortages have altered the level and pattern of import demand dictated by the structure of the economy. In the more developed territories, the import substitution strategy has proceeded much further than in the OECS and Belize. The result of this policy is that the share of consumer goods in total imports has tended to fall. Concomitantly, the share of intermediate and capital goods has increased. For instance, in the case of Barbados, the share of consumer goods in total imports dropped from 49% to 31% between 1964 and 1984.

(*See* Table 5.3). In the same period intermediate goods increased from 27% to 45%. One reason for this change has been the rapid development of the clothing and assembly industries during the 1970s. Between 1969 and 1984 the value of intermediate products (including construction materials) increased more than ten times.

Unlike Barbados and Trinidad and Tobago which produce oil, the figures for the other territories have been distorted by the significant increases in international oil prices since 1973. While Trinidad meets most of its requirements from domestic sources, Barbados' production now amounts to about half of its requirements. For this latter country imported fuel in 1984 amounted to about 6% of the value of total imports, as compared to 4% in 1973 and 2% in 1964. In the case of Guyana, however, fuel imports accounted for over 40% of total imports in 1983 as compared to 13% in 1973. In Jamaica the proportions were almost 30% in 1984 as compared to less than 10% in the early 1970s. The fuel bill for Guyana amounted to 58% of domestic exports in 1983 and 48% for Jamaica in 1984.

An important observation that is often made with respect to the import structure of Commonwealth Caribbean countries is that although the share of food imports in total imports may have fallen, in absolute terms the food bill has increased rapidly over the years. For the MDCs i.e. Barbados, Guyana, Jamaica and Trinidad and Tobago, the food bill climbed from US$76 million in 1955 to US$628 million in 1983. This amounts to an average annual increase of 7.8%. In the same period food imports into the OECS countries and Belize jumped from about US$13 million in the earlier year to US$151 million in the later year. Total food imports into the CARICOM region (including the Bahamas) in 1983 was around US$910 million. For countries that are basically agricultural in nature, this is a highly undesirable trend. Paradoxically food products amount to a significant proportion of domestic exports. In this situation a large part of the foreign exchange earned would flow out again in the form of payments for food imports.

An examination of the import structure of the OECS and Belize supports some of the observations made with respect to that of MDCs. In particular, one can note the falling share of food imports and the increasing share of fuels, though the absolute levels of both categories have increased. (*See* Table 5.4). Food imports still account for over 20% of the total imports of these countries, and this indicates the scope for greater domestic production. The growth of tourism is partly responsible for the rapid rise in the food bill.

The increase in the fuel bill is the result of both a higher

Table 5.2 Commonwealth Caribbean: Major exports as a percentage of total domestic exports, selected years

Countries	Year	Main exports	Total
Antigua	1960	sugar (83.4%)	83.4
	1983	manufactured goods (72%)	72.0
Bahamas	1973	hormones (32%); cement (24.1%); rum (22.9%); salt (4.3%)	83.3
	1985	hormones (10.3%); cement (0.8%); crawfish (6.5%); rum (5.4%)	23.0
Barbados	1960	sugar and by-products (92.5%)	92.5
	1985	sugar and by-products (13.9%); manufactured goods (85.5%)	99.4
Belize	1960	sugar (19.9%); citrus products (30.4%); wood (35.0%)	85.3
	1984	sugar (45.7%); citrus concentrates (13.7%); garments (20.8%)	80.2
Dominica	1958	bananas (55.5%); fruit juice (17.6%); essential oils (9.7%)	82.8
	1984	bananas (43.6%); soap (21.6%)	65.2
Grenada	1960	bananas (20.7%); raw cocoa (31.2%); nutmeg (35.2%); mace (7.5%)	94.6
	1984	bananas (18.4%); cocoa (27.2%); nutmegs (12.8%); fresh fruits (30.7%)	89.1

Guyana	1960	sugar (46.0%); rum (2.4%); molasses (2.2%); rice (12.3%); bauxite (23.6%)	86.5
	1984	sugar (33.6%); rum (2.0%); molasses (0.4%); rice (10.0%); bauxite & alumina (44.4%)	90.4
Jamaica	1960	bauxite (19.5%); alumina (29.8%); sugar (23.3%); bananas (8.6%)	81.2
	1984	bauxite (24.8%); alumina (41.7%); sugar (9.0%); bananas (0.2%)	76.1
Montserrat	1967	fruits and vegetables (98.0%)	98.0
	1984	manufactured goods (88.0%)	88.0
St Christopher-Nevis	1958	sugar and molasses; (88.5%)	88.5
	1983	sugar and molasses; (59.9%); manufactured goods (30.0%)	89.9
St Lucia	1962	bananas (77.9%); copra (9.5%)	87.4
	1984	bananas (50.0%); coconut oil (6.6%) clothing (15.2%); paper & paper board (10.2%)	82.0
St Vincent	1960	bananas (48.6%); arrowroot (24.8%); copra (14.7%); cotton (1.8%)	89.9
	1984	bananas (27.0%); flour (16.8%)	48.8
Trinidad & Tobago	1960	petroleum & petroleum products (82.4%); sugar (7.9%)	90.3
	1984	petroleum & petroleum products (83.5%); sugar (1.0%); fertilisers (7.0%)	91.5

Sources: Official Trade Reports; ECLA, *Economic Activity in Caribbean Countries*, Various Issues.

Table 5.3 MDCs: Composition of imports, selected years (percentages)

Categories	Barbados 1964	Barbados 1984	Guyana 1968	Guyana 1983	Jamaica 1964	Jamaica 1984	Trinidad & Tobago[b] 1967	Trinidad & Tobago[b] 1984
Consumer goods	49.1	31.3	38.0	8.9	45.2	13.8	52.1	47.1
Food	28.8	14.3	13.0	2.8	19.1	8.4	23.0	17.4
Other non-durable	7.7	9.2	5.0	2.1	11.1	3.6	12.8	10.5
Durables & semi-durables	12.6	7.8	20.0	4.0	15.5	1.8	16.3	19.2
Intermediate goods	27.5	45.4	31.1	72.3	29.1	61.9	19.4	15.5
Fuels	1.9	6.0	9.7	43.2	11.3	29.5	1.5	0.7
Other	25.6	39.4	21.4	29.1	17.8	32.4	17.9	14.8
Capital goods	19.8	21.8	30.9	17.8	25.2	24.3	27.1	30.0
Construction materials	6.9	5.2	9.3	4.6	9.6	5.7	9.4	9.5
Transport equipment	[a]	[a]	[a]	2.9	4.4	3.5	5.6	5.5
Other machinery & equipment	12.4	15.7	20.6	10.3	11.2	14.4	12.1	14.9
Other capital	0.5	0.9	1.0	—	—	(0.7)	—	—
Other	3.6	1.5	—	1.0	—	—	1.3	7.5
Total	100.0	100.0	100.0	100.0	100.0	100.0	100.0	100.0

Note: Because of differences in interpretation as to what should be included in each category, the percentages for the various countries are not strictly comparable.

[a] Included in 'other machinery and equipment'.
[b] Excludes petroleum imported under the processing agreement.

Sources: Official Trade and Statistical Reports; ECLA, *Economic Activity in Caribbean Countries*, Various Issues.

Table 5.4 OECS and Belize: Composition of imports, 1955 and 1983

SITC Sections	1955 US$mn.	%	1983p US$mn.	%
0 Food	11.0	28.2	135.2	23.8
1 Beverages and tobacco	1.8	4.6	16.1	2.8
2 Crude materials, inedible except fuels	1.4	3.6	15.6	2.7
3 Mineral fuels, lubricants and related materials	2.2	5.6	74.0	13.0
4 Animal and vegetable oils and fats	0.4	1.0	3.8	0.7
5 Chemicals	3.2	8.2	50.7	8.9
6&8 Manufactured goods	12.6	32.3	149.0	26.3
7 Machinery and transport equipment	5.6	14.4	108.0	19.0
9 Miscellaneous transactions	1.7	2.1	15.6	2.8
Total	39.9	100.0	567.6	100.0

p. Provisional
Sources: Official Trade Reports; Statistical Departments.

volume of imports and higher prices. The decline in oil prices in recent years should have a favourable effect not only on the balance of payments position of these countries, but on domestic prices, if the benefits are passed on to the consumer. In Commonwealth Caribbean countries generally, imported fuels are not only critical to transport, but to electricity generation which provides the bulk of the energy required for domestic and commercial purposes. In 1983, for example, it was almost 20% for Belize, 12% for St Lucia, 11% for Grenada and 8% for St Vincent. These ratios are generally lower than those of Guyana and Jamaica whose economies are apparently much more dependent on imported fuels.

With respect to the other categories of imports, the assembly-type operations which have been set up in OECS countries and Belize to take advantage of the relatively low labour costs explain a large part of the increases that have taken place in the importation of intermediate and capital goods. The manufacturing sector in these countries is still in a very rudimentary stage and the importation of chemicals is critical to their agricultural production, which may explain the tendency of this category to maintain its share. The proportion of machinery and transport equipment has increased over time, accounting for almost 20% of total imports in 1983. The growth of income and tourism largely explain this development.

Direction of trade

As part of the British Empire (later to become the British Commonwealth of Nations), the trade of the British territories in the Caribbean was for long oriented towards the UK and associated territories. Initially this was as a result of British trade policy by which Britain traded her manufactures in return for raw materials and foodstuffs, but subsequently and perhaps more importantly it was as a result of the system of preferential duties which member countries granted to each other's goods. Essentially the arrangement provided for the preferential treatment of the exports of the Caribbean in the UK and Canadian markets in return for granting of preferential treatment to Caribbean imports originating in the Commonwealth. This system of imperial preferences had its origin in the early part of the century, and reached its zenith in the late 1930s following the Ottawa Conference of 1932, which gave formal blessing to discrimination in favour of Commonwealth trade in response to the growing protectionism that was sweeping the world. Since then, the system has been on the wane and the margin of preference accorded many categories of Commonwealth exports in the UK market was considerably reduced over time as a result of several factors. The most important of these were British participation in the GATT deliberations and her membership of the European Free Trade Association (EFTA) which was formed in 1960. Her entry into the EEC (now EC) in 1973 literally brought to an end the system of Commonwealth preference which had continued to govern Commonwealth trade, even after independence was attained by the British colonies. It should be pointed out, however, that certain selected agricultural exports such as sugar and bananas, continue to enjoy preferential treatment in the British market under the Lomé Convention.

For Commonwealth Caribbean countries, the UK remains their most important trading partner among EC countries. Their proportion of trade with her, however, has been declining. For instance, the share of Jamaica's exports going to the UK fell from about 31% in 1960 to 13% in 1984. Over the same period Trinidad and Tobago's share also declined from 31% to less than 10% as did Barbados' from 61% to 29%, and Guyana's from 37% to 30%. For the OECS countries, the proportion of their exports going to the UK has also tended to fall, though less sharply than that of the more developed territories. This is no doubt partly explained by the continued dominance of sugar and bananas in their export trade and the dependence on the special treatment accorded these products under the Lomé Convention. In the 1960s the UK accounted for over 80% of Dominica's exports, but by 1982−83 this had dropped to around 43%. Only about 30−35% of Grenada's domestic exports have been going to the UK in recent years, as compared to an average of 45−50% in the early 1960s. In the case of Belize, there has been a reverse trend with the share of domestic exports sold in the UK market actually increasing since 1960, when the proportion recorded was 12%. By the late 1970s/early 1980s this had increased to over 40%.

As far as imports from the UK are concerned, there has also been a declining trend which has been assisted no doubt by the dismantling of the Sterling Area arrangements and the integration movement in the Caribbean. The search for cheaper sources nearer home has no doubt also had an effect. In the early 1960s generally, the UK accounted for over 30% of the imports of Commonwealth Caribbean countries. In the case of Trinidad and Tobago the proportion fell from 30% in 1960 to 10% in 1984. Over the same period, the comparable figure for Jamaica declined from 34% to 5%; for Barbados from 39% to 8%; for Guyana from 39% to 10%; and for Belize from 32% to 10%. For the OECS countries the UK has also fallen in importance as a source of supply, but the decline has not been as sharp. For instance, between 1979 and 1983 the UK still supplied on average 20% of Dominica's import requirements, as compared to over 30% in the early 1960s.

For countries such as Trinidad and Tobago, Jamaica and Barbados, the US has emerged as the most important single market in recent years. In the case of Jamaica, the US took an average of 39% of this country's total exports in the 1982−84 period as compared to 36% in the 1961−63 period. Over the same period the figure for Barbados increased from 7% to 49%, for Trinidad and Tobago from 26% to 56% and for Guyana from 19% to 24%. The proportion for the Bahamas has continued to remain high at over 85%. In the 1970s Belize sold about 50% of its exports (on average) in the US market, and continues to do so, though the figure can fluctuate from year to year. For the OECS countries, the US tends to be less important as a market than the UK which, as indicated earlier, continues to buy their major agricultural exports under special arrangements. The exception is St Kitts-Nevis which sells a significant part of its sugar production in the US and this no doubt explains the higher proportion associated with the US.

With respect to imports, the US with its diversified production structure has grown increasingly important as a source of supply. At one extreme it provides the Bahamas with over 75% of its import requirements while at the other extreme only about 20% of Guyana's imports have been originating in that market in recent years, which proportion incidentally, is only slightly less than that which obtained in the early 1960s. Most Commonwealth Caribbean countries now procure over 30% (a few over 45%) of their import requirements in the US market, as compared to less than 20% in most cases during the early 1960s.

The growth of trade with Canada has been disappointing. In 1928 Canada supplied as much as 19% of West Indian imports and took around 25% of West Indian exports.[1] As can be seen in Table 5.5 Canada now generally accounts for less than 5% of the region's trade. With respect to exports, trade with Jamaica and Guyana has been strongest in recent years, the main items traded being bauxite and alumina. In 1960 Jamaica sold 25% of her exports in the Canadian market, but by 1984 this had fallen to 14%. In the same period Guyana's exports to Canada declined from 25% to 4%. Trinidad and Tobago's proportion also fell from an average of 5% in the early 1960s to less than 1% in recent years, as has Barbados' from around 10% to around 2% in recent years. The share of imports from Canada has also generally been falling, partly no doubt as a result of an inability to compete with US sources. Countries like Jamaica, Barbados and Guyana, which derived about 10% of their imports from Canada in the 1960s now buy around 5%. Even in the case of the OECS, Canada has found it difficult to hold or increase its share of these countries' imports obtaining in the 1960s. This trend is in some ways surprising, given the extremely good relations that exist between Canada and Commonwealth Caribbean countries.

Canada has long been involved in the economies of these countries. Some of the oldest financial institutions operating in the area are of Canadian origin. Canada's technical and financial assistance continues to play a part in the development of the region. To reverse the trade trends mentioned earlier, the Canadian government, in early 1986, announced a plan similar to that of the US' CBI. CARIBCAN, as the scheme is called, is intended to increase the range of goods eligible for duty-free entry into Canada. Like

Trade and economic relations 129

Table 5.5 Commonwealth Caribbean: Direction of trade, 1984 (Percentages)

Countries	Domestic exports						Imports					
	US	Canada	EC	CARICOM	Other	Total	US	Canada	EC	CARICOM	Other	Total
Antigua	0.4	0.0	2.8	59.8	37.4	100.0	49.8	4.4	18.6	9.6	17.6	100.0
Bahamas[1]	31.1	7.3	18.8	0.0	42.8	100.0	78.2	2.9	8.3	0.0	10.6	100.0
Barbados[2]	27.6	1.6	8.1	22.3	40.4	100.0	47.8	5.6	12.0	11.7	22.9	100.0
Belize[2]	49.7	2.1	21.2	7.5	19.5	100.0	45.8	2.8	22.2	2.3	26.9	100.0
Dominica	1.6	0.0	51.4	45.0	2.0	100.0	26.6	7.7	29.6	21.0	15.1	100.0
Grenada	5.6	3.0	53.0	35.7	2.7	100.0	24.6	4.4	24.3	24.7	22.0	100.0
Guyana[3]	18.0	4.2	42.0	13.8	22.0	100.0	18.0	3.2	14.3	41.1	23.4	100.0
Jamaica	48.2	14.4	14.7	7.2	15.5	100.0	45.6	5.4	9.6	3.2	36.2	100.0
Montserrat[3]	25.7	0.0	7.5	65.0	1.8	100.0	38.5	3.6	20.0	21.4	16.5	100.0
St Kitts-Nevis	45.6	1.0	27.8	22.0	3.6	100.0	39.6	4.4	16.4	19.5	20.1	100.0
St Lucia	17.4	0.0	53.1	26.5	3.0	100.0	36.7	4.2	20.7	16.8	21.6	100.0
St Vincent	10.7	0.7	24.2	64.2	0.2	100.0	37.0	3.1	24.4	19.3	16.2	100.0
Trinidad & Tobago	57.7	0.6	15.2	9.2	17.3	100.0	37.9	6.9	19.3	7.3	28.6	100.0

[1] Export and import figures refer only to non-oil trade.
[2] The figures for exports include re-exports.
[3] Domestic exports relate to 1983.

Sources: Official Trade Reports; OECS, Statistical Pocket Digest, 1985; IMF, Direction of Trade Statistics, Yearbook, 1986.

the CBI, however, certain key items of interest to the Caribbean such as textiles, clothing, footwear, luggage and leather goods, lubricating oils and methanol, are excluded from the scheme.

Despite its distance, imports from Japan have been growing at a faster rate than imports from Latin America which is considerably nearer geographically. The trade balance is heavily in favour of Japan which buys relatively little from the Caribbean. In 1966 imports from Japan accounted for 1.3% of Trinidad and Tobago's imports. By 1984 this had grown to 11%. In the same period the trade deficit with Japan increased from US$9.4 million to US$212 million. In 1984 Jamaica's trade deficit with Japan amounted to US$26 million as compared to US$25 million for Barbados and US$2.90 million for Guyana. In some OECS states imports from Japan already amount to over 5% of their total imports. With little or no export taking place the trade deficit is likely to increase. The bulk of the imports from Japan comprise manufactured goods, particularly machinery and transport equipment. Some food products (e.g. canned fish) are also imported. Exports from Caribbean countries consist largely of chemical products from Trinidad and Jamaica.

In 1985 intra-regional imports in CARICOM amounted to about 10% of total imports. It is estimated that this proportion fell to about 7.5% in 1986. Despite the continuing decline in intra-regional commerce in recent years, CARICOM is by no means an insignificant market for member states. Generally a greater proportion of OECS' exports goes to the CARICOM market than is the case with countries such as Belize, Guyana, Jamaica or Trinidad. For instance, with respect to St Vincent more than 45% of its export trade in recent years has been with CARICOM countries, with Trinidad and Tobago being its major market. For the latter country CARICOM accounted for only about 9% of its exports in 1984, as compared to 7% for Jamaica, 14% for Guyana, 22% for Barbados and 7.5% for Belize. Bahamas' trade with CARICOM is negligible. With respect to imports it is estimated (based on 1985 figures) that the OECS countries derived about 26% of their imports from CARICOM countries. For Trinidad, Belize Barbados, Jamaica, and Antigua, the proportion in 1985 varied between 2.3% and 11.7%

Even though commodities like rice and oil tend to account for a large part of CARICOM trade, the regional market is not without significance to the region's agricultural and manufacturing sectors. With respect to the latter, a large part of its output is dependent on the regional market, given its inability to compete in extra-regional markets because of the high costs and in some cases poor quality associated with the products turned out. In the case of Trinidad and Tobago, for instance, some 42% of manufactured goods classified chiefly by material (SITC 6) was sold in the CARICOM market in 1985.

Following the attainment of political independence by Commonwealth Caribbean states, it was widely hoped that a stronger trading relationship would have developed between these countries and Latin American nations, given the factor of geographical proximity and the desire to improve relations by policy-makers on both sides. Trade, however, has not developed to any significant extent. A major part of the commerce that takes place is confined to a few countries and tends to be concentrated on a limited range of products. On balance, the Commonwealth Caribbean buys a great deal more from Latin America than it sells. The main sources are Brazil, Colombia, Venezuela, Mexico and Honduras. Lumber from the latter country and oil products and manufactured goods from the others feature high in this trade.

In the 1960s the share of Trinidad and Tobago's total imports originating in Latin America ranged between 25% and 50%. The bulk of this, however, was accounted for by imports of crude oil from Venezuela for refining. Between 1960 and 1970 Venezuela supplied (on average) almost 60% of the value of Trinidad and Tobago's total imports of crude and semi-refined oil imports. This trade began declining as far back as the early 1970s as oil companies began shifting their sources of supply to Africa and the Middle East. It has now virtually completely disappeared. In recent years, imports from Venezuela have been accounting for less than 1% of Trinidad and Tobago's total imports. In 1984 Spanish South America plus Brazil and Mexico together supplied less than 5%, the Central American Common Market countries (viz. Guatemala, Honduras, Nicaragua, Costa Rica and El Salvador) 1.5% and the rest of Latin America (viz. Cuba, the Dominican Republic, Haiti and Puerto Rico) less than 1%. In other words less than 10% of Trinidad and Tobago's imports comes from Latin America. Lumber from Honduras and oil exports to this country account for most of the trade with Central America.

With respect to the rest of Latin America, Brazil is by far the most important supplier (2.8% of total imports in 1984) followed by Venezuela (0.5%) Colombia (0.3%) and Argentina (0.2%). About 30% of imports from Latin America consists of manufactured goods, as compared to 20% for food, and 40% for crude materials. With respect to exports, less than 5% goes to Latin America. This trade tends to fluctuate from year to year, both in value terms and as a proportion of total exports. Between 1980 and 1984 the proportion of total exports to Brazil averaged 0.25%, to Venezuela 0.15%, to Colombia 0.03%, to Argentina 0.5% and to Honduras 1.6%. While exports to Honduras, Haiti, and the Dominican Republic largely take the form of petroleum products, a significant part of its export trade with Latin America consists of chemical products.

In 1984 14% of Jamaica's imports originated in Latin America. Of this, more than half was accounted for by oil imports from Venezuela. Oil and oil products from Colombia, Ecuador, Mexico, and Panama accounted for another 26%. In terms of exports, less than 5% are sold in Latin American countries. With respect to other Commonwealth Caribbean countries, more or less the same pattern can be observed. Imports from Latin America tend to be greater than exports, but this trade generally accounts for less than 3% of total imports. Recently because of its inability to find foreign exchange to buy oil from Trinidad (its traditional source) Guyana has entered into a barter trade system with Venezuela with whom relations have not traditionally been good because of a still unresolved border dispute, and this has contributed to the drop in intra-regional imports in CARICOM.

Commonwealth Caribbean trade is still highly metropolitan-oriented. As a result of the integration effort the share of intra-regional trade in total trade has increased, but the regional market has not served to stimulate a vibrant manufacturing sector. A few traditional products still dominate. Manufactured goods traded include a large proportion of assembly and packaging type products in which the local value-added tends to be small. Balance of payments problems in recent years have encouraged the adoption of trade restriction measures which have resulted in a decline in intra-regional trade.

With respect to Latin America, the growth of trade appears to be affected by a number of factors. National markets are still highly protected in the region, despite an increasing recognition that if regional states are to become more export-oriented there is need for a new approach towards protection. Importers accustomed to certain sources or familiar with certain brand names are often unwilling to switch to new products or new suppliers, even when the new product appears competitive both in price and quality. Scarcity of information with respect to what is available, quality and price is another factor that can hamper the growth of commerce. In the case of the Caribbean and Latin America the language barrier can exacerbate this problem. More trade displays may be one way to deal with this issue. Inadequate transport facilities (which in itself may be the result of the lack of a substantial amount of trade) is a major impediment to stimulating a greater interchange of goods. Insufficient export credit facilities and the absence of financial links tend to militate against the development of new trading relationships.

Given this situation it is difficult to see how the volume of trade could be increased outside a comprehensive co-operative framework touching a wide range of issues relating to development strategy, use of resources, transfer of technology, barriers to trade, transport, problems of the sea, financial co-operation, investment, etc. The past approach of single country to country interfacing and the setting up of numerous committees and commissions is fraught with difficulties in an area with several sub-regional co-operative endeavours. In the past, political issues like membership of the OAS by the small Caribbean states, the Belize-Guatemala territorial dispute and the Guyana/Venezuela border problem tended to impair the pursuit of stronger economic ties. There was also some fear on the part of the small Caribbean states of putting themselves in a disadvantaged position *vis-à-vis* their larger Latin American neighbours whose motives were often seen in purely political terms. There was also an unwillingness to expose the budding integration movement in the Caribbean to the possible disintegrative forces that could have resulted from a broader geographical linkage, particularly in respect to an area that was seen to be characterised by a great deal of instability. With the growth of confidence, and given the problems facing CARICOM, there is now a greater willingness to explore avenues of co-operation, particularly in the context of the increasing protectionist tendencies that have emerged in some industrial countries.

Economic relations between Commonwealth Caribbean countries and Western Europe on the one hand, and between Commonwealth Caribbean countries and the US on the other take place within the framework of two separate sets of arrangements. Since a major purpose of these arrangements is to protect existing markets in certain traditional products and encourage trade in new items, it is necessary that we discuss them in this chapter.

Commonwealth Caribbean-Western European economic relations

The Lomé Convention which currently governs economic co-operation between a select group of African, Caribbean and Pacific countries has its roots in France's desire during the discussions leading up to the formation of the EEC to preserve its economic ties with her colonies. At French insistence and despite some opposition by Germany and the Netherlands, Part IV, Articles 131−136 was included in the Rome Treaty which was signed in 1958. By including this section, the original six members of the Community multilaterally agreed to associate their overseas countries and territories. With French persuasion, the first European Development Fund (EDF) was also set up in 1958 for a five-year period to provide assistance to the overseas territories which then numbered about twenty. In the years immediately following the signing of the Rome Treaty, most of the associated states sought and obtained their independence, and this necessitated a new framework of co-operation, since the newly independent countries wanted to preserve the old ties which gave them privileged access to the European market, as well as financial assistance.

In 1963 a new five-year agreement was signed at Yaoundé (the capital of Cameroon) and this came to be known as the First Yaoundé Convention. The agreement was renewed again in 1969, with little change. In a declaration of intent adopted by the Council of Ministers in 1963, third world countries with economic and production structures comparable to those of the Associated States of Africa and Madagascar (AASM) were offered three options: (1) accession to the Yaoundé Convention; (b) association *sui-generis*; and (c) a preferential trade agreement. An association agreement was signed with Nigeria in 1966 but never became operational. Likewise the first Arusha Agreement signed with Kenya, Tanzania and Uganda never came into being, though a second one (signed in 1969) took effect in 1971. The enlargement of the Community from six to nine in 1973 and the fact that by this time a large number of colonies scattered in various parts of the world had not only attained their independence, but had begun to articulate common positions on a number of issues, demanded a new look at the relationship between Europe and the developing world. Britain's membership in particular required a broader approach to co-operation, given the strong ties with her numerous colonies and former colonies in Africa, the Caribbean and the Pacific. With Britain's entry into the EC not only were twenty independent countries in Africa, the Caribbean and the Pacific invited to negotiate association agreements with the EC, but other countries in Africa with similar production structures were also required to do so.

Rather than seek separate arrangements, the Yaoundé members and the new associable countries chose to explore the possibility of an overall co-operation agreement with the EC. Out of these negotiations grew the first Lomé Convention which was signed in Lomé (the capital of Togo) on 26 February, 1975 by the EC and 46 independent states of Africa, the Caribbean and the Pacific (ACP). The Convention was renewed a second time on 31 October, 1979, but this time there were 57 ACP members. The current Convention (Lomé III) was signed on 8 December, 1984, by the ten EC countries[2] and sixty-five ACP states. Four months later, Angola joined the pact bringing the number of ACP states to sixty-six.

Besides the Lomé Convention, the EC has a number of co-operation agreements with other countries. It is the Lomé Agreement, however, which is hailed by many as a 'model' for governing relations between developed and developing countries. Although it is the economic arrangements which attract attention, the political implications are by no means lost, as can be seen in the following statement:

> To varying degrees, Europe and the Third World have been relegated to the sidelines by the super-powers, without being safe from any tension, or conflict between them. By co-operating, Europe and the Third World can gradually strengthen their independence and help create poles of stability in the world.[3]

To be sure, Lomé does have its critics, some of whom see it as a perpetuation of neo-colonialism. Some of the developing countries (e.g. Latin American states) which are not party to the agreement see it as discriminating against them. Though Lomé III itself is an improvement on its predecessors, ACP states have not hesitated to express their dissatisfaction with some of its provisions and with the amount of aid provided. In the following section we outline the main provisions of the Lomé III Convention.

As indicated earlier, Lomé III brings together ten EC members[4] with a total population of 273 million (1984) and 45 states in Africa, 13 in the Caribbean and 8 in the Pacific, with a total population approaching 400 million. The ACP countries vary widely in terms of size, per capita income, resources and levels of development. The contracting parties, which number 76, represent almost half the membership of the UN and contain a population of over 6 hundred million. With a total GNP of US$2371 billion at current market prices, and an average per capita GNP of over US$8500 in 1985, the EC is the world's major economic power. Between them the 66 ACP states and the 10 EC states account for 17% of the world's surface and 13% of its population.

The contracting parties see the Convention as not only aimed at promoting and expediting the economic, cultural and social development of the ACP states, but also as a commitment to intensifying their efforts to create, with a view to a more just and balanced international economic order, a model for relations between developed and developing states. The contracting parties agree that ACP-EC co-operation should be guided by principles which recognise equality between partners, respect for their sovereignty, mutual interest and interdependence. The right of each state to determine its own political, social and cultural and economic policy options is also underlined. The need for more balanced development is recognised and the parties pledge themselves to the promotion of rural development, food security for the people and the revival and strengthening of agricultural production potential in the ACP states. The Convention also expresses support for regional groupings and recognises the need for special treatment for the least-developed ACP states and the specific difficulties confronting landlocked and island states. The development of services such as tourism and maritime transport have been recognised as important areas for greater emphasis in Lomé III.

Undoubtedly, from the ACP's point of view one of the most important benefits provided by the Convention is access to the European market for both agricultural and manufactured goods. Under the Yaoundé Convention, associated states were required to grant reciprocal trading concessions to the EC. Under Lomé this is not the case. ACP countries are only required to grant EC countries trading arrangements no less favourable than those extended to other countries (except ACP or other developing countries). With respect to the expansion of EC-ACP trade, the effectiveness of the Lomé Conventions has been widely questioned in the context of the trends that have emerged. Available data for recent years indicate that in value terms exports from Commonwealth Caribbean countries to the EC increased from 558 million ECU in 1976 to 1274 million ECU in 1985 or by 128%. If refined oil products from the Bahamas are excluded the percentage increase would be 135%. On average, Commonwealth Caribbean exports to the EC increased by 31% between Lomé I (1976-80) and Lomé II (1981–85). Again if the Bahamas is excluded on the basis that oil trade could not strictly be defined as domestic exports, the increase would be in the region of 78%. The bulk of the trade with the EC is accounted for by traditional products such as sugar, molasses, rum, bananas, refined petroleum products, bauxite, alumina, cocoa, etc. Sugar, rum and bananas are traded under special protocols and, therefore, do not fall under the general rules of the Community. As far as non-traditional exports (including manufactured goods) are concerned the EC remains an insignificant market.

There may be several explanations for this situation, some having to do with production problems, while others relate to marketing issues. Generally, as we have indicated before, Caribbean countries have not been able to develop a significant export capacity either in industrial goods or non-traditional agricultural products which could compete abroad in terms of quality or price. A major proportion of those currently produced would have difficulty meeting the value-added criterion.[5] Distance would also be a factor, since this would add to the c.i.f. cost of the product. Even though Commonwealth Caribbean countries have preferential access to the European market, the operation of a Generalised System of Preferences would have eroded some of the advantages enjoyed, and this would, therefore, have called for a greater degree of competitiveness on the part of Caribbean producers. Lack of knowledge of the European market and the high cost of introducing Caribbean products to consumers have also acted as a deterrent. ACP countries supplied only 3.3% of total EC imports in 1985. The proportion, however, varied from one member state to another between a range of 0.8% and 6.5%. With respect to exports only 2.1% of the EC's exports went to ACP countries in 1985.

The Lomé Convention is not only about trade. Technical and financial assistance form an important aspect of the Agreement. Without a production capability, trade preferences are of little significance. The negotiators were particularly aware of this in the discussion leading up to Lomé III, given their experience with the previous Conventions. Lomé III provides for a total financial package of 8500 million ECU.[6] Of this, 7400 million ECU will come from the European Development Fund (EDF) and are allocated as follows:

(a) 6060 million ECU for general technical and financial cooperation:
   • 4860 million ECU will take the form of grants
   • 600 million ECU will take the form of special loans
   • 600 million ECU will take the form of risk capital

(b) 925 million ECU will take the form of transfers under the STABEX arrangement

(c) 415 million ECU is allocated to the Sysmin scheme.

In addition to these resources, the European Investment Bank (EIB) will be asked to make loans of up to 1000 million in accordance with terms and conditions provided for in its Statute.

The financial assistance offered by the EC falls below the minimum requested by the ACP states. These funds, however, are available for both programmes and projects and for rehabilitation, repair, and maintenance as much as for new investments. The ACP states were also able to get improvements in a number of areas. Recognising the heavy dependence of these countries on agricultural activities, greater emphasis is placed on co-operation relating to agricultural and rural development. The objectives include, *interalia*: greater self-sufficiency in production, reinforcing food security at national, regional and international level, guaranteeing the rural population incomes that will significantly improve their standard of living, improving rural productivity, ensuring a balance between food crops and export crops; improving production by on-the-spot processing of the products of agriculture, including livestock farming, fisheries and forestry; and protecting the national environment. The development of services such as tourism and maritime transport as indicated earlier, are to receive greater emphasis. An entire title of the Convention is devoted to the development of fisheries. STABEX has also been improved by reducing the thresholds and by instituting clearer management and reporting procedures on the use of transfers.

Since ACP countries are largely agricultural producers, it was not surprising that the STABEX associated with Lomé I covered mainly agricultural commodities. Only one mineral product was included and that was iron ore, so countries such as Zambia and Zaïre who depended heavily on mineral exports felt discriminated against. To deal with this shortcoming Sysmin was introduced under Lomé II and kept under Lomé III. It is not an export earning stabilisation scheme, but a special financing facility designed to help economies dependent on the mining sector. Its main purpose is to maintain or re-establish existing production capacity, when export earnings have fallen as a result of a decline in production. The products covered include copper (and cobalt), phosphates, manganese, bauxite and alumina, tin and iron ore. Under Lomé III, the system has a fund of 415 million ECU. Countries eligible for assistance are those where any one of the listed products represent 15% or more of export earnings; or where all mining products together (except oil, gas and precious minerals) represent at least 20% of total export earnings. For the least developed land-locked or island ACP states, these proportions are 10% and 12% respectively. Sysmin financing is available when there is a fall of at least 10% in production or export capacity. Loans are repayable over forty years at 1%.

While ACP states continue to praise the Lomé Convention as a useful partnership arrangement, they have not failed to register their disappointment over the amount of benefits they have received under previous Conventions. With respect to trade, some countries have increased and diversified their exports to the EC markets. Others, however, have stuck to traditional exports. Because some of the EC aid has gone into these traditional areas, there is a belief in some quarters that this may have discouraged stronger moves towards economic diversification. ACP states also cite the safeguard clause (which the EC could invoke to protect sectors of its economy threatened by foreign competition), as a deterrent to the development of exports in areas where they might have a comparative advantage. Though the rules of origin of the Lomé Convention appear to be more generous and flexible than those in the Generalized System of Preference, ACP states have expressed a desire for greater leniency. They have also made repeated calls for more of their agricultural exports to be allowed into the EC where the agricultural sector is the most protected of all activities. With respect to financial aid, one study[7] points to a wide range of factors which have contributed to this form of assistance not being as effective as might have been the case if there had been more careful selection and design of projects, and if greater attention had been paid to implementation and viability considerations. In many cases the institutional and policy support at the local level was lacking.

The US Caribbean Basin Initiative (CBI)

The Caribbean Basin Economic Recovery Act which provides the legal basis for the so-called Caribbean Basin Initiative (CBI) was signed into law on 5 August, 1983 and came into effect on 1 January, 1984. The CBI, unlike the Lomé Convention is not a negotiated agreement. Unlike Lomé, too, which is reviewed every five years, the CBI has a life of twelve years, i.e. it comes to an end in 1995. There is no commitment to renew.

The CBI revolves around a programme of trade, economic assistance and tax measures which are intended to help in the 'economic recovery' of 'Caribbean Basin' countries. This includes an initial US$350 million aid package (mainly for the private sector), legislative measures to allow US citizens to deduct for tax purposes expenses of business conventions held in eligible Caribbean Basin countries; special measures to support the economic development of Puerto Rico, the Virgin Islands and other insular possessions and a one-way free trade arrangement providing duty-free access to the US market over a period of twelve years for almost all products originating in Caribbean Basin countries. The excluded items include textiles and apparel, canned tuna, petroleum and petroleum products, certain leather products and footwear, watches and watch parts. To qualify, goods must be exported directly to the US and a minimum of 35% of their value must be locally-added (though 15% may be of US origin).

The eligible states number 27,[8] including the thirteen CARICOM countries, plus Anguilla, the Dominican Republic, Haiti, the Cayman Islands, Netherlands Antilles, Turks and Caicos Islands, the British Virgin Islands, and Aruba in the Caribbean, Surinam in South America and Costa Rica, El Salvador, Guatemala, Honduras, Nicaragua and Panama in Central America. For any of the eligible countries to benefit from the programme the President has to designate a country as a beneficiary. The Caribbean Basin Recovery Act lists the criteria which would not allow a country to qualify. The President may not designate a country if it:
(a) is a communist country;
(b) fails to meet certain criteria with respect to the nationalisation or expropriation of US property;
(c) does not take adequate steps to co-operate with the US to prevent narcotic drugs from entering the US;
(d) fails to recognise arbitral awards to US citizens;
(e) provides preferential treatment to the products of another developed country which adversely affects trade with the US;
(f) engages in the broadcast of US copyrighted materials without the consent of the owner; or
(g) has not entered into an extradition treaty with the US.

In designating a country, the President has to be guided by some further criteria. These include, *inter alia*, trade policies and practices, the extent of assurance to the US of reasonable access to its market and resources, living standards of its inhabitants and policies towards workers. At present, six of the 28 eligible countries have failed to meet the designation criteria. These are: Anguilla, the Cayman Islands, Guyana, Nicaragua, Surinam, and Turks and Caicos Islands.

The CBI has been criticised from several angles. As indicated earlier, even before the CBI came into being the share of Commonwealth Caribbean trade with the US was increasing. Under the Generalised System of Preferences Scheme some 80% of the region's exports to the US already entered duty free. The CBI arrangement would increase the proportion by about 15%. From the Caribbean countries' point of view, the concern is with some of the excluded products such as textiles and apparel articles which they feel they are capable of exporting. During 1984 and 1985 the CBI had no noticeable impact on the region's exports to the US. In fact, between 1984 and 1985 there was a reduction in US imports from Caribbean Basin countries, but this was largely explained by a drop in oil imports. In response to this situation, President Reagan announced a new scheme (not part of the CBI) in February 1986 to permit higher access levels for garment exports from the Caribbean. The scheme allows garments made from cloth woven and cut in the US to enjoy guaranteed minimum access levels, although not on a completely duty free basis.[9] It should be noted that the US already operates a programme (under US Tariff Schedule Item 807.0) applicable to all countries and embracing all products capable of assembly which affords partial duty exemption on value on US components assembled abroad. Despite this move the recent cuts in US sugar quotas for Caribbean countries to protect domestic growers and the duties imposed on cut flowers from Costa Rica have raised serious doubts about the US' intentions to bolster the CBI.

President Reagan has also announced his support for a proposal made during 1985 by the Governor of Puerto Rico to use government development funds for investment under the CBI.[10] The plan involves the creation of twin plant manufacturing ventures, in which Caribbean countries would supply low cost labour for the assembly of items manufactured in Puerto Rico and the US. To qualify, a CBI country must have in effect a bilateral tax information exchange agreement.[11] In order to encourage investment abroad US companies have, since 1 January, 1985, also been allowed to form Foreign Sales Corporations (FSCs) in countries outside of the US customs zone. Permitted places include US Virgin Islands, other US possessions excluding Puerto Rico, and foreign jurisdictions especially approved by the US government. The operations of such corporations allow US companies to earn some exempt and non-taxable income on their exports from the US.

A second area of criticism relates to the lifespan of the CBI, which is generally felt to be too short to allow investors to recover their investments. In order to encourage investment, regional governments see the need for a commitment that the programme would be extended, particularly against the fact that the 10% tax credit on new investments that was proposed did not form part of the final arrangements. With respect to investments, there is a further observation. The fact that the President has the power to suspend duty-free treatment of an eligible article, and impose a duty on it, means that an enterprise initiated under CBI incentives could find its products blocked from entering the US market if they pose a threat to a domestic industry. This situation is not likely to encourage investment. Yet a third area of disappointment among Commonwealth Caribbean countries has stemmed from the overall quantum of financial assistance provided under the programme, and in particular the distribution of the initial US$350 million, which strongly favoured certain countries in Central America.

Some critics see the CBI as having little to do with economic development and a great deal to do with political and security considerations. The contention here is that for minimal economic benefits, Caribbean Basin countries are being pressured to move in a particular ideological direction and to adopt certain foreign policy stances favoured by the US.

> The CBI reflects the administration's interest in military security, political loyalty, and advantages for US firms, rather than US concern for the region's long term development.[12]

It is further claimed that the programme ignores the structural characteristics of these countries. It is argued that the emphasis on private sector development as the key to development is misplaced.[13] A further area of concern is the fear that the CBI could encourage a series of bi-lateral arrangements with the US which could impact adversely on the integration movement in the Caribbean. In such an event far from helping development, the CBI could perpetuate fragmentation and lead to increased dependency.

Notes

1. See H. Brewster and C.Y. Thomas, 'The Development, Structure and Terms of West Indian Trade with Canada', in *West Indies − Canada Economic Relations*, Selected papers prepared by the University of the West Indies in Connection with the Canada-Commonwealth Caribbean Conference, July, 1966, Mona, I.S.E.R., 1967.
2. The ten EC members are Belgium, Denmark, West Germany, France, Ireland, Italy, Luxembourg, Netherlands, The United Kingdom and Greece (which became a member in 1981). Spain and Portugal were admitted as members in 1986, but they are still in a transitional stage.
3. Taken from an undated EC Commission document dealing with the history of the Lomé Convention.
4. See footnote 2.
5. The general value-added criterion is 50%, though in some cases it is higher.
6. Under Lomé I total financial resources provided amounted to 3457.8 million ECU. Of this figure (which includes the running costs of the

Commission delegations in the ACP countries), all Caribbean countries got 202.4 million ECU or 17.0%. Under Lomé II the Caribbean figure was 318.8 million ECU (5.8%) out of a total of 5530 million ECU.
7 German Development Institute, *Evaluation of the Co-operation between the European Community and the Caribbean ACP States*, Berlin, November 1985.
8 Aruba was added subsequently, making the number 28.
9 To date, four countries (the Dominican Republic, Haiti, Jamaica and Trinidad and Tobago) have signed agreements.
10 This required a revision of Section 936 of the US Internal Revenue Code to allow qualifying CBI countries to be eligible as sites. It is estimated that as much as $100 million annually in new investment could be generated.
11 At the time of writing only Barbados and Jamaica had such an agreement.
12 A.F. Lowenthal, 'The Caribbean Basin Initiative', in *Foreign Policy*, Summer 1982.
13 See James Petras, 'A Military Policy in Search of an Economic Rationale: Reagan's Caribbean Basin Aid Program', *Comercio Exterior*, November 1982.

CHAPTER 6

Factors influencing Commonwealth Caribbean production structure and trade policy

Commonwealth Caribbean countries recognise that trade is essential to their well being. They, therefore, take a particular interest in discussions aimed at reducing or removing trade barriers, and increasing access to foreign markets. As colonies of Britain, they were required to operate a two-tier tariff system, one applicable to Commonwealth goods, and the other to non-Commonwealth trade. With independence, this system has disappeared. The present import regime which comprises tariffs and non-tariff barriers is informed by revenue considerations, the need to protect infant industries, the desire to assist the balance of payments, and to foster industrial development.[1]

The decision taken to promote regional economic integration is also reflected in the tariff and protective structure. Generally, rates tend to be lower on raw materials, intermediate inputs and capital goods than on final consumer products. Credit, tax and price preferences can also have a significant effect on the allocation of resources among productive activities and on the bias in favour of exporting or import substitution.[2] The effective rate of protection for the manufacturing sector tends to be much higher than the nominal rates would suggest.[3] Incidentally, preferential treatment in foreign markets for a country's exports can also influence its domestic production structure. The protective role of the import regime in the Commonwealth Caribbean, as indicated earlier, is related to the strategy of industrialisation which presumes that in the early stages of their life, new industries require protection from competition. Failure of such 'infant' enterprises to mature in many cases has resulted in the emergence of an uncompetitive environment, and the perpetuation of comparatively high levels of protection. This in turn has had an adverse impact on the balance of payments performance. Unintentionally, the industrial strategy pursued has had a built-in bias against export. Despite the opportunities that have been offered in the markets of certain industrial countries, Commonwealth Caribbean countries have not been able to increase significantly non-traditional production, and therefore have not been able to take advantage or be part of the new trends and development in the international trading system.

One of the salient features of the post-war period has been a growing inter-dependence in the world economy. A major dimension of this inter-dependence has been the expansion of international trade as a result of the lowering of trade barriers. Poor countries not only export to the industrial nations, but they themselves now take a substantial part of the latter's exports. 'The developing countries have been buoyant and dynamic markets and now account for well over 20% of the exports of the industrial world. Today, the US sells about one-third of its exports to the non-oil developing countries — roughly the same amount as it sells to the EC and Japan combined. Some forecasts envisage the developing countries accounting for between two-fifths and one-half of the growth of the industrial country exports in the 1980s — provided, of course, the developing countries can find markets for their own exports.'[4]

Despite the progress that has been made in reducing or dismantling many of the trade barriers set up in the pre-war years, this remains an important issue in international trade relations. In fact, in recent years the resurgence of protectionism and bi-lateralism has added to this concern. The fact is that in both developed and developing countries particular industries or sectors are protected, though perhaps for different reasons. The advantages of a free market economy, however, remain a powerful attraction. The irony is that while the industrial nations indulge in the most strident form of protectionism, the weaker countries in the system are often put under pressure to dismantle their trade restrictions. The argument, of course, is that free trade eliminates inefficiency and promotes an efficient allocation of resources at the global level. The fact that the real world situation is often quite different from simplistic text book models is often conveniently ignored. Since international trade theory still exerts a significant influence on policy, in the following section we examine the nature of this theory. We then take a look at the global institutional framework governing international trade. In the final section we outline the basis and elements of Commonwealth Caribbean trade policy.

The relevance of trade theory

Modern trade theory has its roots in the 'absolute advantage' theory propounded by the English economist, Adam Smith (1723–90) in his famous book *An inquiry into the nature and causes of the wealth of nations* published in 1776. Smith's views were a direct reaction to the mercantilist thinking prevalent in Europe in the period between the mid-fifteenth and the middle of the eighteenth century. The mercantilists had argued that a nation's wealth (and power) could be measured in terms of its stock of precious metals, mostly gold. Nations wishing to become wealthy and powerful, therefore, needed to encourage exports (which would stimulate industry) and discourage imports which were seen to drain bullion. Given the system of exchange and international settlements at the time, a surplus of exports over imports would have resulted in an inflow of precious metals. In a situation where the existing stock of gold was fixed, surplus nations stood to gain at the expense of deficit countries. The strong economic nationalism which this view was intended to foster fitted well into the climate of political and military conflicts among European states at the time.

Smith's vision was much broader. He saw wealth in terms of output or production and envisaged a situation where all countries could gain from international trade (rather than some at the expense of others) if each specialised in the production of commodities in which it had an absolute advantage (or could produce more efficiently than others), and exchange the excess production for goods which it could not produce as efficiently as other countries. Specialisation at the international level in a context of free trade was seen by Smith as the best way to maximise global welfare. David Ricardo (1772–1833) took Smith's ideas a bit further and argued that even in a situation where one country had an absolute advantage over another in the production of two commodities it would still be beneficial to both, if each specialised in the production of the commodity in which it had a comparative advantage and import the product in which it had a comparative disadvantage. Both Smith and Ricardo assumed labour to be the only factor of production and to be homogeneous, i.e. all of the same type.

The Ricardian analysis in particular is based on a number of implicit and explicit assumptions, some of which are critical to the validity of the conclusions and the policy implications that flow from them. While the analysis was carried out within the framework of two commodities and two countries, no doubt for ease of exposition, it should be pointed out that the conclusions derived from such a model may not necessarily be valid in an expanded framework. The other major explicit and implicit assumptions were as follows:

(a) cost (price) of a commodity could be inferred from the amount of labour time that went into its production (the labour theory

of value). Implicit in this theory is the assumption that labour is the only factor of production, or is used in the same fixed proportion in the production of all commodities and that it is homogeneous i.e. it is only of one type in each nation
(b) no transport costs and the absence of obstacles (e.g. tariffs) to trade
(c) labour was assumed to be mobile within individual nations but completely immobile between countries
(d) perfect competition in all factor and product markets
(e) constant costs of production. Implicit in this assumption is that the scale of operations has no effect on costs
(f) no technological change
(g) trade is assumed to be by barter. Money is neutral and acts simply as a medium of exchange
(h) unchanged factor supply and
(i) full employment.

In Ricardian theory, comparative advantage and disadvantage is based on differences in labour productivity between nations. Demand differences are largely ignored. Only one factor of production is assumed to exist — labour. The neo-classical theory expounded by the two Swedish economists Eli Heckscher (1879—1952) and Bertil Ohlin (1899—1979) argues that factor prices may be the critical factors determining specialisation. In other words, they assume more than one factor of production. The Heckscher-Ohlin theory states that each country will tend to produce and export the commodity which uses more of its abundant and cheap factor, and import the commodity in which a great deal of its scarce and expensive factor is used. The Heckscher-Ohlin theory is heavily supply biased, in that it seeks to explain trade principles in terms of differences in factor endowment (which is taken as fixed and homogeneous) and factor prices. Tastes (identical consumption patterns) and technology are assumed to be the same in all countries, while constant returns to scale is assumed to prevail.

In the Ricardian model production functions are assumed to differ between countries. In the Heckscher-Ohlin theory production functions are taken to be similar across nations, though they differ between commodities. The analysis also abstracts from transport costs and takes the Ricardian assumptions of perfect competition and international immobility and national mobility of production factors. Given the assumption of national mobility of factors, trade under certain very restrictive assumptions will lead to the equalisation of factor prices between trading countries, i.e. remove the pre-trade differences in factor prices. Two of these assumptions are that trade must be completely free so that the prices of traded products will be equated in all countries and prices of commodities must accurately reflect the cost of producing them.[5] Since in practice trade is never completely free, factor prices between countries are not likely to be equal. In fact some factor prices (particularly those like capital or skilled labour which are internationally mobile) will be less unequal than others.[6] It should be pointed out that the analysis in the neo-classical model tends to be in terms of money rather than real costs.

The factor price equalisation theorem is not essential to an acceptance of the Heckscher-Ohlin approach.[7] Nor does it require non-specialisation, 'and it would presumably survive if technologies were similar though not identical'. If like all models it is seen as a way of 'representing reality that picks out certain features as crucial and enables us to understand their implications' in the context 'where the features modelled are in fact the crucial ones', the model can be useful.[8]

The theories discussed above have not been able to provide a completely satisfactory or convincing explanation of the pattern of international trade. Some of the empirical work undertaken provides partial support for the hypotheses enunciated. In others the findings appear to contradict the predictions.[9] For example, MacDougall and Kravis found some evidence in support of differences in labour productivity as a major influence on the pattern of international trade. Belassa, too, in a study of the UK and US found a high correlation between productivity and export performance. On the other hand, Wassily Leontief in a 1954 study of a number of US industries concluded that 'American participation in the international division of labour is based on its specialisation in labour intensive rather than capital intensive lines of production. In other words, this country resorts to foreign trade in order to economise its capital and dispose of its surplus labour, rather than vice-versa'.[10] Since the US is assumed to be better supplied with capital than its trading partners, this was a startling result which generated a great deal of controversy. Some attributed it to the statistical and methodological approach employed. Others sought more plausible explanations. Leontief himself thought America's relative superiority in capital may be overstated. He felt the superior effectiveness of American labour provides the country with a greater labour supply than is commonly believed. Buchanan thought that Leontief's neglect of natural resources may have been a crucial factor affecting his results. Venek was to argue later that the US could not make full use of its capital, because the country was not well supplied with natural resources. The latter is needed to complement capital in the production process.

It has become increasingly recognised in recent years that the complexity of international trade and the fact that countries do not have equal access to the same production technology make it difficult to explain trade patterns by one theory or model. The classical and neo-classical explanations are constantly being supplemented by explanations which appear to be partial rather than a complete framework of analyses. One explanation known as the 'technological gap' hypothesis argues that the industrial countries, because of their technological sophistication, are pioneers in the development of new products and this gives them easy access to foreign markets in the early stages of manufacture. At a later stage, production may shift to other countries who may be able to develop an export potential in the particular products based on some cost advantage. The product cycle theory[11] explains trade patterns in terms of changes in input requirements as products move through the production phases of 'new', 'growth' and 'mature.' In its 'new' phase the product will be in a period of experimentation which would be associated with a high degree of skill labour input. Production in this phase is likely to be for the home market. As the product becomes standardised and accepted, producers are likely to seek out foreign markets and the product moves into a stage of mass production and consumption. By the time this 'mature' phase is reached the level of skill required is likely to be less. Once the product becomes established other countries may find it possible to produce the goods perhaps more effectively than the innovators.

Another hypothesis known as the 'preference similarity' hypothesis argues that a country will tend to export those goods it produces for the home market. The act of producing at home to satisfy the needs of the majority is assumed to lead to a degree of efficiency which allows producers to venture into foreign markets. The needs of the minority at home which cannot be satisfied by local producers could be satisfied by producers in countries where the tastes of the majority are similar. Yet another argument relates exports to the size of the home market. In situations where the home market permits economies of scale the lower costs will encourage producers to enter foreign markets.

In the early post-war years, it became increasingly apparent in the developing world that development would not just happen. It had to be initiated, nurtured and managed. Goals would have to be defined and institutions and policies formulated to achieve these. In the 1950s and 1960s it was found necessary by a large number of developing countries to write development plans which not only served to provide a perspective on development objectives and strategy, but also defined financial needs. The exercise of planning for development required a theoretical framework, and since poverty was seen to be closely associated with the colonial legacy of production and trade, the theoreticians in the developing countries found a direct challenge in theories and models which sought to validate the inherited production and trade structure. Given the long history of integration of developing countries in the international economy, it was not surprising the critics first sought to question the link between the nineteenth century pattern of trade and development. Even though the relevance of classical and neo-classical theory to developing countries may have been a separate issue, the question could not escape scrutiny in a context where theory tended to be used to justify phenomena due to historical and political factors, rather than strict economic rationale.

The most severe attack was not unexpectedly directed at the assumptions of the classical and neo-classical theories. Both groups of theories sought an explanation for trade patterns in price differences. The theory of comparative costs assumes that prices in international trade reflect cost differences. 'Under the assumptions of full employment and perfect competition,[12] the opportunity cost of a commodity, which is the value of the factors used to produce it in their best alternative employment, is equal to its market value. Market prices of factors and commodities can therefore be used to determine comparative advantage under competitive conditions.[13]

In the real world, prices are a reflection of both demand and supply factors. Perfect competition exists neither in the product market nor in the factor market. Large transnational firms with branches spread across many nations dominate the production processes in many countries. Trade unions are known to exert considerable influence in the labour market. Some commodity prices are also influenced by the existence of commodity agreements. In practice, transport in certain situations can be a significant factor in costs and the location of an activity. The assumption that factors of production are fixed in quantity and constant in quality across nations and are fully employed bear little relationship to reality. This is one of the static assumptions of traditional trade theory. In the past this assumption led to the conclusion that since developing countries had a large amount of unskilled labour, they should concentrate on the production of goods requiring large amounts of unskilled labour and little capital. In practice, nations can accumulate capital and change their factor endowment situation. New resources may also be discovered with the same result. Labour can be trained to acquire new skills and this can bear on the comparative advantage positions of particular countries. Many countries spend large sums of money on research and education with the purpose of enlarging the productive capacity of their economies.

The assumption in classical theory that labour is the only factor of production or is homogeneous is difficult to justify. Later economists were to demonstrate however, that this assumption is not critical to Ricardo's comparative advantage theory. Godfried Haberler (b. 1900) in 1930 used the concept of 'opportunity cost' to get around the problem raised by the labour theory of value. Employing the construct of a production possibility curve to delineate the production possibilities open to a country based on its resources, he argued that the cost of a commodity could be measured in terms of the amount of another commodity that must be given up to produce an additional unit of the first commodity. The cost of the first commodity could be calculated in terms of resources released by the amount of the second commodity given up.

The classical theory assumed that technology was fixed while the neo-classical theory took the position that it was similar, or that even if it changed it was freely available to all countries. In the real world technology has not only been changing rapidly, but its spread has been very uneven. The fact that the transnational corporations located in the developed countries spend significant sums on research and development lead them to guard very closely the fruits of their research. Another assumption implicit in the theory of comparative advantage is that 'the benefits of technical progress tend to be distributed alike over the whole community, either by the lowering of prices or the corresponding raising of incomes.'[14] It has been argued that the benefits of increased productivity stemming from technical progress have been confined largely to the industrialised nations, and this is reflected in the gap in the standard of living between the latter and the underdeveloped nations. The argument here is that since technical progress seems to have been greater in industry than in primary production (which characterises underdeveloped countries) the fall in prices should have been greater in manufactures than in primary products to the extent that lower prices reflect increased productivity. It has been argued (not without controversy) that the opposite has been the case. The benefits of technical progress have been expropriated in the form of higher incomes in the industrial nations.[15]

The assumption of immobility of factors of production implies that factors of production are owned by nationals. In classical and neo-classical theories it is taken for granted that all the benefits of trade accrue to nationals of the particular countries. In a world of foreign investment and the movement of people, part of the domestic production will accrue to foreign factors. While traditional theory assumes away the existence of governments, the latter are major actors in the international economy. Governments use a range of devices such as tariffs, licences, subsidies, etc., to influence trade, out of deference for certain social and economic objectives at the domestic level. Free trade tends to be the exception rather than the rule.

The question of internal mobility of factors in response to external market forces is one that cannot be taken for granted in developing countries where production structures tend to be rigid in the short term. A great deal of the investments in these countries is of a specific nature with its own servicing infrastructure. For example, the resources tied up in sugar or bananas cannot easily be shifted in the short term to other areas of activity, if there was a fall in demand for these products resulting from, let us say, high costs. The fact, too, that corporations tend to specialise in certain lines of activity often makes them unwilling to move into new areas of production, when the old ones are threatened by more efficient production. Producers and trade unionists are often able successfully to lobby their governments to obtain increased protection or subsidy in a particular area in which the country may have lost its comparative advantage. This is true of developed countries as much as of developing. Movement into new areas of activity often require retraining of workers and this may take time. The point is that the simple movement from one line of production to another or from one commodity-mix to another portrayed by the smooth curves in the text books has no counterpart in reality. In practice, change could be painful since social and political forces may come into play.

In the light of the forgoing discussions, it is not surprising that developing countries have tended to pay little attention to the policy prescriptions stemming from trade theory and instead have concentrated on issues of growth and growth theory. The latter 'either ignores comparative advantage and the possibilities of trade completely, or it considers mainly the dynamic aspects, such as the stimulus that an increase in exports provides to the development of related sectors or the function of imports as a carrier of new products and advanced technology.[16] With the increasing problems that have come to be associated with the import substitution strategy in many developing countries, the link between domestic production and international trade policy has become increasingly recognised. A few traditionally poor countries in the Far East have shown that limited natural resources is no impediment to a significant expansion of non-traditional exports. This has inspired other nations to look at their development strategies and how these are influenced by global trade policy. In the following we look at the policy/institutional framework of international trade.

The global policy/institutional framework

A large number of the elements in present day international trade policy have their beginnings in the early post-war years. The goals and objectives of this policy as well as the institutional framework were already established before the majority of developing countries in the world today attained their constitutional independence. The process of international acceptance literally called for membership of organisations such as the General Agreement on Tariff and Trade (GATT), the International Monetary Fund (IMF) and the International Bank for Reconstruction and Development (IBRD). Membership of these institutions (from which countries with Centrally Planned Economies have generally been excluded)[17] implies not only the acceptance of certain obligations and responsibilities, but adherence to rules, regulations and operational procedures over which they had, with a few subsequent exceptions, little influence in shaping.

The last three institutions (which are sometimes referred to as the Bretton Woods System) grew out of the Bretton Woods Conference of 1944 and were intended to complement each other. The IMF was conceived as the centre of a new international monetary system following the disorder of the 1930s and early 1940s. The World Bank was set up to encourage the flow of foreign capital. One of its immediate tasks was to help in the reconstruction of a devastated Europe. The GATT was established in recognition of the need for institutions to help in the removal of discriminatory practices affecting international trade. The GATT, however, was intended to be a temporary arrangement pending the establishment of the International Trade Organisation (ITO) whose objectives were much broader, extending as they did to cover employment, commodity agreements, etc. The ITO, however, never came into being, and as a result the GATT continues to provide the framework for the conduct of international trade. For various reasons there are several countries besides most of the Soviet Bloc states which have opted to stay out of GATT.[18]

Membership of GATT means the acceptance of certain contractual obligations. With the disintegration of the world economy in the 1930s, bilateral agreements and protectionism had assumed major dimensions. The aim of GATT was to remove discrimination in international trade. Towards this end the most favoured nation clause was made the cornerstone of the Agreement. Essentially, what this provision requires is that trade concessions agreed to between a member state of GATT and a third country have to be extended to other contracting states. As stated in the Agreement, the principle of reciprocity is built into the clause. It was recognised that equality of treatment in a world of unequal nations did not make such practical sense. Initially, provision was made for the use of protective measures in the interest of development or for balance of payments reasons. The Agreement also allowed for the formation of free trade areas and customs union, once certain conditions were met. Despite these exception clauses, developing countries increasingly felt that in a situation where countries were vastly different in economic strength, there was need for more special treatment of poor nations. To meet this complaint, a new Part IV was added to the GATT in 1965. Under this section provision was made for an exemption from the requirement for reciprocity in tariff concessions. Since, however, discussions among the developed countries revolved around goods that were not of particular significance to developing countries, the latter saw the need for further measures if they were to expand their export trade. In 1971 member states of GATT agreed to a waiver from the most favoured nation rules in order to permit the introduction of Generalised System of Preferences (GSP) schemes. These permitted access to the markets of certain developed countries for a wide range of products without requiring developing countries to reciprocate.[19]

While the level of tariffs have been reduced in the post-war period, trade restrictions are still very much in evidence today. Quotas, licensing and negative lists are still widely used. In the developed countries trade restrictions take more subtle forms such as labelling and packaging requirements, health standards, etc. In recent years sector arrangements (e.g. automobiles, electronics) in the form of 'voluntary' restraint agreements have not only increased the number of traditionally protected areas, but have contributed to the increasing share of international trade being conducted outside of GATT rules. Both in the developed and developing countries restrictions are often used to protect inefficient industries. In the developed states lobbyists often have little difficulty in convincing legislators of the need for protective measures in areas of the economy facing strong external competition, particularly when unemployment is high or the industries concerned are seen as strategic. In the developing countries the need to protect jobs is also a dominant concern. One of the more common arguments for protection, however, revolves around the infant industry concept which contends that in the early stages of development young industries need to be protected from the foreign, established ones. The experience in many countries has shown that protection once installed is often difficult to remove. Under protection many 'infants' assume monopoly position and in a situation devoid of competition often show little tendency to grow up.

Some current issues

With the eight multilateral rounds of trade negotiations (the so-called Uruguay Round) in the GATT underway, a great deal of attention has come to focus on services. One of the items on the agenda is a US sponsored proposal to make trade in services subject to rules similar to those governing trade in goods. Up to now GATT discussions have focused largely on goods trade. With a few minor exceptions, GATT itself does not deal with services which between 1970 and 1982 grew at an annual rate of 14.7% as compared to 15.4% for trade in goods. In 1984 world services exports (excluding investment income) was estimated to be 384 000 million SDRs, or about 20% of merchandise exports.[20]

Services form an increasingly important part of the economic activity in both developed and developing countries. 'In the US, for example, almost 67% of gross national product (GNP) and 74% of civilian non-agricultural employment is in services. By contrast, the share of services in GNP in LDCs ranges from 29% for low-income economies, to 49% for medium-income and 52% for upper-middle-income LDCs.'[21] Services in fact have been growing at a faster rate in LDCs than in industrial economies. 'Between 1973 and 1983, the average annual growth rate for services was 2.1% in the industrial nations, 1.3% in the higher-income LDCs, and 5.3% and 5% respectively, in the middle-and low-income LDCs.'[22] With respect to the export of services the industrial countries accounted for 74% in 1984 as compared to 81% in 1975. The US is the largest exporter of services in the world followed by the EC and Japan. The balance of payments performance of the service sector varies from country to country. Some high-debt countries like Brazil and Mexico tend to have large deficits because of debt service payments. Others like the Bahamas, Singapore and Barbados tend to have larger surpluses in the 'invisible' account. In the Commonwealth Caribbean, tourism is the major service export, earnings from which tend to offset a significant part of the trade deficit in a number of countries. In a few cases (e.g. Trinidad and Tobago, Jamaica, Barbados, Guyana) where air or sea carriage services are provided, foreign exchange is also earned from the transport of goods and people.

On the payments side, foreign debt service payments account for a significant part of the deficits on the services account of Guyana and Jamaica, and more recently for Trinidad and Tobago. The factor service payments accounts relating to direct foreign investment are generally negative. Commonwealth Caribbean countries also import a wide range of services relating to management, professional and technical services, commissions, royalties, patents, advertising, film rentals and insurance. Between 1976 and 1985, for instance, Trinidad and Tobago paid abroad US$1601 million as service fees.

Services are important to development, and there is concern among developing countries that liberalisation of certain types of services could adversely affect the growth of such services in their own economies including those that are in their infant stages. The main argument is that they do not have a comparative advantage in services that are traded. The proponents for liberalisation contend that the removal of barriers to the free movement of services would lead not only to greater efficiency and lower costs, but would increase the flow of investment which would make possible greater access to modern technology. Developing countries are also concerned that liberalisation would not only lead to increased dependence on the industrialised countries for critical services, but would impinge on national security and sovereignty. 'They believe that negotiating access to communication, transportation, or financial networks is tantamount to bargaining over a nation's ability to manage its own development strategy and safeguard its national security.'[23]

The buoyant growth of world exports in the period between the end of World War II and 1973 was in a large measure the result of the trade liberalisation process that took place in this period. In recent years the growth of world exports has slowed considerably, and this is widely blamed on the resurgence of protectionism in the world economy. Terms like 'neo-mercantilist' and 'beggar-thy-neighbour' are once more being used with increasing frequency to describe the trade policies of some members of the world community.

Restrictions in international trade were never really completely dismantled, and may never be. In fact, while some of the more traditional forms (like tariffs) were being reduced under the auspices of international organisations, more subtle and less discernible ones were being put into place. The question is, why is there this growth in protectionist sentiment, despite the widely acknowledged benefits of freer international trade?

A conclusion strongly influencing the early post-war discussions on the international economy was that for countries to import, they must be able to export. The flaw in the mercantilist argument that countries should strive to increase their wealth by emphasising exports and restricting imports was widely recognised. For political reasons, mercantilist sentiments will always be around, but for obvious reasons, they tend to be more appealing in times of economic crises like those that plagued the world system in the 1970s and early 1980s. The resurgence of protectionism is partly the result of the politico-economic changes experienced by the global system in the post-war period. The reduced economic dominance of the US, the emergence of the EC and Japan as economic powers, and the development of significant export-oriented manufacturing sectors by a number of developing countries have changed the pattern and structure of international economic relations. In the absence of international mechanisms for restoring trade balance, countries react individually introducing their own measures to deal with any perceived threats to domestic employment or standards of living.

There is no doubt that because of its size and purchasing power, the US market has been a major target for other countries' export thrust. The US economy itself has been slow in adapting to changes taking place in the world economy. Many of its industries have become inefficient as a result of obsolete technologies, low labour productivity and varying levels of protectionism. A slowing up in the growth of foreign earnings accompanied by increasing imports and massive foreign expenditures related to its military ventures abroad has considerably weakened its external position. The US found itself in the 1960s and 1970s facing not only a rapidly recovering Europe, but a vibrant Japanese economy based on modern technology and organisation. The US also found itself targeted by some developing countries who have been able to develop significant industrial sectors through the clever use of domestic policies and lower labour costs. At the same time, strong control has been kept by these emergent exporters over their own markets, employing a number of devices to restrict imports from other countries.

The significant increase in oil prices during the 1970s had a severe impact on the external position of oil-importing countries, some of which were already experiencing balance of payments problems. Since the late 1970s, the payments problem has been exacerbated by depressed prices for certain major commodities such as sugar and bauxite. For oil-exporting countries, the falling oil prices since the early 1980s has considerably weakened their external position. With problems facing their export sectors, several countries have found it increasingly burdensome to service their debt. In this situation measures to restrict imports are easy to rationalise.

Developments in the industrialised countries inevitably have repercussions on developing countries in a world that has grown increasingly inter-dependent. Buoyant economic conditions in rich countries tend to lead to greater exports from the developing nations, or at least to a less restrictive import policy. Poor economic performance on the other hand quickly gives rise to protection, and lower import levels. Even in the absence of economic crises, commercial policies in the developed countries are often dictated by political and strategic considerations. Policies contrary to broad national economic interests are often put in train to satisfy interest groups who may be seen as providing critical political support for legislators. Agriculture has been one of the most highly protected sectors in the developed countries, and while this may be partly related to the political clout of the farm community, it is also the result of a policy aimed at food self-sufficiency which is often seen as a strategic need. The desire not to deplete stocks of critical raw materials also exerts a strong influence on commercial policy relating to the imports of competing raw materials. In recent times we have seen trade policy being used to punish some offending state, or to reward those offering moral or policy support.

The advantages of policies based on free trade have been strongly argued in the theoretical literature. Indiscriminate protection, it is argued, leads to resource misallocation and results in inefficiency and high costs of production. On the one hand high costs adversely affect a country's ability to export. On the other hand domestic consumers are forced to pay higher prices for a product that would be available for a lower cost under more liberal trade policies. Inability to export, of course, also affects the country's ability to import. Not surprisingly the theory of free trade is often used as a point of reference by international organisations set up to prevent the mistakes of the pre-war years and to improve the workings of the international economic system.

In recent years there has been an increasing amount of conflict between such institutions as the IMF and the World Bank and developing countries who have sought their assistance. A great deal of this conflict arises from the greater government intervention required in conditions of underdevelopment and in situations where there are commitments to certain nationalistic objectives. In these countries trade policies must of necessity be development policies. When developing countries are asked to pursue less protective policies in the context of a situation where the industrialised nations are protecting inefficient sectors of their economies, they not surprisingly see an inconsistency in the administration of world trade policy, and question the international commitment to development. The products afforded greatest protection are invariably those which developing countries are capable of producing competitively, such as textiles.

There are a number of special arrangements which have been enacted with the avowed aim of promoting exports from developing countries generally, or from a select group of poor countries. The most prominent among these arrangements (which have all been discussed earlier) are the Generalised System of Preferences Schemes, the Caribbean Basin Initiative (CBI) the Lomé Convention, and more recently CARIBCAN, the arrangement involving Canada and the Caribbean states. While these arrangements do not generally insist on reciprocal concessions, it has been found in practice that the access they offer to the markets of the developed countries tends to be effectively limited by non-tariff barriers like packaging, labelling and health requirements, import levies, quota restrictions, etc. All of them have safeguard clauses which permit the granting states to resort to protective measures in the event of a domestic industry being threatened by foreign competition. This obviously would make prospective investors in developing countries very wary.

Elements in Commonwealth Caribbean trade policy

The legacy of the colonial economy is still very evident as Commonwealth Caribbean countries, as indicated earlier, continue to rely on traditional exports such as oil, bauxite, sugar, rice, bananas, etc. for foreign exchange earnings. In several countries tourism has emerged as an important activity. This is not surprising, given the abundant natural resources of sun, sea and sand. Despite the efforts that have been made to encourage the growth of an industrial sector, manufactured exports have been slow in emerging. The decline in earnings of many traditional exports, stemming from both a decline in production and marketing problems, have in many cases strengthened protectionist tendencies in the face of a rising import bill that was greatly affected in most cases by the steep increases in the price of oil during the 1970s. Even intra-regional trade which is governed by the CARICOM Agreement has been greatly affected by the protectionist trends that have emerged in the early 1980s in response to the foreign exchange crisis. Some of the measures put in force have been of a retaliatory nature and seem to be devoid of any economic rationale.

The economic policies pursued during the 1950s, 1960s and 1970s were largely of an import substitution nature. The foreign exchange required came from traditional exports. With the changes taking place both in the international economy and in the domestic structure, the need for an export bias is now widely recognised. Many countries in the region are now offering special incentives for export performance. To increase competitiveness certain national currencies have been devalued, while greater attention is being paid to productivity and the requirements of foreign markets.

Foreign trade, as indicated before, is important to these nations. As countries with small markets, exports have to be an indispensable element in any development strategy. Since the 1950s, however, the emphasis has been on creating jobs, with encouragement being given to the local assembly of previously imported final goods. The restrictions on the latter were increased, while intermediate products and capital goods attracted lower or zero duties. Paradoxically, the latter policy negated the employment objective since it encouraged capital intensive techniques. The burden for earning the foreign exchange again fell on the traditional sectors. Mechanism and policies aimed at moving from import substitution to export development received little or no attention. It was simply hoped this would materialise by itself. There was a significant intellectual failure to grasp the strategies at work by the suppliers of final goods in terms of the way they dealt with nationalistic policies and the imperatives of their own survival.

One effect of the import substitution strategy was that resources moved into activities that were offered protection, rather than those that promised to be efficient. Protection was easily justified on the infant industry argument. With the small domestic markets and the duplication taking place in neighbouring territories, the effects of economies of scale were lost. While manufacturing enterprises were afforded protection, there was little pressure to divert resources from the traditional agricultural export sectors towards more food crop production. The fact that sugar and bananas, two of the region's most important exports, have been protected in the UK market may have served to delay the rationalisation of agriculture. The failure of new export activities to emerge in a significant way may also have been a factor in the failure to reorientate agriculture.

Despite the intention to diversify their economies, the achievements in this direction have been limited. This has not only been the result of defective or inadequate internal policies, but the postures adopted by foreign governments. While the oil importing countries of the region were faced with higher import bills, Trinidad and Tobago's net foreign reserves position increased by over 1000% between 1973 and 1981. Based partly on oil revenue, and partly on borrowed funds or the participation of foreign companies, the decision was taken to set up a number of energy based industries aimed essentially at foreign markets. One of these plants was the Iron and Steel Company (ISCOTT) which is 100% owned by the Trinidad and Tobago government. This company produces steel rods, and despite a small amount of exports, has found itself in difficulty with steel producers both in the EC and US markets.

The desire, it seems, to break out of the mould of suppliers of food and raw materials and importers of industrial goods continues to be challenging. Even with respect to a primary export like sugar, the US quota from the region has been falling, as protection increases for high cost domestic sugar producers and artificial sweeteners. This is one example where domestic political considerations have taken precedence over economic considerations or over foreign policy dictates. Faced with restrictions for products in which they have a comparative advantage, it is easy to see why developing countries often reject the resource allocation arguments that arise when they try to set up industries for which they may not be particularly suited.

The failure of the manufacturing activities to emerge as a significant sector either in terms of providing jobs or earning foreign exchange has given rise to the need for a critical evaluation of existing policies. Certainly, there is a need for an import substitution strategy. A greater measure of efficiency, however, has to be aimed at and this has to be reflected in the structure of incentives. An export-oriented strategy does not preclude this. Products which can be produced competitively for local consumption may also be able to compete in foreign markets. An import substitution strategy also has to be aimed at increasing local value-added and encompass arrangements with foreign supplies which lead to an effective transfer of technology over time. An export oriented strategy requires a proper co-ordination of all policies that bear on costs and production.

In an effort to increase their competitiveness in the context of other measures being instituted to deal with balance of payments problems, some countries in the region have already begun to pay attention to areas which have long been neglected. One of these is the exchange rate. In the region generally, costs have tended to rise faster than those in competing states, making it difficult for these countries to compete in foreign markets. Both Guyana and Jamaica have had to undertake significant devaluations of their respective currencies in recent years following agreements with the IMF. Trinidad and Tobago also on its own accord devalued its currency by 50% in December 1985 in an attempt to deal with fiscal and foreign payments problems which had emerged following the decline in oil prices. Essentially, what a devaluation does is reduce the foreign currency price of exports and increases the price of imports in terms of local currency. This is expected to stimulate exports and discourage imports thus improving the trade balance. Trade barriers in foreign markets are assumed away. Increased opportunities for domestic production are provided. Given the structure and functioning of Caribbean economies, experience has shown that while it may pre-empt the need for administrative measures, devaluations in themselves will not have a significant impact on productive capacity, in the absence of a wide range of other measures. In the long term, of course, the most effective way to deal with high costs is to increase productivity.

It would be a mistake if Commonwealth Caribbean countries were to allow their production structure to be dictated purely by available natural resources. With abundant human resources, there is a need for policies to encourage products with high skill and technology content and for which there is a demand in international markets. While factor endowment does explain part of international trade, comparative advantage in a world of rapid communication and transportation is being increasingly determined by the ability of states to gauge trends in the international economy, to access information and knowledge, to mobilise skills and management and to build flexible production structures capable of responding to the needs of a changing market. At the regional level co-operation in production and marketing has been minimal with the effect that insular development strategies have taken a predominance which resists rationalisation aimed at securing a more efficient use of resources. The same point could be made with respect to the major service export of the region viz. tourism which is a relatively high cost product. Existing structural weaknesses in Caribbean economies is partly the result of the conceptualisation of and approach to the national development strategies adopted. In this situation, these countries have not only left themselves open to exploitation, but they have also been unable to take full advantage of opportunities offered them in international markets. Failure to develop a vibrant export trade which could finance their development needs explains the continued heavy dependence on foreign financial assistance.

Notes

1. Protective devices take different forms. Some of the more common in the Caribbean are *ad-valorem* tariffs (which are levied on the basis of the value of the imported product), specific duties, surcharges, import licensing, and outright bans on certain products. Various forms of government assistance can also help to give a domestic product an advantage over an imported one.
2. Mahmood Ali Ayub, *Made in Jamaica: The Development of the Manufacturing Sector*, Baltimore: The Johns Hopkins University Press, 1981, p.71.
3. *Ibid*. p.80.
4. J. de Larosière, *The World Economy in 1984: Problems, Policies and Prospects*, Washington, D.C., IMF, 1984, p.13.
5. See, H.R. Heller, *International Trade: Theory and Empirical Evidence*, New Jersey: Prentice Hall, Inc., 1973, p.125.
6. See J.R. Williamson, *The Open Economy and the World Economy*, New York: Basic Books, Inc., 1983, p.57.
7. *Ibid*.
8. *Ibid*., p.58.
9. For a summary of these works, see S.J. Wells, *International Economics*, London: George Allen and Unwin Ltd., 1969, pp.23–25. See also John Williamson, *op. cit*. See also M.A.G. van Meerhaeghe, *International Economics*, New York: Crane, Russak & Co., Inc., 1972, pp.20–58.
10. Quoted in Wells, *op. cit.* p.50.
11. This theory is most closely associated with the name of Raymond Vernon. See 'International Trade and Investment in the Product Cycle', in *Quarterly Journal of Economics*, 80, 1966.
12. The Heckscher-Ohlin version of the comparative cost doctrine provides a measure of comparative advantage that does not depend on the existence of perfect competition and initial equilibrium. See H.B. Chenery, 'Comparative Advantage and Development Policy', *American Economic Review*, Vol. 51, 1961.
13. *Ibid*.
14. See Raul Prebisch, 'The Economic Development of Latin America and its Principal Problems', *op. cit.*
15. *Ibid*.
16. H.B. Chenery, *op. cit.*
17. GATT principles are premised on the existence of decentralised or market economies. Despite this, however, countries such as Cuba,

Hungary, Romania, Poland, Czechoslovakia and Yugoslavia have been admitted as members. On August 15, 1986 the Soviet Union formally applied for permission to participate in the 'Uruguay Round', of GATT, but the request was rejected. Incidentally the Soviet Union is now the world's sixth largest exporter of merchandise trade.
Yugoslavia, Romania and Hungary are members of the World Bank and the IMF.
18 Among them are several Latin American countries (e.g. Ecuador, Bolivia, Paraguay, Panama and Venezuela).
19 For a discussion of these schemes see Tracy Murray, *Trade Preferences for Developing Countries*, London: Macmillan Publishers Ltd., 1977.
20 See J.J. Schott and J. Mazza, 'Trade in Services and Developing Countries', in *Economic Impact*, 1987/2.
21 *Ibid.*
22 *Ibid.*
23 *Ibid.*

CHAPTER 7

Aspects of the integration experience in the Commonwealth Caribbean

The signing of the Treaty of Rome in 1957 by six European nations to bring into being the European Economic Community (EEC) was a significant event in the post-war international economy. The six countries involved were Belgium, Luxembourg, Netherlands, France, Italy and West Germany. The total population of these countries in 1958 was around 170 million as compared to 175 million for the US and 92 million for Japan. Part of the significance lay in the fact that by some standards, most of the countries in the grouping were themselves large. The preamble to the Treaty of Rome included among its basic objectives the establishment of the foundations for an 'ever closer union' among European peoples, the improvement of their working and living conditions, and the progressive abolition of overseas countries. The initial steps towards the attainment of these objectives were the creation of a customs union by abolition of internal tariffs and other barriers to trade, the establishment of a common internal tariff, the development of a common policy for agriculture, and the introduction of measures to establish the free movement of labour, capital and services. Provision was made for the overseas countries which had special links with member countries to have an associate status with the EEC.

Parallel with this movement was the formation of the European Free Trade Association (EFTA) in 1960 by Austria, Britain, Denmark, Norway, Portugal, Sweden and Switzerland. The total population of these countries in 1960 was about 90 million. An association agreement was signed with Finland in 1961, while Iceland became a member in 1970. The association involved an industrial free trade area in which members undertook to progressively dismantle the barriers to trade on industrial goods between themselves, but maintain their own tariffs and their own independent commercial policies towards the rest of the world. In 1973 Britain and Denmark, along with the Irish Republic, became members of the EEC. Since then Greece (1981) and Portugal (1986) and Spain (1986) have also joined. In 1984 the population of the enlarged EEC, now the European Community (EC), would have numbered around 320 million with an average per capita GNP of over US$8000. In the same year the population of the US was estimated to be 237 million and its per capita income over US$15 000. The comparable figures for Japan were 120 million for population and US$10 400 for per capita income.

The formation of these groupings in Europe had a demonstration effect in developing countries, particularly in Africa and Latin America. Some of these countries, particularly in the latter, had long enjoyed political independence, but remained underdeveloped and heavily dependent on the metropole. The desire to industrialise as a means of bringing about structural changes in their economies made integration an attractive option, even though orthodox economic theory was not certain about the degree of benefits that could be derived from integration among non-industrial countries.

Since the mid-1960s Commonwealth Caribbean countries have also been engaged in efforts to attain a greater measure of economic integration among themselves. These efforts have so far met with limited success, as has been the case in other developing areas. Some of the problems being confronted appear to be common to the various groupings. In this chapter we shall undertake a brief discussion of the Commonwealth Caribbean integration experience against the backdrop of the experience in other parts of the developing world. We begin by examining the theory of economic integration and its relevance to developing countries.

Integration theory

The theory of economic intergration is essentially an extension of neo-classical international trade theory. Though there are several levels of integration, the discussion tends to be carried out largely around the concept of the customs union, i.e. a free trade area with a common external tariff. Prior to the publication of Jacob Viner's book *The Customs Union Issue*[1] in 1950, the formation of a customs union was seen as a movement towards free trade and this would therefore bring about an increase in world welfare.[2] Viner argued that in certain circumstances welfare could be reduced. The two critical concepts employed in customs analysis are 'trade creation' and 'trade diversion.' Trade creation describes a situation where trade is shifted from a high cost producer within the union to a lower cost producer within the grouping. On the other hand, trade diversion refers to the situation where trade is diverted from lower cost producers outside the union to higher cost suppliers within the area. In this analytical framework if trade creation exceeds trade diversion, a case for forming a customs union exists. The analysis is essentially static and is concerned with the efficient allocation of resources in a situation of full employment and given inputs of resources. Orthodox theory is concerned with the gains that may be derived from changes in the existing pattern of trade.[3] Apart 'from the tariff, domestic prices are assumed to reflect opportunity costs, so that the chief domestic grounds for interference of resources do not arise. The orthodox theory was evolved with the developed countries of Europe in mind and expressly for the purpose of throwing light on the problem of integration in Western Europe.[4]

Since in developing countries external trade in relation to domestic production tends to be large, and intra-regional trade tends to be small in relation to total trade, it would be easy to dismiss a case for integration among such countries on grounds that the opportunities for trade creation are limited. Critics, not surprisingly, have argued that while developing countries must also be concerned with the efficiency question, the existence of unemployed resources and development imperatives should lead poor countries to view integration from a different perspective.[5] The concern should not so much be with the immediate benefits of integration, but with changing the existing pattern of trade and production.[6] Promoting inter-sectoral linkages and growth may be more important than efficiency consideration.

For countries lacking a regional and industrial base, regional protection tends to provide enhanced market opportunities which would not otherwise be available. A larger market, of course, makes possible economies of scale, which should not only stimulate local and foreign investment, but lead to lower prices for consumers. There are limits to the industrialisation process in small national markets where import substitution can be pushed to a certain point without becoming a costly affair. Integration, too, by allowing competition between firms in the area may encourage greater efficiency and productivity, thus laying the basis for extra-regional exports of manufactured goods. The growth of the industrial sector should also assist in the development of entrepreneurship which is often in scarce supply in developing areas.

Depending on the supporting policies adopted, integration may avoid waste by leading to a more rational division of both domestic and foreign resources. The exchange of information among participating governments and a greater measure of collaboration with respect to foreign investment policies, can result in the transfer of more relevant technologies to the area, and also increase the benefits of foreign capital. Integration may also make possible projects which individual governments could not undertake on their own, and which may be of a kind that could attract foreign financial support, both from governments and multi-lateral agencies. Integration can also result in improved terms of trade, if countries use their enhanced bargaining position to get better prices for their exports and intensify the co-ordination of trade policies and practices.

In short, it is argued that in a development context, integration ought to be seen in dynamic terms. Precisely the conditions and environments that are taken for granted in industrial countries form part of the development challenge in poor countries. In developing states economic objectives are often seen as forming only one part of the integration effort. Co-operation in non-economic or non-trade areas (functional co-operation) is often an integral part of the overall integration package. There is also a political element in almost all economic integration schemes. Increasingly, there is a security rationale as well, that also tends to have an economic dimension. In recent years, for example, there has been increasing concern with food security which could best be tackled on a regional basis.

Integration in developing countries

Since 1960 at least ten integration schemes have been formed among developing countries. Such efforts, however, have not met with outstanding success. While some schemes still survive, integration objectives are not actively pursued in most of them. That legislation has not been enacted to put an end formally to the moribund movements may reflect the fact that the dream still remains. For small states in the present world community, there are not many options to closer economic and political co-operation. Small countries and even large poor countries realise that there are certain distinct advantages to be derived from the integration of markets. Additional benefits can flow from the pooling of resources and skills, and increased bargaining strength in international negotiations. In the context of modern technology, certain types of enterprises require large markets to be viable, and are therefore more easily attracted to integration areas.

Despite the advantages of economic integration, why have integration movements met with such limited success in developing countries? The answer lies both in internal and external factors. The desire in some cases to guard too jealously the newly won political sovereignty, particularly in the early post-independence years may have been too strong to accommodate the economic arrangements which integration dictated. Perhaps these ambitions came too early after independence when countries were still formulating and consolidating domestic arrangements. The legal framework too, may have been too imitative of that adopted by the developed countries, and, therefore, almost completely ignored the historical experience and the social, economic and political situations in the regions. Some of the treaties, though lucid in language and brilliant in rhetoric, proved inadequate for dealing with such crucial issues as the distribution of benefits, polarisation, allocation of industries, policy towards foreign investors, loss of revenues resulting from removal of tariffs, etc. Certain complementary policies are required to make free trade arrangements work and these have proved difficult to adopt in the face of different ideological outlook, over-indulgent nationalism and lack of political will.

With respect to external factors, it is clear that balance of payments problems arising from depressed commodity prices, trade barriers in the developed countries, increasing prices of imports, servicing of the foreign debt and reduced capital inflows have adversely affected postures of individual units. In almost all the schemes in developing countries intra-regional commerce has tended to account for a small part of total trade. The developed countries themselves as well as multi-lateral agencies have not provided a great deal of support for integration efforts in developing countries. On the contrary, in certain cases industrial countries have blatantly encouraged bi-lateral arrangements in the context of trying to influence the positions of individual member states.

Economic integration in the Commonwealth Caribbean

Existing arrangements for the economic integration of the Commonwealth Caribbean have their beginnings in the 1960s, following the collapse of the West Indies Federation in 1962.[7] The Caribbean Community (CARICOM) which has its basis in the Treaty of Chaguaramas signed in 1973 seeks to deepen the process of integration started some years earlier by promoting co-operation in both economic and non-economic areas. The main aim behind the establishment of the Community, as one of its architects has pointed out, is not only the economic development of each single member country

and of the region as a whole, but the enhancement of the effective sovereignty of the member states of the region and the self-determination of its peoples.[8] To achieve these aims the signatories of the Treaty of Chaguaramas commit themselves to co-operate in three major areas:
   (a) Economic integration (through the common market) involving:
      - Market integration
      - Co-ordination of joint actions in production
      - Joint actions in extra-regional trade and other economic transactions
      - A special regime for the Less Developed Countries (LDCs)
   (b) Co-operation and common services in non-economic areas such as health, education, transport, etc. (so-called Functional Co-operation)
   (c) The co-ordination of the foreign policies of member-states.

Market integration involves not only the removal of barriers to intra-regional trade, but the establishment of a common external tariff and protective policy. Though the economic arrangements are referred to as a 'common market', there is no explicit commitment to the free movement of factors of production. Member states are asked to give preferential treatment to citizens of other member states with respect to the provision of certain types of services and to examine ways and means for the introduction of a scheme for the regulated movement of capital within the region, giving particular attention to the needs of the LDCs. CARICOM, therefore does not fit neatly into traditional schemes of integration. While it lacks some of the arrangements of a common market, it includes other fields of co-operation in functional and other areas.

Article 17 of the Treaty requires member states to 'aim at the fullest possible co-ordination of their foreign policies' and 'to adopt as far as possible common positions in major international issues.' Article 34 requires member states to 'seek a progressive co-ordination of their trade relations with third countries or groups of third countries.' A decision taken by the Heads of Government in 1985 also called on member states to consult with each other before concluding trade and economic agreements with third countries and groups of third countries. The Treaty also requires member states 'to adopt a scheme for the rationalisation of agricultural production within the Common Market with a view to promoting complementarity in national agricultural programmes and providing special opportunities for the development of agriculture in the Less Developed Countries.'

With respect to tourism, the Treaty calls on member states to collaborate in the promotion and development of industry. Recognising the need to gain greater control over economic decision-making, member states are urged to work towards increasing national ownership of their resources and 'the adoption as far as possible of a common policy on foreign investment.' In drawing-up national development plans member states are asked to consult with each other in order to promote 'maximum complementarity between industries and economic sectors.' They also agree to work jointly towards the formulation of a long term Common Market Perspective Plan as a framework for co-ordinating development efforts.

In the 1960s there was considerable discussion over the approach that the integration movement should take. Fearing loss of newly-won political sovereignty, the politicians were more inclined towards the simple approach of removal of barriers to intra-regional trade. The academics felt that the removal of trade barriers in itself was not likely to have much effect on the growth of intra-regional trade since restrictions were already insignificant as a result of the obligations dictated by the Commonwealth System of Preferences under which goods originating in Commonwealth countries received special treatment. It was also felt that in a Caribbean context simple trade liberalisation was likely to result in increased polarisation among Caribbean states. Integration in the Caribbean, they argued, should go beyond the concern of the more efficient use of resources. Trade production and development should be the main focus of integration strategy in the region. In this respect the pooling of resources and regional industrial programming were essential if real gains were to be derived from the integration effort.[9] In recognition of the points raised by the academics, the Chaguaramas Treaty underlined the need for industrial programming not only to secure an equitable distribution of benefits, but to encourage greater use of the region's raw materials, to create production linkages and generally to make more efficient use of the region's resources.

The approach suggested in the Treaty of Chaguaramas is one that recognises the constraints on the small Caribbean states and the disadvantages that could flow from policies of competition and unplanned development. The Treaty was intended to provide a framework for regional development and is not a substitution for efforts at the national level. By the late 1970s it had become evident that integration was not proceeding as was envisaged, and in the light of issues relating to the question of ideological pluralism, a group of Caribbean experts was set up in March 1980 by the Sixteenth Meeting of the Council of Ministers of the Caribbean Common

Market to prepare a strategy for the Caribbean Integration Movement during the decade of the 1980s.[10] The experts found that while some modest gains were made in the area of trade and functional co-operation, very little progress was made towards the achievement of major objectives outlined in the Treaty. These included co-ordinated or joint actions in production, harmonisation of monetary and external payments policies, and a scheme for the regulated movement of capital within the Common Market. In the areas of consultation on economic policies or the co-ordination of development planning very little had been achieved. Because of delays in decision-making at the national level certain regional projects, particularly in the field of agriculture could not be implemented. In the area of foreign policy co-ordination they found existing practice far from satisfactory and stressed the need for more effective machinery and mechanisms.

More than seven years after the expert group reported, there has been little improvement in the situation on both the economic and functional fronts. In fact intra-regional trade restrictions intensified following the deterioration of Trinidad and Tobago's economic position since 1981. The clearing facility which was set up in 1969 to facilitate the settlement of claims among members suspended operations in March 1983. In the area of air and sea transportation there have been no major breakthroughs. Deadlines for the removal of trade trestrictions come and go. A Common External Tariff and a Common Protective Policy against third countries is yet to be fully established. Two encouraging recent developments have been the setting up of an export credit facility to encourage the growth of regional and extra-regional trade and a CARICOM Enterprise Regime which is intended to encourage regional investment.

An assessment of CARICOM

Given the structure of CARICOM, it would not be correct to judge the success of the movement in terms of the growth of intra-regional trade. Yet increasing regional trade forms an important part of the exercise. One can gauge the importance attached to the trade aspect from the fact that all other areas of integration have been affected as a result of failure to resolve satisfactorily restrictions imposed by certain major member states to deal with balance of payments problems and the retaliation by others to this move. It would be instructive therefore to examine recent trends in intra-regional trade.

In the late 1960s intra-regional exports amounted to about 6%

of total exports. The proportion for intra-regional imports was slightly less. Since then these proportions have increased, but intra-regional trade still accounts for only a small part of total trade — around 9 to 10% at its peak in the early 1980s. This proportion has now fallen back to about 7 to 8%. Not all countries are dependent to the same extent on the regional market. Generally, the LDCs sell a large share of their exports to CARICOM and derive a larger share of their supplies from this market than do the MDCs. In 1984 the CARICOM region took only about 7% of Jamaica's exports as compared to 14% for Guyana, 22% for Barbados and 9% for Trinidad and Tobago. Jamaica also obtains a smaller proportion of her import requirements from the CARICOM region than the other MDCs. With respect to the LDCs, over 25% of their exports in most cases are sold in the CARICOM market. Generally, around 15—20% of their imports come from this source. Though Belize is classified as an LDC, its trade direction, no doubt because of its location, is different from that of the OECS countries. Belize's domestic exports to CARICOM have averaged less than 5% in recent years, while the share of imports has tended to be even lower.

The decline in the value of intra-regional trade in recent years has been a source of concern to those who view integration as an important part of the strategy of Caribbean development. The decline of this trade is related to several factors. In the late 1970s both Guyana and Jamaica imposed restrictions on imports from other CARICOM states as part of a package of measures to deal with their balance of payments problems stemming from the significant increases in the cost of oil, falling commodity prices, recession in the world economy and production problems at home. The Treaty of Chaguaramas makes provision for a member state to introduce quantitative restrictions on imports to safeguard its balance of payments position. There was a feeling in some quarters that the safeguard provisions were abused by both Guyana and Jamaica. The government of Trinidad and Tobago took no retaliatory action while the oil boom was in progress, but with the rapid economic decline since 1981, following the drop in oil prices, this country has adopted defensive measures of her own. As the most important single market in CARICOM, this move exacerbated the trading problems in the region. The significant increase in income in Trinidad and Tobago during the boom years encouraged a rapid increase in the level of imports from both regional and extra-regional sources. The manufacturing sector in other CARICOM states came to depend critically on the Trinidad and Tobago market. Reduction in access to this market, therefore, had an immediate impact on income and employment in the other territories. Despite the efforts made to remove intra-regional trade barriers, prevailing high levels of unemployment, falling incomes and persistent balance of payments problems continue to provide a rationale for retaining the barriers. In this situation uncompetitive and inefficient enterprises have no difficulty in perpetuating their protection.

Between 1973 and 1981 intra-regional trade in current values increased by an average of almost 24% per year. It is estimated to have declined by 2.6% in 1982, 12.5% in 1983, 10.9% in 1984 and 3.3% in 1985. Preliminary data indicate a further fall in 1986. The value of intra-regional trade in 1985 was 28% below the 1981 level. Not all countries have been affected to the same extent. Barbados' domestic exports to CARICOM declined from almost US$59 million in 1982 to US$35 million in 1985 — or by more than 40%. Exports from Jamaica fell by 37% between 1982 and 1984. Barbados' imports from CARICOM declined by 24% between 1980 and 1982, but have shown a tendency to rise since. Jamaica's CARICOM imports dropped by more than 50% between 1980 and 1984. The data for Trinidad and Tobago also indicate a sharp fall in the value of CARICOM trade in recent years. The value of domestic exports to CARICOM declined by 20% between 1980 and 1985. If petroleum products are excluded, the decline would be in the region of 50%. On the other hand the value of imports increased steadily until 1983 when it reached almost US$186 million (or 7.2% of total imports). Between 1983 and 1985 imports from CARICOM dropped by 4.7%. Agricultural products from the LDCs have apparently not been affected to the same extent as their manufactured goods which compete with those produced in the MDCs.[11] Many of the manufacturing enterprises set up in the LDCs had targeted the markets of the MDCs, and particularly that of Trinidad and Tobago.

Despite the current problems affecting regional trade, CARICOM governments have repeatedly affirmed their commitment to the integration movement in the Caribbean. Action, however, has not matched this commitment. Political will has been lacking and this has affected the march of the integration movement in the Caribbean. Even when decisions are taken, implementation is a slow process. Time, it seems, is not important. But as time passes, not only does disenchantment grow, but opportunities are missed. Structures come into being, which are difficult to remodel or remove. It is clear that politicians often find it difficult to reconcile national interest with that of the region as a whole. Even though the long term benefits of a regional approach to an issue may be apparent, once it is perceived that the national interest (however defined) may suffer in the short term there is often a reluctance to abandon insular policies, whatever long term costs may be associated with such policies.

In some non-economic areas a certain amount of functional co-operation has been attained. In many vital areas, however, meaningful integration continues to elude the region. For instance, while the role of air and sea transport has been recognised as critical, the rationalisation and reorganisation of existing services are yet to be accomplished. With respect to industrial development, it has long been recognised that because of the small national markets and limited resources, a complementary rather than a competitive approach would be much more beneficial to the region. To accomplish this would have required a certain amount of regional planning and the co-ordination of national policies, including policies on foreign investment. The tendency of regional governments to see themselves in competition with each other has led to a tremendous amount of duplication of facilities, and consequently a wastage of capital. The benefits of economies of scale have been limited, and this may partly explain the high costs of many categories of goods produced in the region. National protection also tends to remove the pressures to improve quality. As indicated earlier, the industrial sector has little depth. Most of the operations are final touch industries involving assembling and packaging of foreign manufactured inputs. Value-added tends to be minimal. The complementary use of the region's natural resources as a basis for industry which has long been advocated, has so far received scant attention. We thus have a situation where valuable capital resources are not optimally used and the operation of policies which presumes a critical shortage of capital funds. Governments have not only offered a wide range of incentives to attract private foreign capital, but have also borrowed abroad to finance consumption and to help generate income and employment. Such policies have led to increasing reliance on foreign resources.

The failure to transform agriculture has also resulted in a situation where the region is critically dependent on foreign sources for food supplies. Twenty-five years after the process of independence started in the Commonwealth Caribbean, the region continues to produce what it does not consume, and consume what it does not produce. The fact that the Caribbean is well endowed with agricultural resources and has a tradition of agriculture points to the absence of adequate policies as the factor which has contributed most to the present situation. Lack of relevant research, land tenure problems, inadequate transport, marketing, and credit facilities, inept macro-economic policies and deficiencies in organisation have contributed significantly to the decline of agriculture in the region. The long rooted Regional Food Plan, designed to increase food production, has been slow in implementation, despite a rising food import bill.

With a market of only five to six million people CARICOM trade policies have, of necessity, to be outward looking. National import substitution with respect to light manufactures has virtually reached its limits in certain territories. The framework of development must be more explicitly export oriented. There is no choice. The pace at which these countries develop depends critically on their ability to earn foreign exchange. Not only has concessional finance declined in recent years, but regional states would find it increasingly difficult to borrow in the light of their current balance of payments problems and developments in the international financial environment.

In the Georgetown Declaration of 1986, the Heads of CARICOM states recognised the need to accelerate the development of economic ties with neighbouring states in the Caribbean and Latin America. This would inevitably involve reciprocal arrangements. Since such arrangements can impede the deepening of CARICOM itself, CARICOM governments ought to work more assiduously at attaining common positions on as wide a range of trade and investment issues as possible. Failure to do so would encourage the bilateral approach to foreign economic relations which may work counter to the objectives of CARICOM.

At another level, CARICOM countries need to take greater advantage of the opportunities offered by the US CBI, the Lomé Convention and the Canadian CARIBCAN. The tendency has been to wait for foreign investors to lead the way. The 'one-stop shopping' arrangement aimed at facilitating decision-making, however desirable, is not enough. The process of identifying areas where these countries can develop a comparative advantage and produce competitively has to become more deliberate and organised. The experience in other countries and particularly those in the Far East has shown that limited natural resources are not a hindrance to competitive export development. Developing marketing strategies are crucial. In this effort the resources of the state, including diplomatic missions abroad, have to be more supportive in this thrust. The research institutions would need to be strengthened in order to play a more active role in product development and technology adaptation. Private firms would have to be given greater incentives to divert more of their resources to the research effort. In this outward looking strategy which will entail changes in production and organisational structures, productivity objectives would need to rank high. Retraining of workers and improving management techniques have to become an ongoing process.

On the question of co-ordination of foreign policies, there are certain instances (e.g. the negotiation of the Lomé Convention) where member states of CARICOM have been able to take a common position *vis-à-vis* outside actors. Generally, however, the bi-lateral approach has been dominant as certain member states have tried to advance their own interests by entering into arrangements with third countries without consulting other partner states, and without fully examining the implications for the integration movement. To be sure, the co-ordination of foreign policies does not imply the pursuit of identical policies. What it does call for is a degree of consultation to prevent commitments to arrangements which could impede the attainment of integration objectives, or weaken the bargaining power of the group as a whole.

It is clear from what we have said earlier that not all CARICOM states attach the same degree of importance to CARICOM or the potential it holds for regional development. There has long been an unspoken scepticism in some quarters, which one suspects has been behind the approach of not to become 'too integrated too quickly.' This scepticism has been reinforced by concerns that the benefits from integration may not be shared as equally as may be desired, given the failure to implement certain mechanisms and policies designed to reduce polarisation. The trading problems of recent years have tended to reinforce this 'distanced involvement' and to underline the view that CARICOM is useful for certain limited purposes only. Given the size and resources of CARICOM, the latter certainly is not an alternative of, or substitute for, a broad-based outward looking strategy drawing on the resources and potential of the international economy. CARICOM ought to be used by member states to formulate the terms of their political and economic linkage with the outside world. While there is scope for increasing self-reliance, autarchic policies are not a viable option.

The question of increasing dependency naturally emerges to the forefront of concerns whenever the move toward more open policies, or increased participation in the international economy is discussed. Control over natural resources and economic decision-making in the context of post-independence nation building remain valid issues. The region, however, cannot isolate itself from the trends towards increasing interdependence in the world economy. There is a need to review constantly policies and strategies. Present approaches must not only draw on the experience and results of the past, but must be carefully thought out in terms of their economic and social consequences. In recent years, for instance, there has been a tendency for some states to take a more open position on private foreign investment. The feeling is that there is now a greater understanding of transnational corporations, and national governments could now bargain more effectively with respect to their participation in national economies and in preserving national sovereignty. The poor economic management of some countries in the recent past may in fact have resulted in 'weaker knees' and a greater inclination to capitulate to almost any type of arrangement, however dubious may be the benefits. Certainly, private foreign capital has a role to play in Caribbean development by supplementing national resources. Unless there is a regional policy, however, clearly defining the areas, scope, terms and conditions of participation, and differences in individual approaches, could interfere with integration objectives.

A final point is worth noting. In the early years of the integration movement, a dichotomy was made between the more developed countries (MDCs) in the grouping and the less developed states (LDCs). The latter were accorded certain special privileges to avoid the emergence of a polarisation problem. In recent years, however, economic performance in some of the LDC's has surpassed that of the MDCs and this has given rise to calls for abolition of the dichotomy and some of the prerogatives accorded to LDCs. It has also intensified the movement for the complete freeing of trade in 1988 — a step the LDCs are reportedly resisting.

Notes

1. J. Viner, *The Customs Union Issue*, New York: Carnegie Endowment for International Peace, 1950.
2. M.O. Clements *et al*, *Theoretical Issues in International Economics*, New York: Houghton Mifflin and Co., 1967, p.175.
3. See Peter Robson, *The Economics of International Integration*, London: George Allen and Unwin, 1984, p.150.
4. *Ibid.*
5. See, for example, Sidney Dell, *Trade Blocs and Common Markets*, London: Constable & Co. Ltd., 1983, p.162. See also W. Demas, 'Planning and the Price Mechanism in the Context of Caribbean Economic Integration', in W. Demas, *Essays on Caribbean Integration and Development*, Mona: I.S.E.R., 1976.
6. See Robson, *op. cit.* p.151.
7. For chronological history of the integration efforts in this period see

CARICOM Secretariat, *Carifta and the New Caribbean*, Georgetown, 1971.
8   W. Demas, *Essays on Caribbean Integration and Development*, Mona: I.S.E.R., 1976, p.117.
9   For a further discussion of these views see H. Brewster and C.Y. Thomas, *The Dynamics of West Indian Economic Integration*, Mona: I.S.E.R., 1967.
10 The Report which is called *The Caribbean Community in the 1980s* was submitted in 1981. The document is a publication of the CARICOM Secretariat, Georgetown, Guyana.
11 In 1985, St Vincent accounted for 24% of Trinidad and Tobago's imports from CARICOM as compared to 2.8% in 1981.

CHAPTER 8

External performance, capital movements and the growth of the foreign debt

There is a strong tendency in Commonwealth Caribbean countries for the import of goods and services to exceed the export of goods and services. In most cases a positive balance of trade is a rare occurrence. Even though for some countries the services balance tends to be positive (in most cases because of the earnings from tourism), these are often outweighed by the negative trade balances. Capital inflows (both private and public) therefore play a major part in sustaining the current high levels of imports.

Between 1970 and 1985 Jamaica had a positive trade balance in only two years, 1977 and 1978. Despite a fairly significant tourism sector, the 'invisibles' or services account was negative throughout the period. Two of the major sources of outflows were the profit remittances relating to foreign investment in the country, and the servicing of foreign debt. The latter in particular has taken on significant proportions in recent years. In the period 1980−84, total interest payments (cash) on the external debt amounted to US$943 million or 24% of the earnings from the export of goods and services in the period. Unilateral transfers have tended to be positive. Between 1979 and 1984 the latter (which includes gifts and remittances from abroad) averaged US$112.3 million per year, as compared to US$22.0 million per year between 1970 and 1978. The current account balance was consistently negative. The cumulative deficits in the 1979−84 period amounted to US$3252 million which gives an average of US$216.8 million per year. Between 1981 and 1984 the deficits averaged 12% of GDP. The deterioration in the economy in recent years has been accompanied by a marked reduction in the inflows of private long-term capital. Between 1970 and 1976 there was a net inflow of US$656 million. Between 1977 and 1984, however, there was a net outflow of US$431 million. With the exception of four years in the period, inflows of private short-term capital tended to be larger than outflows. To deal with the foreign exchange crisis the government has resorted to large-scale foreign borrowing to complement the concessional funds received. Between 1978 and 1984 official inflows totalled US$1720 million as compared to US$350 million between 1970 and 1977. Despite these borrowings, the overall balance was negative in ten of the fifteen years between 1970 and 1984. The net foreign assets of the country declined from US$156.7 million at the end of 1971 to minus US$543.1 million at the end of 1980 to minus US$1299 million at the end of June, 1985.

The whole economic situation of Jamaica must have deteriorated dramatically, though, following the devastation caused by Hurricane Gilbert which hit the island in September 1988. The effects of the hurricane on the economy have yet to be calculated but it must have worsened an already deteriorating trade balance.

In the case of Barbados, the trade balance was negative in every year between 1970 and 1985. Because of the important place of tourism in the economy, the services account tends to be positive, but these balances have not been large enough (except in 1984 and 1985) to offset the negative trade balances. The result is a situation of persistent current account deficits. Net direct investment flows have generally been positive. Between 1970 and 1984 these totalled US$110 million. In the same period outflows of direct investment income amounted to US$81 million. Portfolio capital outflows in recent years have exceeded inflows. Public sector external borrowing has increased significantly since the mid-1970s. Between 1977 and 1984 public sector long-term inflows totalled US$151 million or 29% of the cumulative current account deficit in the period. The servicing of this debt, as we shall see later, has itself generated capital outflows in the form of interest and principal repayments. Between 1981 and 1984 interest payments on the external debt averaged over US$10 million as compared to less than US$2.5 million in the 1970–80 period. Since 1978 the country has had an overall deficit in only one year (1981). This situation, however, is largely due to the inflows of capital associated with the government's borrowing activities which no doubt has tended to cover up deficiencies in economic performance.

Between 1970 and 1973 Trinidad and Tobago experienced deficits in both the trade and current accounts. As an oil exporter the increase in international oil prices during the 1970s had an extremely favourable effect on its external position. Between 1974 and 1981 the country experienced a cumulative trade surplus of US$2625 million and a cumulative current account surplus of US$965 million. As a result of the fall in oil prices, the picture has changed since 1981. Despite positive trade balances in 1984 and 1985 (largely as a result of the fall in imports), the country experienced a cumulative current account deficit of US$2890 million between 1982 and 1985. The capital account balance (non-monetary sector) was generally positive. A major influence was the inflows of foreign private direct investment (FPDI). Between 1970 and 1984 there was a total inflow of US$1923 million giving an average annual flow of US$120.2 million. The immediate foreign exchange impact of FPDI, however, has to be measured against the outflows of direct investment income which totalled US$3152 million in the period, the average per year being US$210 million. Other private inflows have varied greatly from year to year. In the period 1979−84 there was a net inflow of US$330 million.

Official capital movements have also tended to have a favourable impact on the positive capital balances. Despite the positive current balances and the increasing foreign reserves position during most years of the 1970s, the government of the country still thought it necessary to borrow. The government also made loans to some of its neighbours in the boom years of the 1970s. In the period 1970 to 1984, there was a total net official inflow of US$469.2 million. Between 1974 and 1981, the overall balance was positive, the cumulative total amounting to US$3148.3 million. As a result, the net foreign reserves of the country increased from US$28 million at the end of 1973 to US$3203 million at the end of 1981. In the period since 1981 the decline in oil prices has impacted unfavourably on the current account, and even though the capital account balance has been positive it has not been able to offset the current account deficits. As a result, the net foreign reserves of the country declined to US$1188 million at the end of 1984. At the end of 1985 it stood at US$994 million or at 31% of the 1981 level.

Between 1970 and 1984 Guyana's trade balance was positive only in five years. The current account balance was negative throughout. The net cumulative current account deficit in the period was US$1167 million. The capital account was generally positive, but this was largely as a result of official receipts from abroad. Private direct investment declined substantially from the mid-1970s, as a response no doubt to the nationalistic policy being pursued and the downturn in the economy. Between 1970 and 1984 the overall balance was negative in nine years, the total net deficits amounting to US$306 million. The net foreign assets of the country declined from US$79.1 million at the end of 1975 to minus US$529 million at the end of 1985.

In the OECS countries, although tourism has become increasingly important in recent years, and remittances from nationals living abroad tend to be fairly significant, these flows have not been able to offset the persistent negative trade balances. Traditionally, official transfers have played a major role in helping to finance the current account deficits. In recent years these transfers have proved inadequate in the face of the scope of the development programmes adopted, and the governments of some of these territories have found themselves in a position where they have to depend increasingly on foreign borrowing on commercial terms. As we shall see later, this development has resulted in debt servicing problems in a number of cases.

Between 1979 and 1983 the current account deficits in Antigua amounted to US$145 million. Official transfers (gifts) financed less than 10% of this as compared to 23% for official borrowing. Foreign private investment and commercial bank flows accounted for the bulk of the rest. In the case of Dominica public grants have played a more important role in financing the current account deficits. Of the total current account deficits of US$121 million in the period 1976−84, public grants amounted to almost 70%, while public borrowing covered 23%. In the case of Grenada, grants financed 67% of the total current account balances incurred in the period 1980−84, while net public borrowings amounted to roughly 30%. In St Lucia capital inflows in the period 1977−84 amounted to US$227.1 million, of which only 13% was project related grants and 8% public borrowing. Private direct investment (mainly investment relating to the construction of the Hess Oil Terminal) contributed more than 75%. The completion of the terminal has resulted in a dramatic reduction in the inflows of private foreign capital. In St Vincent, public sector inflows have been larger than private flows in recent years. Between 1977 and 1983 the latter are estimated to have totalled (in net terms) less than US$10 million, as compared to US$45 million for the public sector. Of the latter figure, official transfers contributed almost 60%. In St Kitts-Nevis, official transfers financed 30% (on average) of the current account deficit in the 1980−84 period. In Belize, public sector inflows have financed over 80% of the current account deficit in recent years.

The negative trade balances are explained by several factors. On the export side these countries have traditionally depended, and continue to depend, on a narrow range of activities for their earnings. Diversification has been slow in coming. For various reasons the level of production of major export commodities (e.g. sugar, bauxite, oil) has been falling. The prices received also fluctuate greatly or rise very slowly − in some cases at a slower pace than the cost of production. For instance, with respect to sugar most of the sugar-producing countries in the region are now selling sugar in export markets below the cost of production. On the import side, increasing incomes and the failure of the domestic markets to meet the rising demand for consumer goods have led to increasing reliance on foreign sources. The development strategy pursued, too, has resulted in a critical dependence on external markets for raw materials and capital goods. While Trinidad and Tobago benefited greatly from the oil prices during the 1970s, the other territories suffered from having to direct a significant proportion of their foreign exchange earnings towards payment for oil. For instance, Jamaica's oil bill increased from US$63.6 million (9.1% of total imports and 14.8% of total exports) in 1972 to US$274.4 million (33.2% of total imports and 50.7% of export earnings) in 1981. In the case of Guyana the fuel bill increased from US$13.5 million (9.4% of total imports) in 1972 to US$153.1 million (35.6% of total imports) in 1981.

Two types of capital flows closely associated with balance of payments performance in the Caribbean are government borrowing and foreign private direct investment. In the following section we examine the external debt situation in the world and the experience of Commonwealth Caribbean countries. This is followed by a discussion on some issues relating to foreign direct investment flows.

The external debt

The international situation

In recent years the external debt of developing countries has emerged as a major issue in international economic relations. The World Bank has estimated that the total external liabilities of developing countries in 1985 was in the region of US$950 billion as compared to US$632 billion in 1980. Of this US$950 billion outstanding at the end of 1985, US$764 billion or 80% were long term. With respect to sources, 36% of the long-term debt was from official sources while 64% was from private sources. Short-term debt (i.e. debt with an original maturity of no more than one year) accounted for 16% of the total. The outstanding amount of short-term debt has been declining since 1982. On the other hand the use of IMF credit has been increasing. In 1980 outstanding IMF credit to developing countries amounted to US$9 billion or to a little over 1% of the outstanding debt. By 1985 this had grown to US$38 billion or to 4% of the total.[1]

The structure of the external debt of developing countries has undergone a remarkable change in recent years as can be seen to some extent in Table 8.1. In 1970 official creditors held 68% of the

Table 8.1 Public and publicly guaranteed long-term debt, 1970 and 1984 (Debt disbursed & outstanding)

Sources	1970 US$mn.	%	1984 US$mn.	%
Official Creditors	33 569	67.8	231 985	41.9
Multilateral	7 698	15.6	93 179	16.8
(IBRD)	(4 676)	(9.4)	(42 834)	(7.7)
(IDA)	(1 832)	(3.7)	(20 645)	(3.7)
Bilateral	25 871	52.2	138 806	25.1
Private Creditors	15 918	32.2	320 976	58.0
Suppliers	6 708	13.6	22 047	4.0
Financial Markets	9 210	18.6	298 929	54.0
Total	49 487	100.0	552 962	100.0

Source: World Bank, Development and Debt Service: Dilemma of the 1980s, 1986.

long-term debt outstanding as compared to 32% for private creditors. By 1984 the former's share had dropped to 42%, while the latter's had increased to 58%. Largely responsible for this substantial increase was the increasing dependence by developing countries on private financing markets for loan funds. Another factor was the inadequacy of funds available from official sources. A third factor was the conditionality attached to resources from both multilateral and bilateral sources. Even though the funds from private financial markets were generally associated with harder terms with respect to grace and repayment periods as well as interest rates, they were free of the political and economic conditions associated with a large proportion of official funds. The substantial increase in resources available to money centre banks and the aggressive lending policies pursued also helped in increasing the share of private finance.

The disbursed external debt varies widely from country to country in terms of the amount outstanding. The external liabilities of 107 countries reporting to the World Bank, under the Debtor Reporting System (DRS) was estimated to be US$865 billion in 1982.[2] The OECD has estimated that the total external debt outstanding for 155 developing and COMECON countries at the end of 1985 was US$1151 billion.[3] Of this figure, the fifteen most heavily indebted countries (Table 8.2) accounted for US$500.6 billion, while another 45 'troubled' debtors contributed US$585 billion. Five Latin American countries (viz. Brazil, Mexico, Argentina, Venezuela and Chile are among the ten biggest debtor countries. While attention is often focused on Latin American countries, a number of developing countries in other parts of the world are also facing a debt crisis which in certain cases is even more grave than that facing middle-income borrowers. For instance, at the end of 1984 the debt of low-income countries in Africa stood at about US$45 billion. This debt represented three-quarters of their GNP and three and a half-times their exports. In 1984 scheduled debt service was around one third the value of their debt service, but for certain individual cases the figure was much higher.[4]

While the absolute amount of debt outstanding gives an indication of magnitude, its economic significance has to be gauged from its relationship to other variables. For instance, a country may have a smaller debt than another country with respect to the total outstanding, but because of the size of this country, the level of development and the resources available to it, this debt may be more burdensome than that of the country with the larger debt. For example, Jamaica's external debt in 1985 was estimated to be US$3.4 billion, but this was more than 200% of GNP. Servicing of this debt was taking more than 20% of earnings from exports of goods and services. Brazil's debt outstanding amounted to about half of GNP in 1985, while in the case of Mexico the figure was 61%. Debt servicing also has to be looked at from the point of view of the government's revenue, so that what may appear to be a small outstanding debt compared to that of other states could be burdensome, if servicing payments absorb a significant part of public revenue.

The accumulation of debt over the years has given rise to substantial annual service payments. Debt service payments for DRS countries increased from less than US$25 billion in 1975 to US$74 billion in 1980 and US$100.1 billion in 1984. Of this latter figure, US$46.3 billion represented principal repayments and US$53.8 billion interest payments. In 1978 interest payments absorbed 16% of Latin America's earnings from the export of goods and services. By 1982 this had increased to 41%, but the preliminary estimate for 1985 indicates that the figure for 1985 may have fallen to around 36%. For the non-oil developing countries as a whole, debt service payments increased fivefold between 1973 and 1981. As a proportion of exports of goods and services, these payments have averaged over 20% since 1980. With such levels of debt service payments, and given the declining trends in annual disbursements, there has been a tendency for net transfers to developing countries to fall. Net transfers to DRS countries declined from US$34.4 billion in 1981 to US$3.6 billion in 1983. In 1984 the figure was negative, US$13.7 billion and in 1985 the estimate was also negative.

A substantial proportion of existing debt was incurred in a time of booming prices in certain commodity markets and a high rate of domestic growth in some cases. Oil exporting countries borrowed to finance expensive industrial projects, assuming a continued upward increase in the price of oil. Oil importing nations, on the other hand, needed external resources to finance balance of payments current account deficits resulting from the oil price increases. The total external debt of non-oil developing countries increased from US$130 billion at the end of 1973 to US$731 billion at the end of 1984.

The debt crisis had been building up for some years, but came to the forefront of world attention in mid-1982 when Mexico declared a 90-day suspension of service payments due on her external debt. President Garcia of Peru later followed by deciding to limit debt servicing to 10% of export proceeds. Towards the end of 1982 at least 30 countries were in arrears on their debt. Among them were some of the largest debtors such as Brazil, Mexico and Argentina. In February, 1987 Brazil suspended interest payment on its medium and long-term debt to banks. A large number of loans outstanding have had to be renegotiated and rescheduled. Between 1975 and 1982, 42 developing countries were involved in 144 renegotiations involving over US$200 million.[5] In an effort to deal with their debt situation some countries (e.g. Chile, Costa Rica, Ecuador, Mexico, Brazil, Argentina), have established debt-equity conversion programmes. In order to prevent these programmes being used for speculative purchase, the type of investment for which conversions may be used tends to be restricted. In some cases the exchange rate is used to channel investment into priority areas.[6]

While the Mexican debt crisis was precipitated by a shortfall in oil revenues, at the general level several factors have contributed. While the oil exporting countries have been affected by the drop in oil prices, non-oil nations have suffered both from depressed prices for major commodity exports, and falling production levels. Poor growth performances in the industrial countries and protectionism have had the effect of reducing imports from the developing countries. Declining private capital flows, short repayment periods and high interest rates have also contributed to the problem, as have inappropriate domestic policies, inadequate external debt management, and overlending by commercial banks.[7]

188 The Commonwealth Caribbean

Table 8.2 Fifteen biggest debtors at end of 1985

Countries	(1) Total debt US$ billion	(2) Owed to banks US$ billion	(3) (2) as a % of (1)	Interest to export ratios[1] 1982	1986
Ten biggest					
Brazil	104.6	74.6	71.3	53	40
Mexico	94.4	75.3	79.8	44	35
Argentina	53.7	42.0	78.2	50	47
Venezuela	34.3	32.7	95.3	18	29
Egypt	31.2	6.9	22.1	n.a.	n.a.
Poland	29.7	6.6	22.2	n.a.	n.a.
Philippines	28.6	12.9	45.1	24	33
Chile	24.4	20.1	82.4	44	36
Yugoslavia	23.9	13.8	57.7	n.a.	n.a.
Nigeria	15.9	6.5	40.9	8	15
Sub-total	440.7	291.6	66.2		

External performance

Five next biggest		
Peru	15.7	6.6	42.0	24	31
Morocco	14.9	4.0	26.8	n.a.	n.a.
Colombia	13.4	6.2	46.3	22	16
Ecuador	9.2	6.1	66.3	30	28
Ivory Coast	7.2	2.9	40.3	n.a.	n.a.
2 Sub-total	54.9	25.8	43.1		
Total 1+2	500.6	317.4	63.4		

n.a. not available

[1] scheduled interest payments as a percent of exports of goods, services and private transfers.

Source: OECD, *External Debt Statistics*, February, 1987; Morgan Guaranty Trust Company of New York, *World Financial Markets*, June/July, 1987

Notwithstanding the growing number of reschedulings and some improvement in the balance-of-payments position of some debtor countries the debt situation remains a matter of serious concern. In 1983 and 1984 growth in some of the industrial countries had resulted in increased demand for imports from developing countries. Falling real interest rates in the post-1982 period also served as a mitigating factor. The fall in the growth rates of industrial economies in 1985 and intensification of protectionist tendencies have served to remove some of the optimism for renewed growth in developing countries and an enhanced capacity for servicing their debt. The prospects facing a wide range of commodities remain bleak. As far as the price of oil is concerned falling prices would adversely affect the oil-exporting nations, but oil-importing countries will experience some relief after the increases of the 1970s. The significant fall in external resources available to developing countries is likely to have a counter productive effect. It is widely recognised that the solution to the debt problem lies in increasing the capacity of borrowing countries to service their debt by enabling them to expand their productive base and allowing them access to export markets.

Given the growing interdependence of the world economy, poor economic performance either in the developed or developing countries tends to have a ripple effect. Developing countries not only depend on the market of the industrial nations, but they themselves are significant importers of goods from these countries. As indicated earlier, banks in the major money markets have played a dominant part in channelling resources from surplus to deficit countries. Some of them over-extended themselves and often were guilty of not undertaking adequate risk assessment.[8] The impact of a massive default on the operations of these intermediaries has not been lost on the international community. A number of plans have been put forward in various forms to deal with the debt problem. An extreme solution suggested by Fidel Castro is massive default by developing countries. A more moderate proposal is the Bill Bradley Plan, named after the US Senator who proposed it. Essentially the Bradley Plan calls for the forgiveness of some interest and principal. Bradley suggests the elimination of three percentage points of interest and another three percentage points of principal over three years. Since enforcement of forgiveness would be difficult to legislate, banks would have to do so voluntarily, and this is difficult to envisage. What some of them have done is virtually to write off some of their claims by increasing loan-loss reserves, but retaining the loans on their books.

Perhaps the most widely discussed of the plans proposed is the

Baker Plan named after the Secretary of the US Treasury, James Baker, who unveiled it in October 1985 at the Joint Annual Meeting of the IMF and the World Bank held in Seoul, South Korea. The plan according to its author has three 'essential and mutually reinforcing' elements:

1. The adoption (with the collaboration of the Fund and the World Bank) by principal debtor nations of comprehensive macroeconomic and market-oriented structural adjustment policies to promote growth, reduce inflation, increase domestic savings and investment, induce repatriation of domestic flight capital and attract foreign capital inflows.
2. A 50% increase ($9 billion) over the next three years in World Bank and Inter-American Development Bank lendings to 15 key debtor countries in support of the countries' structural adjustment programmes.
3. Increased new lending ($20 billion over the next three years) by the international banking community to those key debtor countries that commit themselves to policies consistent with the plan.

The approach to the debt problem in recent years has revolved around efforts aimed at mobilising resources to help meet debt payments and negotiating new payment schedules. This has largely been on a country by country basis. The Baker Plan offers a more comprehensive approach to the problem. There are questions, however; and this may explain the lukewarm response in some quarters. One of the foremost of these questions relates to the amount suggested, which works out to about US$10 billion per annum. When seen against the fact that principal repayments of major borrowers was estimated to be about US$26 billion in 1985 while interest payments amounted to US$36 billion, an average of US$10 billion while not miniscule appears to be far from adequate.

Under the plan commercial banks are being asked to provide US$20 billion in new loans over the next three years. After the recent experience, banks have reason to be more cautious and prudent in making new loans. Many of them are already overexposed. In 1982 claims as a percentage of capital for the 24 largest US banks amounted to 200%, and though this had declined to 148% by 1985, it still remained high. It can be argued that failure to reverse the trend of declining private lending could adversely affect existing loans, since borrowing countries would not be able to carry out the kind of programmes necessary to strengthen their debt servicing capacity. Given the fact that many of the countries in need of new funds do not appear creditworthy if conventional indicators are used, banks may have to be provided with incentives such as guarantees and relaxation of loan-loss reserve requirements if they are to play the role being asked of them. Multilateral development banks (in particular the World Bank and the Inter-American Development Bank) are being asked under the plan to provide an additional US$9 billion over the 1986–88 period. In fiscal years 1983 and 1984 the World Bank (IBRD and IDA) alone approved loans averaging around US$15 billion per year. Disbursements amounted to about US$11.1 billion per year. With a lending capacity of about US$14 billion per year, the World Bank should have little difficulty in expanding its disbursements to meet the Baker target.

Another major question concerns the extent to which borrowing countries will be willing to pursue the kind of macro-economic and market-oriented adjustment policies perceived by lenders to be essential to economic stimulation. Many of them have already undertaken adjustment programmes to correct balance of payments problems and to meet the requirements of lending agencies. In some cases this has entailed a reduction in the standard of living. Adoption or continuation of policies suggested will depend not only on domestic perception of their efficacy, but on the possible political and social effects that are likely to be generated. However hard-pressed some countries may be, there may well be limits to what they will bear to secure access to new funding. From an ideological point of view the approach suggested to deal with the problem of growth and development may simply be unacceptable to some states.

There is another issue that needs to be raised here. Even if debtor countries were to agree to the kind of programmes being suggested, persistent and in some cases increasing protectionism in the industrial countries could frustrate the efforts being made at the domestic level. Falling terms of trade could also exert a debilitating effect. For the programme to attain its desired effect industrial countries will have to give some attention to trade policies as they affect developing countries, and in particular the debt-ridden ones.

An assessment of the situation almost two years after the Baker Plan was proposed shows that the objectives are not being met. 'Despite an increase in World Bank activity, overall official financing to the Baker countries[9] has dropped off, because of cutbacks by the regional development banks and net repayments to the IMF. Moreover, despite new money packages, claims of BIS-reporting commercial banks on the Baker countries declined nearly $3 billion last year [1986].'[10] Heavily-indebted countries are also finding it difficult to achieve sustained economic growth as a result of both internal policies and poor economic performance of the industrial countries.

This, combined with increasing protectionism has impacted adversely on the exports of developing countries generally. As a result, the average gross external debt as a percentage of exports, services and private transfers for the 'Baker countries' increased in 1986 over the previous few years. If we take the ten most heavily indebted of these countries, the percentage in 1986 was 385 as compared to 290 in 1984 and 264 in 1982. The overall projection for 1987 is similar to that of 1986, though the position of some countries is expected to increase.[11]

The external debt situation in the Commonwealth Caribbean

Because of the need to develop the social and economic physical infra-structure, the level of public investment tends to be high. In most cases, however, government savings tends to be small or negative. For instance, with respect to Jamaica current central government savings were consistently negative between 1976 and 1984, as was the case in Guyana. This situation has resulted in increasing dependence on foreign savings. For example, foreign inflows averaged 8.4% of GDP in Jamaica between 1976 and 1984, as compared to 8.2% between 1970 and 1975.

In recent years the governments of Commonwealth Caribbean countries have tended to pursue development programmes which call for a higher level of investment than could be financed from domestic savings. Again, in the case of Jamaica, while Gross Fixed Investment as a proportion of GDP averaged 21% in the period 1970-84, Gross Domestic Savings averaged only 14%. The comparable investment ratio for Guyana was 27%, whilst its domestic savings ratio averaged 17%. In Antigua, Gross Domestic Investment ratio in real terms averaged 42% between 1979 and 1983. Gross National Savings at constant prices, however, averaged only 16% of GDP. In Grenada real investment averaged 41% of GDP between 1980 and 1984 as compared to an average of 11% for National Savings.

The debt position in the Commonwealth Caribbean varies widely from country to country. This section is divided into two parts. In the first we discuss the position in the more developed territories, viz., Barbados, Guyana, Jamaica, Trinidad and Tobago and the Bahamas. In the second we look at the recent borrowing experience of the OECS countries and Belize.

The situation in the MDCs

Between 1970 and 1985 the public external debt of Bardados increased from US$15.1 million to US$222.0 million or by almost fifteen times. In 1985 this debt represented 18% of GDP as compared to 9% in 1970. In the latter year interest payments on the debt amounted to US$0.9 million, but fifteen years later this had grown to US$130.4 million. Over the period amortisation increased from US$1.7 million to US$14.7 million. External debt service payments in 1985 amounted to 1.4% of GDP as compared to 1.3% in 1974. As a proportion of exports of goods and services the ratio increased from 0.9% to 3.8% over the 1970–85 period. Guyana's external debt has also shown a strong tendency to increase. The disbursed outstanding debt grew from US$80 million (30% of GDP) in 1970 to US$214 million (50% of GDP) in 1974 and to US$742.7 million (161% of GDP) in 1985. In 1974 the debt outstanding represented about 73% of the exports of goods and non-factor services. By 1984 this proportion had grown to almost 300% not only because of the growth in debt, but as a result of the poor performance of the export sector. Because of the latter factor, debt service has become extremely burdensome. As a percentage of the export of goods and non-factor services, foreign debt service payments increased from 4.8% in 1974 to over 20% in 1981. Since then the average has been just over 15%, but this is largely as a result of the accumulation of arrears. The scheduled debt service in recent years is estimated to amount to more than 30% of the exports of goods and services.

The outstanding external debt of Trinidad and Tobago increased from US$79.1 million at the end of 1970 to US$125.2 million at the end of 1974. It dropped to US$53.7 million at the end of 1976, but has increased steadily since reaching US$975 million at the end of 1985. With the inclusion of the debt of state enterprises the figure stood at US$1856.7 million (38% of GDP) at the end of 1986. As a percentage of GDP, the outstanding external debt declined from about 10% in 1970 to 2% in 1976. Between 1976 and 1981 the ratio averaged around 7%. Since 1981 the ratio has increased steadily reaching 10.2% in 1984 and an estimated 12.4% in 1985. The rising ratio is the result of both greater borrowing and a declining GDP. With respect to the servicing of the external debt, annual interest and capital payments increased from US$9.9 million (1.2% of GDP) in 1970 to almost US$146 million (1.8% of GDP) in 1984 and to an estimated US$169 million (2.1% of GDP) in 1985. Of this latter figure US$84 million represented interest payments. Throughout the period 1970-85 debt service payments amounted to less than 2% of nominal GDP on average. The debt service ratio (i.e. interest and capital repayments expressed as a proportion of the export of goods and non-factor services) fluctuated between less than 1% and 6.4% in the period 1970-82. Since then it has averaged about 6.6%. The Trinidad and Tobago government chose to increase its foreign debt during the 1970s and early 1980s despite a strong foreign reserves position.[12] Some of the borrowing was undertaken not so much out of need, but apparently to establish creditworthiness.[13] The decline in oil prices in recent years has made debt servicing burdensome in the context of the government's large current expenditure and the ownership of a large number of unprofitable enterprises. External debt service payments in 1986 amounted to US$218 million or over 15% of recurrent revenue and over 12% of earnings from exports of goods and services, as compared to 6.2% in the previous year.

With respect to Jamaica the total outstanding external debt (including debt guaranteed by the central government) increased from US$154 million (15.8% of GDP) to US$3499 million (176% of GDP) at the end of 1985. As a proportion of the export of goods and services the former figure represented 28.6%, while the latter amounted to 280.0%. The actual debt service ratio which was around 3% in 1970 averaged 28.7% between 1981 and 1984 and increased to 41% in 1985. In recent years the country has not been able to meet some of its debt servicing obligations and therefore the actual debt service ratios do not reflect the true debt servicing position. On an accrual basis the debt service ratio would have averaged 43.2% between 1980 and 1985, while the actual ratio averaged 29.0%.[14]

The share of commercial loans in the total external debt of Commonwealth Caribbean countries varies widely. At the end of 1972 commercial banks accounted for 12.6% of Barbados' foreign debt as compared to 7% for intergovernmental and zero for international institutions. At the end of 1984, the latter's share had increased to 45%, commercial banks' share to 25%, and intergovernmental to 18%. In the case of Trinidad and Tobago the total external debt outstanding in 1970 had an original maturity of more than ten years. At the end of 1984 this had fallen to 13%. The other 87% were termed medium term, i.e. possessing an original maturity of up to ten years. This change in the structure of the debt reflects the increasing reliance on commercial sources rather than official development assistance.

In the case of Guyana non-commercial sources accounted for 56% of the disbursed external debt outstanding in 1972. By 1984 this had increased to 76%. Outstanding multilateral loans increased from less than US$5 million in 1972 to almost US$250 million in 1984. Bilateral loans increased by more than 200% over the same period. The slower growth rate of commercial debt is no doubt explained not only by the harder terms associated with it, but by the country's declining creditworthiness. For the same reason Jamaica, too, has had to rely increasingly on bilateral and multilateral assistance. In recent years the debt owed to commercial banks has been falling both absolutely and as a percentage of the total. For example, between 1980 and 1985 the share attributable to this source dropped from 25% to 12%. The share of official (bilateral) increased from 27% to 42% over the period, while that of official (multilateral) moved from 36% to 39%.[15] In order to maintain their credit standing in capital markets the IMF and the World Bank do not normally reschedule debts, and this means that their loans have to be serviced as scheduled.

The external debt situation in the OECS and Belize

Taken as a group the disbursed external debt outstanding of OECS member countries increased from US$41.6 million at the end of 1975 to US$241.6 million at the end of 1985 or by 480%. In the case of Belize the foreign debt increased from US$11.6 million to US$98.4 million or by 748% over the same period. While the rate of growth of the external debt varies widely among the countries, in all cases there has been a significant increase in outstanding debt over a very short space of time (*see* Table 8.3). For instance between 1975 and 1985 the external debt of Grenada, Montserrat, St Lucia and St Vincent increased by more than eight times. For the other OECS countries the increase ranged between 3.5 times for Antigua to 6.6 times for Dominica. In the case of Belize, the external debt outstanding at the end of 1985 was over 800% above the 1975 level. As a proportion of GDP (in 1985) two OECS countries had figures of over 50%, while for another two the figure was over 20%. The percentage for Belize was more than 50%.

Generally, the foreign debt has grown at a faster pace than GDP. For the OECS, outstanding external debt in 1985 amounted to 33% in 1985 compared to 18% in 1977. The proportion for Belize moved from 11% to 53% over the same period. Correspondingly, debt service as a proportion of GDP has also tended to grow. For the OECS as a group the ratio increased from less than 1% in 1975 to 4.6% in 1985. The debt service ratio (i.e. principal repayments and interest expressed as a proportion of exports of goods and services) has also shown a strong tendency to increase. An examination of Table 8.3 will show that the ratios themselves (for most states) do not appear large as compared to many other countries in the developing world. For the OECS countries as a group the figure in 1985 was 7.8%. For individual countries the actual figure varied between 2.7% for St Lucia and 20.3% for Grenada. The figure for Belize reached 11.8%. Another relationship that helps us to put the size of the debt in perspective is the proportion of government revenue that has to be diverted towards the servicing of this debt. For the OECS countries, the proportion was 4.9% in 1983 as compared to 6.7% for Belize. As with the debt service ratio this proportion can vary from year to year depending on changes in the size of the aggregates. For instance, in the case of Antigua external debt service took 24% of central government's revenue in 1980 and 42% in 1981. In the case of Grenada the figure was over 30% in 1985, as compared to less than 5% in 1977.

It is difficult to make statements about the burden of the public external debt by merely looking at proportions such as the debt service ratio or the ratio of debt service to government revenue. To begin with, these ratios tend to reflect actual debt service payments and not scheduled payments. Some of these countries are in arrears as far as servicing their external debt is concerned. For example, in the case of Antigua, less than half of accrued debt service obligations falling due in 1982 and 1983 were actually paid.[16] Arrears increased from 9.1% of current revenue in 1979 to 47.4% in 1983. In Grenada, too, the fall of the debt service ratio from 6.3% in 1982 to 4.8% in 1983 was largely as a result of arrears accumulation.

Traditionally, the OECS countries and Belize have tended to finance a substantial part of their public sector investment programme by concessional funds. Increasingly they have been turning to private commercial sources in the context of reduced concessional inflows and ambitious public sector investment programmes. In the case of Belize commercial finance accounted for 24% of total public external debt in 1983 as compared to 16% in 1980. In the case of Antigua debt on commercial terms increased from 71% of the total in 1978 to 77% in 1983. In Grenada commercial bank loans which were negligible before 1981 were accounting for 30% of the outstanding public debt in 1983. As indicated earlier, commercial loans may allow governments to be more flexible, but they generally carry shorter maturities and grace periods and higher interest rates. These conditions increase the debt servicing burden.

Given their weak fiscal positions and the high degree of volatility

Table 8.3 Commonwealth Caribbean: Selected data on external debt,[1] 1970 and 1985

Countries	External debt outstanding US$mn (1) 1970	US$mn (2) 1985	Outstanding debt as a % of GDP (at market prices) (3) 1970	(4) 1985	External debt service payments[2] US$mn (5) 1970	US$mn (6) 1985	Debt service payments as a % of exports of goods and services (7) 1970	(8) 1985
MDCs								
Barbados	15.1	222.0	9.0	17.9	0.9	30.4	0.9	3.8
Guyana	80.0	742.7	30.0	160.7	6.0	25.0[a]	3.3	10.2[a]
Jamaica[3]	154.0	3 499.0	15.8	176.4	14.0	448.4[a]	2.6	40.9[a]
Trinidad and Tobago	79.1	974.5	9.4[b]	12.4[b]	9.9	168.7	2.8	6.2
Bahamas	27.3	146.7	7.0	8.0	3.4	33.8	1.0	3.0
LDCs	1975	1985	1975	1985	1975	1985	1975	1985
Antigua	18.3	64.5	27.9	36.0	0.6	11.0	1.2	8.9
Belize	11.6	98.4	12.1	53.2[b]	2.1	15.5	2.6	11.8
Dominica	6.8	45.0	24.4	51.0	0.6	5.5	4.5	16.0

Grenada	5.5	49.6	13.7	51.4	0.6	10.5	2.7	20.3
Montserrat	0.4	3.7	5.1	10.0	–	0.4	–	9.3
St Kitts-Nevis	5.4	20.4	18.7	30.3	1.2	1.9	6.2	3.7
St Lucia	3.4	28.7	8.5	16.8	0.1	2.5	0.4	2.7
St Vincent	1.8	29.3	4.9	28.9	0.2	2.2	1.9	2.8

Data for LDCs generally refer to external public and publicly guaranteed debt.
[1] End of period disbursed outstanding debt.
[2] Interest and amortisation.
[3] Refers to Central Government debt, debt guaranteed by government and Bank of Jamaica debt
[a] Actual payments; on an accrued basis these figures would be much higher. The debt service ratios are based on actual rather than scheduled payments.
[b] Calculated on GDP at factor cost.

Sources: CDB, *Annual Report, 1986*; Official Publications; CDB, *External Public Debt in the OECS and Belize, 1977–83*.

associated with their foreign exchange earnings, the OECS countries and Belize need to exercise a great deal of caution in expanding their foreign debt, particularly the commercial component. In situations where exports are highly concentrated in a few activities, and where production is easily affected by natural conditions such as disease, pests and the weather, and where prices tend to fluctuate as a result of changes in market conditions or exchange rates, debt service ratios can be a poor guide to foreign borrowing. Given the poor state of their physical infrastructure, the governments in these countries are under pressure to improve domestic facilities in order to attract investment and encourage growth. There is need to finance a greater proportion of domestic investment from local sources. To this end fiscal reform is underway in most of these countries upon insistence of donors and lenders. Even in the face of domestic efforts to increase local savings, however, there will still be a need for external resources. For some of these states further commercial borrowing at this point could damage their credit rating which would undoubtedly impact adversely on future attempts at borrowing.

Some issues relating to direct foreign investment

The fear is often expressed that a large part of the social and economic progress made by Latin America and Caribbean countries in the 1960s and 1970s could be lost in the 1980s, if policies both at the domestic and international levels are not put in place to counter the declining trends of recent years. In 1985, only six countries in the region were able to achieve growth rates of more than 3%. In a number of states per capita income has fallen since the early 1980s. Real wages have also declined, while open unemployment and underemployment have increased. In nearly all countries central government expenditures for social services, health care, education, nutrition and housing – measured on a per capita basis, have declined in real terms.[17]

It is widely recognised that two factors critical to the regaining of lost ground are a reversal of protectionist trends in the industrial countries and an increase in the volume of investment in order to expand productive capacity. The mitigation of neo-protectionist tendencies would depend a great deal on how countries deal with the loss of comparative advantage in certain fields of production and the kinds of policies adopted by surplus countries with respect to exchange rates, trade and investment barriers. With respect to the level of investment in developing countries this has been affected by a decline in both official and private resources from abroad. In fact it has been estimated that as much as one third of capital importing countries have experienced negative resource transfers in recent years. Between 1979 and 1981 the net transfer to capital importing countries averaged US$40.7 billion per year. This figure fell to US$10.4 billion in 1982, and since then there has been a net resource outflow. In 1985 this outflow was estimated to be in the region of US$31 billion. The net transfer (outflow) from Latin America and the Caribbean was US$30 billion in 1985.[18] The factors which have contributed to this phenomenon are: a decline in official development assistance, high levels of debt service payments, a drop in bank lending and a decline in the net flow of private investment. Based on 1983 prices and exchange rates, total resource flows to developing countries were less in 1984 than in 1980 (*see* Table 8.4). Direct investment flows dropped from US$16.77 billion in 1981 to US$9.50 billion in 1984.

To get their economies moving again a large number of developing countries have intensified their efforts to attract private foreign investment. This has resulted partly from their critical debt situations, and partly from an inability or unwillingness to undertake further borrowing. A few countries, as indicated earlier, have established programmes aimed at swapping debt for equity.

Though the pros and cons of various forms of private foreign capital have been extensively discussed in the literature,[19] it remains a controversial subject. In the 1950s and 1960s, it was widely believed that foreign capital was a panacea for all the economic ills plaguing developing countries. Private foreign investment was seen as not only providing resources to supplement domestic savings, but was also associated with the transfer of technology, marketing and managerial skills, development of exports, access to foreign markets, the development of local entrepreneurship, as well as the more effective use of local resources. The key to the transformation of traditional agriculturally-based economies into manufacturing economies, it was fervently believed, lay in the attraction of foreign investment. In this connection, Commonwealth Caribbean countries, as indicated earlier, enacted a wide range of legislative measures to encourage investment generally, but particularly to attract private foreign capital. The effect of these measures on the growth of the manufacturing sector was also discussed earlier, and there is, therefore, no need to repeat that discussion.

While trying to attract foreign investment to promote manufacturing industries, Commonwealth Caribbean governments were

Table 8.4 Total resource flows to developing countries by major types of flow, 1950–84 (US$ billion at 1983 prices and exchange rates)

	1950–55	1960–61	1970	1975	1980	1981	1982	1983	1984
(I) Official development assistance	(8.35)	19.54	22.18	31.59	36.05	36.23	33.69	33.80	35.75
1 Flows from bilateral sources	8.34	18.60	19.38	25.88	28.75	28.52	26.21	26.23	27.35
a DAC countries	8.35	15.87	14.82	14.56	16.99	17.71	18.35	18.53	20.10
b OPEC countries	–	–	1.02	8.44	8.19	7.46	4.56	4.33	3.79
c CHEA countries	–	1.80	2.60	2.23	2.48	2.88	2.86	2.94	2.95
d Non-DAC/OECD	–	0.02	0.01	0.02	0.81	0.21	0.18	0.07	0.10
e LAC donors	–	0.91	0.93	0.63	0.28	0.26	0.26	0.26	0.41
2 Flows from multilateral agencies	–	0.94	2.80	5.71	7.30	7.71	7.48	7.57	8.40
(II) Grants from private agencies	–	–	2.25	1.99	2.17	1.97	2.30	2.34	2.50
(III) Non-concessional flows	7.54	15.29	28.66	51.01	55.66	68.56	60.10	82.10	54.00
1 Official or officially supported	–	6.57	10.36	15.66	22.91	21.55	21.90	19.82	20.00
a Private export credits (DAC)	–	2.03	5.47	6.57	10.43	10.99	7.06	5.50	5.00
b Official export credits (DAC)	–	2.80	1.54	1.78	2.31	1.95	2.65	2.10	2.50
c Multilateral	–	0.80	1.86	3.76	4.55	5.57	6.58	7.22	7.50
d Other official and private flows (DAC)	0.94	0.65	0.68	1.15	1.91	2.62	3.00	3.00	–
e Other donors	–	–	0.84	2.42	3.52	1.13	2.99	2.00	2.00

2 Private	—	8.72	18.30	35.55	32.75	47.01	38.21	62.30	34.00
a Direct investment	—	6.54	9.66	16.89	9.89	16.77	11.81	7.80	9.50
b Bank sector[a]	—	2.18	7.85	17.84	21.57	29.19	25.89	54.00[a]	24.00[a]
c Bond lending	—	—	0.79	0.62	1.29	1.05	0.51	0.50	0.50
Official development finance[a]	8.35	20.34	24.04	35.35	40.60	41.80	40.27	40.92	43.25
Total resource flows (I+II+III)	(15.89)	34.83	53.09	84.59	93.88	106.76	96.09	118.26	92.25

[a] Bank Sector includes for 1983 and 1984, significant amounts of rescheduled short-term debt.
Source: OECD, Twenty-five Years of Development Co-operation: A Review, 1985.

also attempting, in the post-independence period, to bring the 'commanding heights' of their economies (oil, bauxite, sugar, finance) under national control, or at least to increase national participation in areas traditionally dominated by foreign enterprise. Failure to arrive at satisfactory arrangements with the foreign owners in some cases led to outright nationalisation, or unilateral adoption of fiscal measures where attempts to increase benefits to the national economy failed. Such actions resulted in an atmosphere of uncertainty that in some cases have affected private capital flows across the board. Transnational enterprises themselves sensing the nationalist mood in newly independent countries generally have been changing their strategies of foreign operation. In the 1950s and early 1960s foreign direct investment largely took the form of branches or subsidiaries tightly controlled by the parent firms. In more recent years a wide range of arrangements have replaced traditional forms of operation. Joint ventures, licensing agreements, management contracts, turnkey contracts, production sharing contracts (particularly in the petroleum industry) and international subcontracting are more widely used.[20] From the transnationals' point of view, such arrangements not only deal with the issue of nationalisation, but provides them with assured access to markets and resources. Under licensing contracts, fees and payments are also often guaranteed, regardless of the performance of the licensor.

A number of factors have combined to lead Commonwealth Caribbean governments to place greater emphasis on private foreign investment and to change the somewhat ambivalent position taken in the 1970s. As indicated earlier, the serious debt situation facing several of these countries and the heavy debt servicing impact on the balance of payments is one of them. A major advantage associated with private foreign investment is that profit remittances is a function of the commercial success of the venture, and does not involve fixed interest payments, as is the case with borrowing. The poor performance of nationalised enterprises has also raised doubts about management capability in these countries in certain areas. The provision of resources by international organisations such as the IMF and the World Bank tends to be conditioned upon the adoption of more market oriented policies, a reduction of government involvement in the economy and an increased role for private investment. Programmes such as the US Caribbean Basin Initiative also envisage an enhanced role for private investment in participating countries which are expected to adopt the necessary policy measures to permit this. The desire to develop non-traditional exports and cultivate new markets also helps to explain the greater enthusiasm to attract foreign private capital. In addition to these factors, some governments in the region feel that they are now more capable of negotiating with transnationals, given past experience and the enormous amount of information now available.

To attract private foreign capital, Commonwealth Caribbean countries compete not only among themselves but with other developing and developed countries. In order to facilitate the foreign investor several countries in the region have set up 'one stop shopping' offices which could deal with applications quickly and effectively. A few have strengthened or reorganised their diplomatic offices abroad. In certain cases investment protection and double taxation agreements have been signed with foreign governments. Barbados, Guyana, Jamaica and Trinidad and Tobago are among the signatories of the ICSID (International Centre for the Settlement of Investment Disputes) which is an autonomous agency of the World Bank, dealing with the international arbitration of investment disputes. Some states have also drawn up Foreign Investment Codes defining the terms and conditions under which foreign investment would be accepted and the areas where it would be permitted.

Even with all this, the question remains: can Commonwealth Caribbean countries attract private foreign capital on the terms or on the scale desired? In recent years there has been a flight of capital from some states in the region as a result of poor economic performance, depressed international commodity markets, the rise of intra-regional trade restrictions and nationalisation. Though some countries like Japan and the EEC have increased their share of the stock of direct foreign investment in developing countries, the US still remains the most important single source of private foreign capital accounting for around 45% to 50% of DAC total. Table 8.5 shows that the stock of US direct investment in Jamaica and Trinidad and Tobago has fallen significantly since the early 1980s. In Barbados it has not changed appreciably in the last few years. On the other hand, US investment in the newly industrialising countries (e.g. Hong Kong, Singapore, South Korea, and Taiwan) in the Far East has been increasing. This is no doubt explained by the relatively high growth rates experienced by these states in recent years and the general framework of development adopted. US investment in Canada, Europe and Japan has also been increasing. Developing countries now account for less than 25% of the US direct investment stock abroad as compared to almost half in 1950. With respect to the Commonwealth Caribbean (excluding the Bahamas) this area in 1984 accounted for less than 1% of the total and 1.2% of the stock in developing countries taken as a group.

Table 8.5 US Direct Investment Position Abroad[1]: Selected countries 1982-85 (US$ m)

Area/Country	1982	1983	1984	1985
All Countries	207752	207203	212994	232667
Developed Countries, of which	154381	155736	157461	172750
Canada	43511	44339	46830	46435
European Community[2]	71712	70210	69688	82071
Other Europe	20737	21968	22329	24691
Japan	6407	7661	7920	9055
Other[3]	12014	11558	10694	10459
Developing Countries, of which	48058	45746	50131	54474
South America	19834	18748	19006	18625
Central America	10174	9904	9828	10374
Bahamas[4]	3121	3762	3412	3377
Bermuda[4]	11519	11056	13009	14104
Jamaica	386	310	257	141
Netherlands Antilles[4]	−19756	−22956	−24626	−21645
Trinidad & Tobago	931	862	871	480
U. K. Caribbean Islands	1425	1960	3007	3525
Guyana	3	6	3	2
Antigua	3	4	4	(n.a.)
Barbados	55	58	47	52
St Vincent	0	0	1	1
Dominica	0	0	n.a.	n.a.
Hong Kong	2854	3068	3249	3124
Singapore	1720	1821	1943	1897
South Korea	690	589	731	757
Taiwan	544	613	736	754

n.a. not available.
1 US Direct Investment Abroad is defined as the ownership or control, directly or indirectly, by one US person of 10% or more of the voting securities of an incorporated foreign business enterprise or an equivalent interest in an unincorporated foreign business enterprise.
2 Excluding Spain and Portugal.
3 Australia, New Zealand and South Africa.
4 Tax havens/offshore banking centres.
Sources: US Department of Commerce, *Survey of Current Business*, August 1986

Given this situation, what are the prospects for reversing capital flight and attracting a greater volume of private investment? To begin with, some existing regulations which were hastily designed in the 1960s and 1970s would clearly have to be modified in view of the new circumstances. Given the limited time horizon of the US CBI and the safeguard clause[21] associated with both this programme and the Lomé Convention, recent experience indicates that these arrangements have not had any significant impact on the flow of private capital. An important incentive is obviously going to depend on economic performance, and in this connection macro-policies designed to stimulate domestic saving and investment will be crucial. In the Caribbean some countries have better infra-structure than others, and this would tend to give these countries an edge. While generally the Commonwealth Caribbean with its aggressive tradition of trade unionism appears to be a high cost area, the lower labour costs in some states could offset some of the advantages held by other countries with respect to infra-structure and resources.

The traditional foreign investment package is becoming increasingly available in disaggregated form. Some elements can be purchased in the open market and this gives host countries greater flexibility in dealing with foreign direct investment. To the extent that these countries depend on access to technology through licensing agreements, more careful attention would have to be paid to the provisions of these agreements to reduce foreign exchange costs and achieve an effective transfer of technology. In their anxiety to gain foreign know-how in the past, too little attention was paid to the implications of certain stipulations in licensing agreements, particularly those relating to exports, training and availability of improvements to existing techniques.

Concluding observations

Though the standard of living in Commonwealth Caribbean countries has risen in the post-war period, their economies still rest on a very tenous basis. The productive base is still highly concentrated and economic performance is easily affected by factors outside their control. The degree of labour utilisation has been a persistent social problem. Commonwealth Caribbean countries take the view that if they are to build on what has already been achieved, they need to undertake a certain level of investment both in infra-structure and directly productive activities. But this has become increasingly difficult in recent years with unsatisfactory levels of both private and public savings. The servicing of the public debt (local and foreign) has been taking an increasing proportion of public revenue. In the case of the foreign debt, while service payments have not reached critical levels in all cases, an increasing share of earnings from the export of goods and services is being absorbed by these payments.

The external debt burden, as indicated, is not simply the result of an increasing volume of foreign borrowing, but of a rising import bill and a decline in production and export earnings levels. The significant increases in oil prices during the 1970s provided fuel to an already rapidly increasing import bill of the oil importing countries. Faced with a foreign exchange crisis, some states (e.g. Guyana, Belize, Jamaica) were forced to turn to the IMF for help. Jamaica's debt to the Fund at the end of 1986 stood at US$665.3 million or 19.0% of its total external debt. The need for balance of payments support and development assistance have forced Commonwealth Caribbean countries to pay greater attention to the role and functions of international organisations to which they were indifferent up to the mid-1970s. Developing countries have long been expressing complaints in various fora about the operational practices of multilateral institutions like the World Bank and the IMF, and suggesting reforms. While some changes have occurred, albeit slowly and grudgingly, the functioning of these institutions ramains far from satisfactory as far as developing member states (who comprise the majority of members) are concerned. The graduation of some Caribbean countries from the soft loans window of the World Bank on the basis of per capita income and the decision to graduate others have met with strong resistance from these countries who feel that concessional funds are essential to further progress. Borrowing of a kind which could increase their debt service ratio, they feel, would impact negatively on the basic task of expanding productive capacity and providing employment opportunities. The fact is some of them might not even be able to borrow on hard terms. These countries with their fragile economies do not have the access to international capital markets as do the larger developing countries.

Notes

1. See the World Bank, *Development and Debt Service: Dilemma of the 1980s*, Washington, D.C., 1986.
2. *Ibid*. p.ix.
3. OECD, *External Debt Statistics*, Feb. 1987.

4 See 'The Debt Problem of Sub-Saharan Africa', in *Finance and Development*, March, 1987. This is an extract from the World Bank Report, *Adjustment with Growth in Sub-Saharan Africa, 1986–90*, issued in 1986.
5 World Bank, *Development and Debt Service, op. cit..* pp.xiii–xv.
6 Martin Schubert, 'Trading Debt for Equity', in *The Banker*, Feb. 1987.
7 IMF, *Recent Developments in External Debt Restructuring*, Washington, D.C., 1985, p.5.
8 Claims by the 24 largest American banks on oil importing developing countries amounted to 200% of capital in 1982. This has been declining since, however, as some of the major lenders have taken steps to increase their primary capital by increasing loan loss reserves, equity capital and certain subordinated debt.
9 The fifteen most heavily indebted on which Baker feels attention should be focused.
10 Morgan Guaranty Trust Company of New York, *World Financial Markets*, June/July, 1987.
11 *Ibid*.
12 The net foreign reserves of the country increased from US$30.0 million at the end of 1973 to US$3,202 million at the end of 1981. As a result of the drop in oil prices and a continued high level of spending the figure dropped to US$994 million at the end of 1985.
13 See the 1978 *Annual Report* of the Central Bank, p.23.
14 See Owen Jefferson, 'Jamaica's External Debt: Size, Growth, Composition and Economic Consequences'. Paper presented at Symposium on *Jamaica's Foreign Debt: The Crisis and Possible Solutions*, held at Mona, Jamaica on 10 May, 1986.
15 *Ibid*.
16 See World Bank Country Study, *Antigua and Barbuda*, Washington, D.C., 1985, p.13.
17 IDB, *Annual Report 1986*, p.4.
18 See the UN, *World Economic Survey, 1986*, p.74.
19 See, for example, Grant L. Reuber *et al.*, *Private Foreign Investment in Development*, London: Oxford University Press, 1973; see also R. Ramasaran, *US Investment in Latin America and the Caribbean*, New York: St Martin's Press, 1985.
20 For a detailed discussion on these, see OECD, *New Forms of International Investment*, Paris: OECD, 1984.
21 Essentially the safeguard clause in these Agreements permit the US and the EC to restrict the import of a particular product in the event that a local industry is threatened.

CHAPTER 9

The international monetary system and Commonwealth Caribbean countries

Some years ago the Brandt Commission made the following observation: 'The prospects in all areas of world trade, whether in commodities or manufactures, in energy or in the activities of multinational corporations, are greatly influenced by the functioning of the world monetary system. Predictable rates of exchange encourage investment as well as trade: erratic and fluctuating rates discourage both. Stable rates increase the confidence of asset holders, whether surplus oil producers or other potential investors. An adequate flow of international liquidity smooths out cyclical fluctuations, makes protection of domestic markets less necessary and enables commodity producers to ride over deteriorating terms of trade.'[1] This easily explains why both developed and developing countries have such a deep interest in the international monetary system. Though the changes which have taken place since the early 1970s have helped to improve the functioning of the system in the context of the changing international environment, there are many issues still to be resolved. For example, procedures and mechanisms for both surplus and deficit countries in restoring a balance are still to be agreed upon. The question of IMF conditionality remains a controversial issue. As far as reforms are concerned, the developed countries set the pace.

With the emergence of serious balance of payments problems in the 1970s and early 1980s, a number of Commonwealth Caribbean countries have had to turn to the International Monetary Fund (IMF) for assistance (*see* Table 9.1). Jamaica has been by far the heaviest borrower. Out of a total external debt of US$3.2 billion at the end of 1984, US$1.2 billion or 37.5% were due to the IMF. Some of the LDCs (e.g. Belize, Dominica and Grenada) have also had to turn to the Fund for assistance. The process of using Fund resources and subjecting themselves to the Fund discipline has been a new experience for these countries and there has been an element of trauma in certain cases. Despite claims for special treatment, the agreements used in the Caribbean have generally conformed to the Fund's normal operating procedures and methodology. This experience has led Commonwealth Caribbean countries to take a keen interest in the call for a new international economic order, and in particular in discussions aimed at reforming the international monetary system.

The objective in this chapter is twofold. The first aim is to examine the ways in which the Jamaican decisions of 1976 (and the subsequent arrangements flowing out of them) have affected the framework of international monetary co-operation. And the second is to explore the implications for developing countries of monetary developments in certain specific areas of critical concern to this group of nations. Since Commonwealth Caribbean countries share many of the features and problems of other parts of the developing world, they have tended to identify very closely with certain positions reflecting the views of the Less Developed Countries (LDCs), and where possible, this will be pointed out.

Introduction

The early seventies witnessed the collapse of the Bretton woods arrangements which had formed the basis of world monetary and financial relations in the post-war period. This took place against the background of a series of piecemeal measures[2] designed to salvage the system and keep the erosion relevant in the context of the new parameters and conditions which had emerged in the world economy as a result of the liberalisation process initiated in the immediate post-war years. The developments in the international money and capital markets, and the shifts in economic power which have taken place over the last two or three decades, challenged the basic premises of the Bretton Woods system and the operational procedures and practices which had grown out of it. This situation obviously called for a comprehensive and in some ways a radical approach to reform as against the *ad hoc* adjustments which the main protagonists opted for over the years, and which eventually failed to withstand the pressures which grew out of the lack of symmetry in the adjustment processes of the post-war monetary arrangements.

With the complete breakdown[3] of the Bretton Woods system in 1973 (when the major currencies went on float), the need for reform took increased urgency. In July of 1972 a committee ('Committee of the Board of Governors on Reform of the International Monetary System and Related Issues') was set up with the object of making proposals for the reform of the monetary system. Prior to the creation of this committee (sometimes called the Committee of 20 because representation was based on the 20 constituencies that

Table 9.1 Commonwealth Caribbean: Financial standing in IMF's general department at 30 April, 1986 ('000 SDRs)

Countries	Quotas	Fund's holdings of currencies[1] Total	Fund's holdings of currencies[1] Percent of quota	Use of reserve fund tranche resource positions
Antigua	5 000	4 999	100.0	2
Bahamas	66 400	55 496	83.6	10 908
Barbados	34 100	70 452	206.6	2 162
Belize	9 500	17 147	180.5	1 896
Dominica	4 000	12 683	317.1	9
Grenada	6 000	7 714	128.6	–
Guyana	49 200	120 947	245.8	–
Jamaica	145 500	749 736	515.3	–
St Kitts-Nevis	4 500	4 493	99.8	8
St Lucia	7 500	7 500	100.0	a
St Vincent	4 000	4 000	100.0	–
Trinidad and Tobago	170 100	68 822	40.5	–

[1] Includes non-negotiable, non-interest bearing notes which members are entitled to issue in substitution for currency.
a Less than SDR 500.
Source: IMF Annual Report, 1986.

appointed or elected Executive Directors to the Fund) which included developing countries,[4] discussions on international monetary questions were confined largely to the industrial countries, mainly the so-called Group[5] of 10. The C-20 produced two reports: a first *Outline of Reform* published in October, 1973 and a final *Outline of Reform* which was released in June 1974, and ended the work of the Committee.[6] In this chapter we shall be referring to this latter document which contains views closely associated with the position of developing countries, and which (with some changes) many people[7] thought provided a good basis for the reform of the international monetary system. The decisions taken by the Interim Committee of the Board of Governors of the IMF in Jamaica in January, 1976, ignored many of the critical issues raised in *Outline*, particularly those in which developing countries had a strong interest. The substitute arrangements adopted in Jamaica still, however, appeared to have been sufficiently convincing to win the support of the developing nations for amendment of the Fund's Articles,[8] which one writer has speculated may have been a major reason for their inclusion in the reform deliberations in the first place.[9]

The Bretton Woods system and its background

The arrangements which formed the basis of international monetary co-operation until 1971 grew directly out of the currency chaos of the 1930s which was a period characterised by competitive devaluations, lack of convertibility, a great variation in exchange rate practices, discriminatory controls over international transactions, capital flight and bi-lateral agreements of various kinds. The fact that these policies proved to be largely self-defeating pointed to the need for an agreed set of rules (a code) which could guide the conduct of monetary relations among countries. To this end the International Monetary Fund (IMF) was set up in 1944. A major objective of the IMF arrangement was to prevent the emergence of the 'beggar-my-neighbour' type of policies of the 1930s, and this can be clearly seen in the purposes of the organisation which include, among others, the promotion of exchange stability, the maintenance of orderly exchange arrangements among members, the avoidance of competitive exchange depreciation, and assistance in the establishment of a multi-lateral system of payments in respect of current transactions between members and in the elimination of foreign exchange restrictions which hamper the growth of world trade. In other words the intention was to create an atmosphere (with what were perceived to be essential mechanisms as far as the politics of the day would allow), which would permit countries to make orderly balance of payments adjustments without resorting to measures which might impede the international flow of goods and investment. As we shall see later, while it was felt that the movements of speculative capital should be controlled, the liberal framework conceived (albeit in an evolving time frame) was deemed necessary for the expansion of world trade, the rational allocation of resources and the maximisation of world income and welfare. With the incorporation of developing countries in the world's organised monetary system, the basic operating assumptions and objectives were extended to them without modification reflecting their peculiar needs and conditions.

It was realised at the time that the objectives outlined above could not be achieved if attention was focused solely on international payments. The IMF was conceived as part of a larger system which included the International Bank for Reconstruction and Development (IBRD), which would provide long term financial assistance, and the International Trade Organisation (ITO), which would concern itself with the removal of trade restrictions such as tariffs and quotas within a multi-lateral non-discriminatory framework.[10] The ITO never became operational (largely because the US refused to sign the Charter), but the General Agreement on Tariffs and Trade (GATT), which was intended to be a temporary arrangement, has survived to pursue some of the objectives of the ITO which was more embracing in scope.

Since both exchange controls and import restrictions have the same effects in practice, this has necessitated a certain amount of collaboration between the IMF and GATT. Generally, the GATT is a much looser arrangement, not only relying on negotiations among its members for the attainment of its objectives, but permitting the imposition of restrictions for balance of payments purposes under several of its articles. This applies even to countries which are no longer under the protection of the transitional provisions contained in Article XIV of the Fund's Chapter.[11]

As far as developing countries[12] are concerned, besides the general exception available to all members,[13] Article XVIII gives special consideration to their conditions. This Article permits such countries 'to take protective and other measures affecting imports' if these are necessary 'to implement programmes and policies of economic development designed to raise the general standard of living of their people...'. It is worthwhile to note here that while the GATT recognises the need for countries in certain circumstances to employ trade restrictions, it directs no special attention to the export problems facing poor countries. It is also worth pointing out that there is a degree of inconsistency between the authorisation to 'take protective and other measures affecting imports' and the reciprocity rule which requires contracting parties to match concessions in tariff negotiations. Not being in a position to conform to this latter requirement, developing countries generally have benefited relatively little from the GATT negotiations.

Despite the obligatory (legal) nature of both the IMF and GATT, the 'exceptions' provisions of these agreements make possible the operation of a wide range of restrictions and controls in practice. GATT in particular, with the difficulties inherent in its negotiating procedures, has managed to attain only limited success in removing such barriers to trade which fall within the scope of its objectives. Recent events have shown that both the IMF and GATT lack authority to enforce policies in certain critical areas impinging directly on the adjustment process. For example, as Tew has pointed out, 'there is nothing in either the GATT or the IMF Agreement to prevent surplus countries from retaining protective tariffs however much they may be warned of other types of restrictions'.[14]

Tew is right. It is clear, however, that those who framed the IMF Agreement felt that the exchange rate was a sufficiently powerful mechanism to restore equilibrium in international payments, and that member countries would adopt postures in respect of external policy that would have permitted a somewhat equal sharing on the burden of adjustment. Failure in this regard was a major factor in the breakdown of the system.

Exhange rates under the Bretton Woods system

Without a doubt the major arrangements introduced by the IMF Agreement of 1944 centred around the exchange rate mechanism and related policies. During the discussions leading to the establishment of the Fund, the American proposals envisaged a situation whereby this institution would have the power to declare par values. The British refused to support this particular suggestion and the position eventually taken (as reflected in the former Article IV of the IMF Charter) was that member countries would declare their initial par value in terms of gold or the US dollar. These par values could not vary by more than 1%[15] on either side of parity (in the case of spot exchange transactions)[16] without permission from the IMF. Responsibility for maintaining the declared rate rested with the national monetary authority of each country, which was required to intervene in the foreign exchange market as the occasion demanded. Except for a 10% margin of change to par values which members could make on their own initiative, approval for changes generally depended on whether a member's balance of payments was seen to be in 'fundamental disequilibrium'. This latter term was never defined (in fact it seems to have been deliberately left vague), but theoretically it was supposed to mean 'a condition of persistent disequilibrium not amenable to monetary, fiscal and other economic measures, except at the cost of significant unemployment or retarded growth'.[17]

The authority of the Fund derives largely from the credit facilities which it makes available to member countries for meeting short term payments problems in the conviction that such assistance will avoid the need for policies which may be adopted by other countries as retaliatory measures. Access to the Fund's resources are not without limit, and the conditions under which credit is granted take on greater severity with increased or persistent borrowings. Whether initially intended or not, the Fund may condition its loans not only on the basis of a particular exchange rate being observed, but on the modification of the whole range of monetary, fiscal and other economic policies which are thought to be affecting the particular country's external balance and performance. The Fund's perceptions, of course, (which are influenced in no small measure by the economic and philosophical convictions of its dominant members) do not always accord with those of member states, particularly developing members, and this has often been a source of serious conflict.[18] Though the Fund claims to be politically and ideologically neutral, the fact that its prescriptions often lead to social and economic conditions with deep political connotations is now seen as a major reason for a fundamental restructuring of this institution.

While the Bretton Woods system concerned itself with current payments, capital transfers were left largely in the hands of national authorities. Initially there was some controversy about the kind of measures that could be adopted for controlling capital movements, particularly with respect to discriminatory currency arrangements or multiple currency practices. The position apparently taken after some deliberation, was that these could be used so long as they did not interfere with current payments or hamper the transfer of funds in settlement of commitments.[19] The sections of the IMF Agreement dealing with capital movements are not very precise and provide room for considerable controversy. Initially the Fund seemed to have favoured a highly restrictive approach to capital transfers, and this is apparent to some extent in Article IV of the Agreement which states that a 'member may not make net use of the Fund's resources to meet a large or sustained outflow of capital, and the Fund may request a member to exercise controls to prevent such use of the Fund'. The apparently restrictive position reflected in the wording of this Article appeared to have undergone some change by the mid-1960s when a rather more liberal thinking began to emerge. In its 1964 Annual Report, for example, such restrictions were seen to be 'less objectionable' than other exchange restrictions, 'particularly where they are intended to deal with speculative movements'. The report went on to state, however, that 'because of the difficulties and drawbacks attached to such restrictions, it is...preferable to follow, wherever possible, policies aimed at attracting appropriate equilibriating movements of private capital through international co-ordination of interest rates or similar international action, or to offset undue movements, of short term capital through the use of international liquidity'.[20]

On the basis of these views it is clear that at this time the IMF was unable to anticipate the degree and extent of capital mobility that developed in the later sixties and early seventies, which wrought such havoc with the fixed exchange rate system. Basically, as many people have pointed out, fixed exchange rates, free capital movements and independent national monetary policies are not compatible.[21] The problem of control, however, is not a simple one. Capital transfers are responsive to a wide range of factors which are not easy to distinguish in practice; and since certain forms of capital movement are widely considered to be essential to economic growth and development, controls are not easily recommended. In particular circumstances, however, countries have not hesitated to institute measures (exchange controls, dual exchange markets, etc.) with the aim of influencing capital flows against the backdrop of certain specific objectives related to internal or external developments.

The changing context

The Bretton Woods arrangements remained almost wholly intact[22] until 1971 when the US decided to suspend convertibility of the dollar into gold, which was a critical arrangement to the system. Even before this, however, strains in the system had already manifested themselves, and in fact economists were pointing to weaknesses in the arrangements since the late fifties.[23] One of the main points of concern was the dependence on the US balance of payments deficits as a source of international liquidity and the ability of the US to meet its convertibility obligations. To be sure, the IMF articles of Agreement did not require the US to sell gold to monetary authorities at a fixed price, and this condition was not essential to the maintenance of a par value system. As Mikesell has observed, however, the viability of the gold-exchange standard of the kind embraced at Bretton Woods 'depends upon the inter-changeability of the different kinds of reserve assets at par, and the avoidance of massive flights from one reserve asset to another.'[24]

The convention adopted by many countries in the post-war years to maintain their parities in terms of the US dollar, and to hold reserves in the same currency,[25] has its basis in the relative strength of the US economy in the early part of the period and the decision by the US government to buy and sell monetary gold at US$35 an ounce. This latter arrangement while providing a reference point for the par value system certainly enhanced the dollar as a reserve asset. The interest earning aspect of dollar reserves as compared to gold, and the inadequacy or unattractiveness of other reserve assets have also been important factors in this respect. It is worth pointing out, however, that the link between the dollar and gold rested increasingly on the assumption that dollar holders would not exercise their right to convert into gold.

The willingness of countries to hold US dollars has enabled the US to expand its overseas expenditure and investment by running deficits on its balance of payments. These deficits have been a major source of world reserves in the post-war period. The fact that the system imposed certain constraints on the US, particularly in terms of the external value of its currency, which became increasingly over-valued *vis-à-vis* other major currencies, led some observers to view that an 'intolerable burden' was placed on this country.[26] Others, however, feel that a reserve currency country is in a privileged position since it is able to settle external deficits by issuing its own currency.[27]

While there may be some truth in both these positions, the fact remains that the system has been associated with a remarkable growth in world trade. Between 1948 and 1971 the value of world trade (excluding trade of the Centrally Planned Economies) is estimated to have grown from US$53.8 billion to US$314.0 billion (or by almost 500% at an average rate of 8% per annum in nominal terms). The trade of some countries grew faster than others, and this led to a redistribution of economic power which challenged a basic premise in the Bretton Woods system. For example, Japan's share of world exports which amounted to less than 1% in 1948 increased to almost 8% in 1971. West Germany's share also increased from less than 1% to over 12% over the period. On the other hand Britain's share declined from over 12% in 1948 to around 7% in 1971 and that of the US dropped from 23% to 14% over the period. The poor performance of both Britain and the US had an adverse effect on both of them as reserve currency countries.

Faced with a dwindling gold stock and an increasing volume of dollars in the hands of foreign central banks,[28] the US government was forced to put an end to the link between the dollar and gold. This was followed by a readjustment of exchange rates among major industrial countries under the Smithsonian Agreement, which resulted in a weighted average depreciation of the dollar of 12% against the leading currencies. In February, 1973, the dollar was devalued a second time, and a system of floating of major currencies soon followed.

The reformed international monetary system

In January, 1976, the Interim Committee of the Board of Governors of the IMF met in Jamaica and concluded a number of agreements which were intended to form the basis of a new international monetary system. The Jamaica meeting culminated the work started in 1972, with the establishment of the Committee of Twenty.

The Jamaica Agreement covered several areas. The main provisions, however, revolved around exchange rate arrangements and the role of gold in the reformed system. With respect to the latter, a decision was taken to abolish the official price of gold and to eliminate the obligation to use it in transactions with the Fund. With respect to exchange rates, a new Article 1V was proposed for adoption. This article commits a member to collaborate with the Fund and other members 'to assure orderly exchange arrangements and to promote a stable system of exchange rates.' Exchange arrangements may include:

  a the maintenance by a member of a value for its currency in terms of the special drawing rights or other denominator, other than gold, selected by the member; or

  b co-operative arrangements by which members maintain the value of their currencies in relation to the value of the currency or currencies of other members; or

  c other exchange arrangements of a member's choice.

The par value system has not been completely abandoned. At

some future date the 'Fund may determine, by an 85% majority of the total voting power, that international economic conditions permit the introduction of a widespread system of exchange arrangements based on stable but adjustable par values.'

The Fund's role under the new Article 1V is to 'oversee the international monetary system in order to ensure its effective operations...'. In accordance with this function it 'shall exercise firm surveillance over the exchange rate policies of members, and shall adopt specific principles for the guidance of all members with respect to those policies. Each member shall provide the Fund with the information necessary for such surveillance, and, when requested by the Fund, shall consult with it on the member's exchange rate policies.'

At this point there are two questions to which we need to address ourselves if we are to see the present arrangements in perspective. The first question is how have the decisions taken in Jamaica affected the Bretton Woods system; and the second is to what extent do they fall short of what are widely considered to be desirable changes in the context of the observable trends in the international economy.

Let us take the first question. Under the Bretton Woods Articles monetary authorities were forbidden from buying gold at a price higher than the official one. The Jamaica Agreement, by abolishing the official price of gold and eliminating all obligations to use gold in transactions with the Fund, considerably reduces the central role which gold has played in the monetary system since 1944. It does not completely eliminate it however. One effect of the abolition of the official price of gold has been to make this asset the subject of great speculation and consequently less attractive as a reserve asset because of the considerable fluctuation in its value. In the *Outline of Reform* it was stated that the SDR should become the principal reserve asset, though it did not say how this should be achieved. In recent years a number of decisions has been taken with the aim of making the SDR a more practical international currency, and hence more capable of playing a larger role in the international monetary system. These include further allocations of SDRs, the authorisation to use SDRs in swaps and forward arrangements, a simplification of the definition of the SDR, and the imbuing of it with a yield closer to market yields as well as instituting a closer relation between the basket of currencies used to calculate the SDR interest rate and those used to calculate its capital value.

As regards exchange rates, the Jamaica meeting merely legalised what was a *de facto* and irretrievable situation. It had little choice. Member countries are no longer required to peg their currencies either to gold or the US dollar. Under the new arrangements members are given much greater freedom in their exchange rate policies. Those so desiring can let their currencies float subject to their own intervention and to the restraints of the IMF, which latter have now been more fully articulated in a new Article 1V.[29] Countries who wish to peg can do so in relation to another currency, a basket of several currencies (including the SDR basket) or by mutual pegging. Changes in the peg can apparently be made as frequently and in as large amounts as are considered desirable. There are no specific limits, too, on the margins within which countries may wish to operate. It is worth noting that the decisions commit members to help promote 'a stable system of exchange rates' and not 'a system of stable exchange rates.' Should conditions permit the introduction of 'exchange arrangements based on stable but adjustable par values', it is clear that this could only be done with the consent of the developed countries, who have the necessary voting power in the Fund to provide an 85% majority. The US, with over 20% of the voting power, has been given an effective veto.

It needs to be pointed out that the decision by the IMF to legalise the system of managed floating among major currencies does not automatically solve the problem of international adjustment. Certainly, it is better able to deal with the difficulties posed by large and volatile capital movements which now characterise the international financial system, and for which no rules have yet been devised. A crucial question on the efficiency of managed floating hinges on the problem of management. This is all the more significant in view of the fact that a system of floating rates is less amenable to international supervisory control than the parity arrangements. While the exchange rates of the major currencies have experienced wide fluctuations under the floating system, the fears that the latter would adversely affect world trade have not materialised.

Though some observers saw the Jamaica agreements as marking the beginning of a new political and monetary era[30] many academic economists, expressed great disappointment over the limited scope of the reform that was undertaken. In particular, they lamented the lack of attention that was given to such key issues as an effective adjustment mechanism, a framework for dealing with disequilibriating capital flows, international control and management of international liquidity, the composition of reserves and asset settlement. Another important issue receiving relatively little attention was the flow of real resources to developing countries. Since SDRs were created there have been proposals that they should be linked to development assistance in some form or another. These proposals have so far not proved acceptable to the rich countries even though, as Triffin has pointed out, of SDR 100 billion growth of world reserves over the five years 1970-74, about 97% was invested in the developed countries — mostly the US.[32] The support of the LDCs seemed to have been won by the decisions relating to the creation of the trust fund out of proceeds from the sale of part of the Fund's gold stocks, the further liberalisation of the compensatory financing facility, additions to the Fund's resources and perhaps most of all by the prospects that the new arrangements would eventually lead to greater stability in the monetary system, which is one of the LDCs' major concerns. The distribution of voting power and decision-making in the IMF was also left untouched, as was the practice of using standard stabilisation packages to deal with adjustment problems in the LDCs.

On the question of capital movements which wrought such havoc with the par value system, the reform said virtually nothing. This, in a sense, was a reflection of the inability of the C-20 to arrive at a consensus with respect to a consistent set of proposals that might form the basis of a framework under a more flexible exchange rate system. A particular difficulty in devising a set of rules for capital movements relates to the problem of identifying capital flows, particularly in a situation where there is 'a strong presumption against the use of controls on current account transactions or payments for balance of payments purposes.[33] It is well known that capital can move in disguised forms through apparent current transactions. Another difficulty arises from the question of distinguishing controls relating to various types of capital movements. The C-20 felt that countries should not use controls over capital transactions for the purpose of maintaining inappropriate exchange rates, or, more generally, of avoiding appropriate adjustments actions.'[34] It is also felt that there should be no obstacles to the flow of capital from MDCs to LDCs. On the other hand the C-20 felt that countries should co-operate in actions designed to limit disequilibriating capital flows and in arrangements to finance and offset them. Actions that countries might choose to adopt could include a more satisfactory degree of harmonisation of monetary policies, subject to the requirements of domestic demand management, prompt adjustment of inappropriate par values, use of wider margins, the adoption of floating rates in particular situations, and the use of administrative controls, including dual exchange markets and fiscal incentives.'[35] This recommendation, of course, was overtaken by events when the

MDCs chose to float as a rule rather than the exception. While theoretically this should lessen the need for controls, the persistence of payments disequilibrium has led to a retention of a wide range of control measures on various types of capital movements.

Monetary reform and the Less Developed Countries (LDCs)

Though, as indicated earlier, developing countries were represented in the C-20 and their views clearly found some acceptance in the *Outline of Reform*, the reforms agreed to in Jamaica not only disregarded a number of key suggestions in this document, but were overwhelmingly influenced by the interest of the developed nations. In fact the decisions with respect to gold and exchange rates were clearly a compromise between the views of the US and France respectively – hence the particular satisfaction emanating from these two sources. The structure of the IMF, of course, gives a dominant position to the richer countries who control the decision making process. This to a large extent explains the significant lack of attention paid by the Jamaica reforms to the expanding and peculiar needs of developing countries, which are now well documented. It has been suggested that to the extent that the arrangements permit the industrial countries to improve their payments position, developing countries will benefit via financial aid and access to commodity and capital markets. It is often pointed out that the reformed system will permit developing countries the same freedom with exchange rates allowed the industrial countries. It is worth noting, however, that under the new arrangements the basis of the IMF's authority has by no means been entirely removed. Floating exchange rates (and particularly the managed system that is prevailing) do not eliminate the need for reserves and IMF assistance since a situation of equilibrium is by no means guaranteed.[36] In fact a country pursuing a policy of pegging its currency to that of a developed country which is floating, may find itself with an increased need for reserves.

Developing countries generally were of the opinion that the Jamaica reforms did not go far enough. Events since 1976 have tended to strengthen this view. To be sure, the greater exchange rate flexibility permitted has enabled the industrialised nations to deal more adequately with their external imbalance problem, and in this sense has played a crucial part in bringing back a measure of stability to the international monetary system. Inflation and bouts of recession from which these countries have suffered in recent years, however, have not only had an adverse effect on the flow of real resources to the developing world, but have given rise to an increase in protectionist tendencies in the former. Seen in the context of higher prices for oil faced by oil importing nations and depressed prices for a wide range of commodities, this development is viewed with extreme concern in poor countries. The payments deficit on current account for non-oil developing countries increased from US$11.5 billion in 1973 to US$32.9 in 1976 and to US$80.6 in 1981. Even though this figure has fallen in recent years, both fuel and non-fuel exporters have experienced consistent deficits as groups since 1982. Borrowing, of course, is one means open to these countries to finance external commitments. Debt servicing for many poor countries, however, is already a serious problem, even if the expansion of the private capital markets offers increased opportunities for borrowing. In fact, in many cases the external public debt has reached such alarming proportions that developing countries tend to feel that this issue should be an integral part of the discussions on monetary reform.

The concern of the LDCs with the state of the international monetary system arises largely from the implications which the latter holds for their development effort. While there are certain issues (e.g. the link between the SDR and the transfer of real resources to LDCs) which hold special significance for them, questions relating to exchange rate regimes, international liquidity and adjustment processes, on which MDCs' attention tends to be focused, are not unimportant to them. Floating exchange rates, for example, introduce a degree of uncertainty with respect to real earnings from exports and real costs of imports, which complicates the problem of planning. To the extent that the availability and distribution of international liquidity can lead to conditions which result in increased demand for LDCs' exports and provide greater accessibility to imports, this issue is also of major interest to poor countries. The terms on which resources are made available is also of crucial concern to LDCs, many of whom have recently gained their political independence. Not only are these countries acutely sensitive to any conditions which appear to be a form of interference in their domestic affairs, but more importantly, they take the view that they are in the best position to assess the nature of their development problem and to formulate appropriate strategies within frameworks of their own choosing. Since LDCs tend to be open economies, subject to influence from a wide range of factors, the availability of external resources mitigates an important constraint on the range of flexibility within which they would like to operate. The terms, as we indicated, are not unimportant to them, and in this connection, the restructuring of the IMF in a way which would enable its less developed members to exert some influence on its *modus-operandi* is an important objective for this group of countries. The mere increasing of the Fund's resources whether through quota changes based on the conventional formula, or through borrowing, is not considered in itself to be an adequate response to LDCs' concern, since they are aware that the terms on which multilateral assistance is made available can be as harsh as those associated with bilateral aid. In the following section we discuss some of the issues raised above in greater detail.

The exchange rate question

One of the major criticisms levelled against the par value system was that it was too rigid in the sense that rates were not altered sufficiently quickly in response to changes in domestic conditions, and as a result the process of international adjustment was affected. It is important to note here that while the par value system did indeed come to be characterised by an excessive amount of rigidity it has been argued by some observers that this was not due to the 'constraints of the international regime but to the inherent characteristics of the national decision-making process on parities.'[37] Changes in exchange rates which were supposed to be economic decisions aimed at facilitating the process of adjustment came to acquire deep political significance. The result was that desirable changes were often delayed, and it was not until the situation assumed crisis proportions that a decision to adjust was taken. One of the anomalies of the Bretton Woods system, as pointed out earlier, was that while pressure could be brought on a country experiencing payments problems to adjust its exchange rates downwards and to institute what were thought to be 'correctional' domestic policies, there was nothing in the arrangements which could force surplus countries to take action at achieving an equilibrium position.[38] This situation was not helped by the fact that the US, which held a key role in the system, could not change its rates without throwing international monetary relations into deep apprehension and disarray.

The par value system clearly did not function as the framers intended, and as a result it became very crisis prone, particularly in the late 1960s and early 1970s with the huge movements in speculative funds, and the absence of any kind of co-ordination in monetary and fiscal policies. Some of the proposals put forward from time to time to overcome this rigidity included a wider band around which par values could fluctuate, and more frequent adjustments of exchange rates to take account of domestic cost/price changes *vis-à-vis* those in other countries. Though many academic economists have often strongly advocated floating rates as a more effective adjustment mechanism, this system has never had strong official appeal. In the *Outline of Reform*, for example, the main feature of international monetary reform was seen to include *inter alia* 'an effective and symmetrical adjustment process, including better functioning of the exchange rate mechanism with the exchange rate regime based on stable but adjustable par values'. Floating rates were recognised as providing a useful technique only in 'particular situations'.

As indicated earlier, the reform undertaken in Jamaica does not lay down any specific regime which a country must follow. As worded the amendment to Article 1V permits a wide range of options. In practice the system varies from one country to another, ranging from independent floating with relatively little attempt to influence market forces to the maintenance of a fixed peg against a single intervention currency.[39] The countries that have resorted to continuous flexibility are mainly the developed nations. There are, however, differences in the extent to which rates are managed. Some countries (e.g. Canada, the US and members of the European common margins arrangements 'have generally refrained from efforts to influence the course of their exchange rates other than smoothing short term disturbances or countering disorderly market conditions'.[40] For a few other countries the extent of management goes beyond this. In fact members of the European 'snake' intervene to keep their respective exchange rates *vis-à-vis* other 'snake' currencies within the agreed margins, and this often leads to heavy borrowings.

There are differences among the developing countries about what the ideal exchange rate system should be. Some seem to favour a system of fixed rates among the developed countries and a freedom on their part to operate with more flexible arrangements. Others (and these include a large cross section) are strongly inclined to support the old system of fixed rates for all countries, but with more flexible procedures for changing parities.[41] Commonwealth Caribbean countries[42] can be placed in this latter group. Within the recent period of floating among the MDCs, only a very few LDCs have experimented with this system. But this does not necessarily mean that they support it. An increasing number has chosen to peg to the SDR or some other composite basket of currencies. A considerable number, however, still continues to peg to one of the major currencies.[43] All CARICOM countries with the exception of Guyana and Jamaica are at present pegged to the US dollar. Guyana is pegged to a basket of her own choosing, while Jamaica uses an auction system that is classified by the IMF as independently floating.

In terms of exchange rate policies, there is no doubt that the attitudes of developing countries are still significantly influenced by tradition in which the domestic currency was pegged to that of the 'mother' country with which the bulk of economic transactions was carried out. Even with changing circumstances the LDCs generally have shown a certain reluctance to depart from a system that does not permit a great deal of fluctuation in the exchange rates of the developed countries *vis-à-vis* one another or with respect to their own currencies. Pegging to a major currency that is floating is not the same as pegging to one within a fixed parity system, and simplicity and administrative convenience may be the strongest attractions to this arrangement. In a situation where a general par value system prevails (as under the Bretton Woods arrangements) pegging to a foreign currency carries with it a degree of certainty which may be beneficial to a LDC in terms of the flow of trade and investment. In such circumstances its operation also probably involves less difficulties than would be encountered in a regime of more flexible rates. On the other hand pegging to a currency that is floating means that movements in a LDC's exchange rate may bear little relationship to the state of a LDC's economy, or its requirements in terms of local developmental objectives or stabilisation policies. Appreciation or depreciation in the intervention currency *vis-à-vis* other major currencies could work counter to the policy aims in the pegging country, since appreciation tends to make its imports cheaper and its exports more expensive at a time when the reverse might be needed. In some instances, of course, appreciation and depreciation can cancel each other out.

In a situation where countries are free to choose their exchange regime, fluctuations in LDCs' exchange rates can originate as much in policies and practices pursued by the MDCs as in the arrangement adopted by the LDCs with respect to their exchange relations with the MDCs. With respect to the former Cline[44] identifies five areas around which LDCs' concern over a more flexible exchange rate system among the MDCs are centred. These are summarised as follows:

1 it would increase uncertainty about real export earnings, import prices, and foreign exchange reserves values;
2 it would lead to greater commodity price fluctuations;

3 it would encourage the formation of currency blocs and might inhibit the diversification of LDC trade from traditional trading partners;
4 it would raise problems for reserve and debt management;
5 it would require the development of forward exchange markets which would be difficult to establish in LDCs.

While these are legitimate concerns some observers feel these fears tend to be exaggerated.[45] For example, it is often pointed out (with strong supporting evidence) that foreign earnings of developing countries tend to fluctuate more in response to demand and supply factors than to changes in exchange rates. With respect to the concern of greater fluctuations in commodity prices which are quoted in the currency of a developed country (e.g. bananas, sugar, coffee, oil), it is often suggested that the effects of a depreciation in the quoted currency for the exporting country have to be measured against the impact on demand in countries whose currency has appreciated concomitantly. This argument is intended to hold particularly in a situation where the demand for the goods is not only price elastic, but where there is no discrimination to its entry in markets of appropriate currencies. Another consideration that needs to be borne in mind is that commodity prices are not fixed irretrievably. Supply and demand factors can easily upset fixed-price arrangements. In the case of oil, suppliers in recent years have been able to increase prices to offset losses suffered through inflation and the depreciating dollar.

As far as the formation of currency blocs are concerned, there is no evidence so far that the tendency in this direction is significantly stronger under a flexible exchange rate regime. A major consideration underlying this particular concern is the fact that a country on the periphery usually has to link the stability of its currency to that of the currency of the centre country 'with which it maintains its principal trade and financial relations'.[46] Fluctuations in the centre currency are seen to impose severe constraints on the periphery country in a number of areas, chief among which is the need to diversify the pattern of foreign economic relations, which is often very highly concentrated. Another consideration that needs to be taken into account is the fact that by pegging to a major currency, a country deprives itself 'of control over the effective exchange rates of its currency *vis-à-vis* other currencies'.[47] Trade with these other countries may not be overwhelmingly significant, but may be of such a kind as to cause serious difficulties in particular sectors and even to disrupt the entire economy.

One option open to developing countries[48] is to peg to the SDR or to any basket of currencies that can serve the needs of the economy. This policy appears to be consistent with the desire to hold a diversified foreign reserve portfolio in order to guarantee against losses resulting from over concentration in one currency in the event of a depreciation *vis-à-vis* other currencies. Such a departure from the traditional approach to foreign exchange pegging and reserves management may require the development of certain types of expertise related to the operation of the foreign exchange and the international money and capital markets. But this may be a minor problem when compared to the disruptions (and the losses) that result from pegging to a single currency operating within an exchange rate regime which the MDCs consider unsuitable to their needs, and to which their reactions remain a constant source for speculation. The concept of a basket represents an attempt to derive an effective exchange rate consistent with a country's international economic relations, since it requires information which is not always readily available; the basket chosen often amounts to an estimate of the effective rate.

In a situation where a group of countries are trying to promote trade among themselves, the likelihood of each state choosing a different basket can give rise to a complex system of cross rates which may lead to difficulties. In cases, however, where there is a similarity in economic problems, trading relationships, production structures, import patterns and so on, choosing a basket should not be such a difficult matter. The SDR has special advantages. It is widely used as a numeraire, it has an international status and its rates are published daily.

There is a prevailing view in some quarters that a system of flexible rates among the developed countries would require LDCs to develop forward exchange markets for their currencies. 'A particular aspect of exchange rate uncertainty that might well involve new cost burdens for developing countries arises from the possibility that greater scope for short term exchange rate fluctuations may increase the need for protection against short term exchange risks through hedging transactions in forward markets. Meeting this need may require development of forward market facilities that are now non-existent or rudimentary in many less developed countries...'[49] This would depend to a great extent on buying and selling practices, and the type of exchange rate policies pursued by LDCs themselves. Experience has shown, however, that in a situation where transactions are largely carried out in major foreign currencies, forward markets are not necessary. 'To the extent that LDC traders wished to hedge against new relative movements of these currencies, they could do so through established forward exchange markets in the financial centres of industrial countries.'[50]

For obvious reasons, poor countries tend to be particularly sensitive to real losses in their reserves. The problem is by no means a new one. Even under the fixed exchange rate system losses could be suffered, as indeed happened in the latter half of the 1960s and early 1970s with the devaluations of the pound and the dollar. Even before floating became a reality, many countries were already diversifying their foreign reserves portfolio (among available assets) in a manner consistent with their foreign trade and foreign debt commitments. With respect to the latter, debt denominated in an appreciating currency will mean a greater real burden and vice versa. A deliberate policy to distribute the debt among major currencies might produce the effect of having gains and losses cancel out. In this connection, there has been a suggestion that developing countries should aim at a debt pattern in terms of foreign currency roughly proportional to the distribution of their foreign currency earnings. 'The result would be that an increased real debt servicing burden on the portion of debt held by an industrial country with an appreciating currency would tend to be covered by increased earnings of export sales to that country, because if the LDC's currency depreciated relative to that of the developed country, there should be a proportionate increase in LDC sales to that country operating on an original trade base proportional to the latter's weight in the debt portfolio.'[51] It should be pointed out, however, that this kind of argument not only assumes a relatively high price elasticity for LDCs exports, but a flexible production structure that could respond to increases and decreases in foreign demand. It also assumes the existence of competitive markets free of discrimination, protectionism and so on. Countries, such as Jamaica and Grenada, heavily dependent on one or two commodities for the bulk of their foreign exchange earnings, particularly in such commodities as sugar or bananas which are marketed under special arrangements, are likely to find such proposals (in normal circumstances) not altogether relevant to their needs.

The issues raised in the above discussion with respect to a more flexible exchange rate system among the MDCs, and the possible implications for the LDCs, have to be seen against the difficulties inherent in arrangements involving less frequent and larger changes in exchange rates. The existing system of managed floating, of course, is far from settled, as is what is the best option for the LDCs. Whether or not the par value system would ever return is a matter for conjecture. Within the present IMF framework which permits a wide scope for exchange rate regimes, the concern of LDCs revolves as much around the state of economic and monetary relations among the MDCs as around the basis of interaction between the latter and themselves. The issues in these respects need to be briefly looked at.

It is widely acknowledged that a system which permits wide and erratic changes in exchange rates operates neither to the benefit of the developed nor developing countries. The global ideal points to a stable but flexible system. With respect to the exchange rate regime pursued by the more developed countries in the circumstances of today's world economy, it is often suggested that there are two essential features which LDCs should desire.[52] One relates to the ability of the system to correct imbalances, and the other to the question of convertibility. Accomplishing the first would mitigate the tendency of developed countries to use restrictive measures on trade and the flow of capital. These are often instituted without distinction between rich and poor nations, with the result that countries whose rate of development hinges critically on these factors are severely affected. With respect to convertibility, it is important that a country whose earnings are gained in one currency should be able to expend these in other markets. The absence of this feature in a currency seriously constrains the choice of countries holding it with respect to prices, quality and suitability. This amounts to the imposition of a real cost similar in almost every respect to that associated with certain forms of tied aid and is an added burden to the LDCs.

While developing countries may not have any control over the exchange rate practices of the industrial countries, the present international legal framework permits them a wide scope in terms of devising exchange rate relations both among themselves and with respect to the MDCs. It is advocated in some quarters (and this is an increasingly prevalent view)[53] that while LDCs should pursue more flexible arrangements than the rigid par value system associated with the Bretton Woods era, any attempt on their part to float would pose serious difficulties for their development, particularly in view of the fact that forward markets do not generally exist for LDCs' currencies. One argument is that since the latter's currencies tend to be overvalued, a system of floating would result in a falling value *vis-à-vis* MDCs currencies which would tend to discourage investment (both local and foreign) since capital values may not rise as much as the depreciation. Another factor seen as militating against a system of floating arises from the greater uncertainty inherent in this arrangement, and the consequences this has for the holding of LDCs' currencies. The same observation, of course, can be made with respect to the MDCs, but they are better equipped to deal (individually and through co-operative arrangements) with sudden rushes by holders to sell their currencies when fear of devaluation arises.

Perhaps the strongest argument to be advanced against the floating proposal for LDCs relates to the scepticism over the ability of changes in the exchange rate to correct external imbalances. The persistence of disequilibrium in the MDCs within a floating regime lends support to this argument. Adjustment through devaluation in LDCs, it is frequently argued, faces even greater difficulties in view of their heavy reliance on imports (including food and essential raw materials) and the problems involved in preventing increased prices (and money incomes) manifesting themselves in the economy generally, and in the export sector in particular. Our limited experience with the use of the exchange rate instrument in the Commonwealth Caribbean shows that the effects of changes in the exchange rate tend to be heavily one sided. Because of the production structure, import and export patterns, internal organisational set-ups and general trading and commercial policies, the direct benefits to these countries from exchange rate changes not only tend to be small, but are quickly wiped out or out-weighed by the adverse repercussions which materialise from the basic conditions.

The Less Developed Countries and the SDR

As indicated earlier, the creation and distribution of international reserves is an issue of importance both to developed and developing countries. Over the last two decades, attention has tended to focus on three separate but related aspects. One is the adequacy (in quantitative terms) of reserves in relation to the growth of international trade. The second is the distribution between developed and developing countries and among individual countries in each group. The third is the nature of reserve assets and the mechanism for their creation. Without wishing to get into a detailed discussion on each of these various dimensions of international liquidity, there are a few observations worth making. With respect to the question of adequacy, the use of different criteria would obviously lead to different requirements levels, and this has often led to a great deal of controversy. The adequacy of liquidity, of course, cannot be discussed in isolation from its distribution, which has tended to favour the industrialised nations whose ratio of reserves to imports tends to be no worse than that of the developing countries. In the 1970s the position of the oil exporting LDCs was improved, but this did not diminish the importance which the group as a whole attaches to the question of reserves creation and distribution, which they see as one of the central issues in discussions pertaining to the reform of the international monetary system. A contention of the LDCs is that greater recognition needs to be taken of the instability in their balance of payments, and the implications this has for the rate of their development. They are also of the view that reserves creation should be under greater international control, and should not depend to such a critical extent on the balance of payments position of particular countries, as has been the case since World War II.

In the post-war period international reserves or liquidity (defined as assets which can be used in international settlements or to defend exchange rates) has largely centred around four elements viz: gold, foreign exchange, reserve position in the Fund and Special Drawing Rights (SDRs). Each of these components has its own advantages and disadvantages as a reserve asset. Gold, for example, has certain inherent features which make it attractive as a means of payment and as a store of value, but it may not be available in sufficient quantities for use in international transactions. Also, its distribution at the global level raises special problems of both an economic and political nature. Though not an ideal asset, in the post-war period certain major currencies (particularly the US dollar) have been used in the role of a means of payment and even as a store of value. In fact the growth of liquidity in this period took place concomitantly with the persistence of the US balance of payments difficulties. During the 1960s, however, there was a noticeable slowing up in the growth of international reserves. Between 1965 and 1968 reserves hardly grew at all. Even before this stage was reached, there was concern about this particular aspect of the world monetary system and the need for a new international asset. It was against this background that the IMF Articles were amended in 1969 to allow for the creation of the Special Drawing Rights, which were long in the discussion stage both in academic and official circles.

At that time the SDR was not intended to replace reserve currencies in international liquidity but to supplement them. Its function was limited to settling balance of payments accounts, and it could not be used to diversify reserves portfolios. Subsequently, the SDR has come to be used as a numeraire, but this was not its original purpose. There was a strong feeling at the time, too, (even while it was still in the discussion stage), that it could be used as a means of providing development assistance to poor nations. The formula eventually used and which failed to consider this latter proposal was based on IMF quotas which gave the developed countries the bulk of the SDR $9.3 billion created between 1970 and 1972. The US alone got a cumulative allocation of SDR$2.3 billion or about 25% of the total. The supporting argument used for this formula was that IMF quotas provided a rough measure of countries' long run reserve demand levels, and in this sense it was neutral.[54]

There is strong support among the LDCs that the SDR should become the primary reserve asset. There is even stronger support for the idea that there should be a link between the SDR and development finance.[55] This was one of their main concerns in the reform deliberations. The C-20 was persuaded to include the proposal[56] in the *Outline of Reform* which contained the view that the distribution of SDRs in favour of LDCs could be done in one of two ways: either directly by giving them a larger proportion of SDR allocations than they would receive on the basis of their share in Fund quotas (the distribution could be done in such a way as to favour the least developed of the developing countries), or by a direct allocation to international and regional development finance institutions of a predetermined share of SDR allocations. Link resources so distributed would be disbursed to developing countries on the basis of development need, and in such a way as to be relatively favourable to the least developed countries. The LDCs appeared to have favoured the first method.

As pointed out earlier, these recommendations proved to be unacceptable when the reform of the monetary system was undertaken. The arguments that a link between the SDR and development finance would not only undermine the 'monetary integrity of the SDR'[57] but 'would be bound to arouse suspicion and concern in the international financial community, and would exacerbate the difficulties of building up confidence in the new system',[58] carried the day. Instead a decision was taken to increase quotas from SDR$29.2 billion to SDR$39.0 or by 33.5%. The increase was done in such a way, that there was a slight redistribution among member states. For example, while Jamaica's share increased from 0.18% of the total to 0.19%, the US proportion dropped from 22.93% to 21.53%. So as not to reduce the voting power of the latter, decisions which formerly required an 80% majority for passage was increased to 85%. Since quotas determine subscriptions, voting power, SDRs allocation and borrowing rights, developing countries tend to argue that if the Fund is to be of greater help to them, the formula for the distribution of quotas would have to take greater account of their particular trading and production structures.

The other measures undertaken to win the support of the LDCs were touched upon earlier. These included the establishment of a trust fund to provide balance of payments assistance on concessionary terms to members with low per capita incomes. (Members initially eligible would be those with per capita incomes in 1973 not in excess of SDR 300). Another was the decision to liberalise further the compensatory financing facility set up in 1963 with the purpose of assisting countries in situations where there is a temporary export shortfall caused by factors beyond a member's control.[59] It was also decided to increase temporarily the size of each credit tranche by 45%. Defenders of the Jamaica reforms also point to the additional IMF facilities to which developing countries have access.[60]

The amended Article gives the SDR new characteristics and uses which are designed 'to contribute to the attainment of the objectives of making the SDR the principal reserve asset in the international monetary system'. If we look at Table 9.2 we shall observe that until 1978 the share of SDRs in total world reserves was falling, reaching a proportion of around 3% in 1978. The main reason for this was that while there were no new allocations of SDRs since 1972, there was an explosive growth in foreign exchange reserves which now account for more than 80% of world liquidity. When the Fund's Articles were amended in 1969 to provide for the creation of SDRs it was projected that by the beginning of 1972, this asset would account for 10% of total reserves and 16% of liquid reserves (reserves excluding gold).[61] It was expected that this proportion would grow over time. Further allocations were clearly forestalled by the growth of foreign exchange liquidity and the fear that further additions to reserves (through SDR creation) might have produced inflationary effects in the world economy. At the end of 1986, if gold were excluded, SDRs would have accounted for 4.7% of world reserves. With the inclusion of gold (at 35 SDR per ounce) this proportion would fall to 4.4%.

In keeping with the resolution to make the SDR the 'principal reserve asset' a decision was taken at a Board of Governors meeting in September, 1978 to strengthen the SDR by allocating SDR$4 billion a year in the period 1979 to 1981. Despite the growth in the absolute amount of SDR reserves since then, an examination of Table 9.2 will show that at the end of 1986 SDRs accounted for 4.4% of world reserves as compared to 7.4% for gold (when valued at 35 SDRs per ounce)[62] and 80.3% for foreign exchange. Failure to agree on a Substitution Account, which would have permitted the substitution of reserve currencies (and perhaps gold) by SDRs, means foreign exchange will continue to play an important role in the world's payments system for some time yet.

Table 9.2 Growth and composition of total world[a] reserves, 1970 to 1986

End of period	Gold[b] Bill SDRS	% of Total	SDRs Bill SDRs	% of Total	Foreign exchange Bill SDRs	% of Total	Reserve position in fund Bill SDRs	% of Total	Total reserve Bill SDRs	Total %
1970	37.0	39.7	3.1	3.3	45.4	48.7	7.7	8.3	93.2	100.0
1971	35.9	29.1	5.9	4.8	75.0	60.9	6.4	5.2	123.2	100.0
1972	35.6	24.3	8.7	5.9	96.1	65.5	6.3	4.3	146.7	100.0
1973	35.6	23.4	8.8	5.8	101.5	66.7	6.2	4.1	152.1	100.0
1974	35.6	19.8	8.9	4.9	126.3	70.4	8.8	4.9	179.6	100.0
1975	35.5	18.3	8.8	4.5	136.9	70.7	12.6	6.5	193.8	100.0
1976	35.3	15.9	8.7	3.9	159.8	72.2	17.7	8.0	221.5	100.0
1977	35.4	13.5	8.1	3.1	200.1	76.5	18.1	6.9	261.7	100.0
1978	35.7	12.8	8.1	2.9	220.8	79.0	14.8	5.3	279.4	100.0
1979	33.0	10.7	12.5	4.1	249.6	81.3	11.8	3.9	306.9	100.0
1980	33.4	9.4	11.8	3.3	292.8	82.6	16.8	4.7	354.8	100.0
1986	33.3	7.4	19.5	4.4	359.1	80.3	35.3	7.9	447.2	100.0

[a] Members of IMF
[b] Valued at 35 SDR per ounce
Source: IMF, Financial Statistics, Various Issues.

The question of conditionality

The decision in September 1978, to augment the allocation of SDRs was accompanied by an agreement to increase IMF quotas by 50%, which would have brought total quotas to SDR$60.0 billion. This followed the agreement in April of that year to increase quotas by 33.5%. It is interesting to note that these decisions came in the wake of no apparent shortage of international liquidity and a persistent reluctance on the part of developing countries (particularly) to make extensive use of the facilities of the Fund. The stiff conditions normally attached to the Fund's credit explains this latter situation. Member states tend to turn to the IMF for assistance as a last resort. Increasingly, countries needing finance for a wide range of purposes have used commercial banks and other private sources which intermediate on a large scale between surplus and deficit countries. In its 1977 Annual Report the Fund noted that 'the development of private international capital markets has led in recent years to a rapid expansion of private institutions into fields where borrowers were formerly dependent on official organisations or the use of their own official reserves. Thus, commercial banks lend to countries encountering balance of payments difficulties, and governments wishing to add to official reserves can do so by holding the equivalent of part of their countries' borrowing in the form of short-term assets abroad'.[63] Not all countries, of course, enjoy these privileges. It is often found that states which need assistance most are the ones who encounter the greatest difficulties in raising finance. A major impediment arises from the fact that private lenders take their cue from the IMF's assessment of a member country's financial position and credit-worthiness. The effect of this is that it often becomes difficult to by-pass the IMF in favour of private institutions for loan funds. In the context of debt rescheduling, creditors also tend to require an agreement between the Fund and debtor countries.

Access to private funds obviously make countries less reliant on the IMF's resources, and therefore more able to pursue policies which may not be consistent with the IMFs perceptions, the way it views the world economic system and its role in trying to preserve a stable monetary order. The IMF's concern over the development of private capital markets and the consequences for its role and functions come out very clearly in its 1977 Annual Report. 'As far as balance of payments finance is concerned, institutions in the private sector do not normally make a practice of applying comprehensive policy conditions when making balance of payments loans to governments. Access to private sources of balance of payments finance may, therefore, in some cases permit countries to postpone the adoption of adequate domestic stabilisation measures. This can exacerbate the problem of correcting payments imbalances, and can lead to adjustments that are politically and socially disruptive when the introduction of stabilisation measures become unavoidable.'[64] If there is a hint here that private lenders should operate in collaboration with the Fund, certain developing countries have made their position on this question quite clear. For example, speaking on behalf of Commonwealth Caribbean countries in the Fund at the 1977 Annual Meeting, Mr O.R. Padmore (Trinidad and Tobago's then Governor on the Fund and the Bank) made the following statement: 'There is no doubt that private commercial banks and other financial institutions have played a tremendous role in providing financial resources both for short-term and medium-term purposes. The countries for which I speak are of the view that these banks have done a magnificent job in this regard acting on their own, and we see no reason for any closer collaboration between them and the Fund. In other words, we feel that the Fund should not provide these organisations with any judgements or opinion except those which may be published.'[65]

The issue raised here is tied up with the larger question of conditionality which is under review in the IMF, and on which developing countries have been particularly outspoken. The LDCs are not averse to certain conditions being attached to IMF assistance. Their concern is with the nature of the conditions and their relevance to the solution of prevailing social and economic problems. One of these conditions is the inflexibility of targets which may be affected by factors outside the country's control (e.g. a rise in interest rates or weather conditions). The Fund argues that acceptance of a stabilisation programme which has certain standard features, should not be viewed as a quid pro quo for access to Fund's resources. The former is an essential complement to the assistance it provides', in helping a country to overcome its balance of payments difficulties.[66] To the extent that the stabilisation measures prove to be 'politically and socially disruptive' in the course of implementation of the programme, the IMF would attribute this to the lateness of the measures rather than to the measures themselves, since the Fund is often brought in after the situation has deteriorated to crisis proportions.[67] Though it is argued that the Fund's intervention is often used as a pretext by member countries to institute unpopular measures and policies which they themselves would have liked to put into operation, it is significant that the dissatisfaction with the terms on which the Fund lends has become particularly evident in recent years. Side by side with the increase in resources, it is felt a genuine effort is needed to come to terms with the peculiar problems faced by developing economies in terms of their operation and the adoption of new approaches for dealing with them, as distinct from the *ad hoc* formulae of the past, which were more of an appeasing nature.

It has often been argued that if the IMF did not exist, it would have had to be created. Certainly, given the experience of the 1930s and the disruptions of the 1970s, one could hardly deny the need for rules to govern countries' behaviour in order to prevent economic chaos and to assist in the expansion of world trade. By continuing to be members of the Fund, developing countries certainly seem to accept this. They also recognise the need for the Fund to adopt measures aimed at ensuring the repayment of its funds. What they have questioned is the analytical basis of the Fund's stabilisation programmes in the light of their peculiar economic and institutional characteristics and the apparent tendency of the Fund to intrude on their sovereignty. The conditions in many developing countries are such that social objectives often take precedence over economic efficiency. The presumption of a well functioning market mechanism which assumes a certain kind of reaction by variables in the system to policy changes often does not apply to many poor countries. There is also a tendency on the part of the Fund to believe that all member countries who come to it for assistance are guilty of incompetent management or inefficiency. It is well known that balance of payments problems may stem from factors outside their control, and this needs to be taken into account in Fund programmes, particularly as they relate to balance of payments targets. The fact that the Fund's stabilisation packages have not been associated with a great deal of success points to the need for a case by case approach to replace a formula assuming a universal set of causal factors.[71]

Rights and obligations in the Fund are based on a system of quotas. The latter in turn are calculated on the basis of a formula reflecting the importance of member states in the world economy. Some of the factors taken into account are the volume of the country's international trade, the importance of trade to the national economy and fluctuations in its balance of payments and level of reserves. Since larger quotas are correlated to voting rights, it means that in cases where a majority vote is needed, a few countries occupy a critical position. In cases where special majorities are needed this position will be even more crucial. As the holder with the largest proportion of votes (19.29% at the end of April 1986) the US is in a powerful position. Next in order was the UK (6.68%), followed by West Germany (5.84%), France (4.85%), Japan (4.57%) and Saudi Arabia (3.47%). Together these six countries account for 44.7% of the votes in an organisation with over 150 members. The Commonwealth Caribbean countries taken together have less than 1% of the total votes. For various reasons (some political, some relating to operational procedures of the Fund) the Soviet Union and East European countries (with the exception of Romania and Yugoslavia) have opted to stay out.

The IMF certainly performs a function and provides a form of assistance in the absence of which there could be greater disruption to the free flow of international trade. The call from many countries is not for the abolition of the IMF, but for its reform to allow developing countries a greater degree of influence in decision making.[72] There is also a feeling that the Fund should have a more international outlook in order to counter the influence of the Western industrial powers. Though the Soviet Union and a few developing countries were present at Bretton Woods, the US and Britain were the major architects of the monetary system that was adopted.

Concluding remarks

Article 1 (i) of the IMF Charter has as one of the Fund's purposes the promotion of 'international monetary co-operation through a permanent institution which provides the machinery for consultation and collaboration on international monetary problems'. For the entire post-war period until 1972, discussions on international monetary problems have largely been carried out among the developed countries outside the framework of the IMF. It was only when serious difficulties developed in the deliberations among the Group of 10 leading to a polarisation in the views of the US and the rest, and when it became increasingly clear that a reform of the system would entail an amendment to the Fund's Articles, that an attempt was made to involve the developing countries in the exercise. The reform eventually undertaken and which managed to win the support of the developing nations fell far short of what was expected in many quarters.

The present international monetary system is often described as a non-system. Important questions have been left hanging in the air. The exchange rate regime which was a key arrangement in the Bretton Woods system remains far from settled, as is the question of symmetry in adjustment, which played a critical role in the breakdown of the post-war system. Issues relating to capital movements, reserve assets, the international management of liquidity and the special position of developing countries in the monetary system are very inadequately dealt with on the pretext that the system will have to evolve into workable arrangements. What influence developing countries are going to have on the direction the system takes is a matter for speculation. As presently constituted, the Fund permits developing nations only a limited impact on policy making which remains the preserve of developed countries, even amidst the international economic and political changes which have taken place since the end of the war. This is reflected very clearly in the fact that while developing countries now form the bulk of the membership of the IMF, they appear impotent to effect any fundamental changes in the operations of this institution, or on the presumptions of its philosophy or ideology which allow for no divergences from a basic capitalist model operating on a smoothly functioning price mechanism.

The LDCs' vulnerability which the recent exchange rate crises have exposed stems in a large measure from the structure of their production and trade, and in a fundamental sense from their development strategies. This is not to understate the role played by defects and shortcomings in international arrangements, or in the functioning of international organisations. Given LDCs' dependence on the world economy, the latter have a crucial part to play in the development process (even if indirectly), but this could only be done by innovative approaches drawing heavily on the LDCs' experience, problems and conditions. The existing structure of international organisations tends to reflect too much the compromises of big power politics, rather than the needs of the evolving world system.

Notes

1 The Brandt Report, also called *North-South: A Program for Survival*, Cambridge, Mass: The MIT Press, 1980, p.201.
2 Starting in 1959 these included such measures as increases in IMF quotas, the creation of the 'Gold Pool' which was designed to stabilise the market price of gold within margins around its official price, the development of multilateral surveillance, the invention of 'Roosa bonds' which were intended to discourage holders of US dollars from converting to gold, the creation of a network of 'swap' agreements among major central banks, the conclusion of the General Agreement to

Borrow (GAB) in late 1961, which gave the IMF greater access to major currencies in an emergency, and later the Smithsonian Agreement which increased the exchange rate margins for the currencies of the industrial countries. See John Williamson, *The failure of World Monetary Reform*, Sunbury-on-Thames: Thomas Nelson and Sons, 1977, pp.18–19.

3 Some observers would argue that the system (for all practical purposes) ended in August, 1971, when the US suspended convertibility of the dollar into gold, which was one of its main pillars.

4 The Committee of Twenty included delegates from Argentina, Australia, Belgium, Brazil, Canada, Ethiopia, France, Germany, India, Indonesia, Iraq, Italy, Japan, Morocco, the Netherlands, Sweden, the United States, the United Kingdom, Venezuela, and Zaire. Most of these delegates represented several countries in addition to their own.

5 The United States, Germany, The United Kingdom, France, Italy, Japan, Canada, the Netherlands, Belgium and Sweden.

6 This Committee was superseded by the Interim Committee of the Board of Governors of the IMF.

7 See, for example, contributions by Fritz Machlup and Robert Triffin in *Reflections on Jamaica*, Princeton Essays in International Finance, No. 115, April, 1976.

8 With certain exceptions an amendment to the Fund's Charter could only be made if three-fifths of the members with four-fifths of the total voting power were in favour.

9 See Williamson, *op. cit.* p.61. This writer also argues that the decision by the US to shift the discussions to an IMF framework arose from that country's increasingly isolated position in the C-20 and from the need to 'wield her influence with greater effect'.

10 It was also intended (as is the GATT) to provide a body of rules to govern commercial relations among contracting parties, while acting at the same time as a forum for the resolution of conflicts arising from trading policies.

11 Section 2 of Article XIV provides that members may 'maintain and adopt to changing circumstances...restrictions on payments and transfers for current international transactions. Members shall, however, have continuous regard in their foreign exchange policies to the purpose of the Fund; and, as soon as conditions permit, they shall take all possible measures to develop such commercial and financial arrangements with other members as will facilitate international payments and the maintenance of exchange stability...'

12 The term 'developing countries' is not clearly defined in the Gatt Agreement. One writer has pointed out that the 'special facilities accorded to a contracting party in the interest of its economic development were paralleled by identical facilities for use by any contracting party engaged in post-war reconstruction.' See J.W. Evans, *The Kennedy Round in American Trade Policy: The Twilight of the GATT*, Cambridge: Harvard University Press, 1971, p.114.

13 Particularly Articles XIX, XX, XII and XIV.

14 See Brian Tew, *International Monetary Co-operation, 1945 to 1970*, London: Hutchinson University Library, 1970, p.100.

15 This was the case for all countries until 1971, when the major industrial nations signed the Smithsonian Agreement which permitted a band of 2.25%.
16 In the case of other exchange transactions the margin permitted could not exceed the margin for spot transactions by more than what the Fund considered reasonable.
17 See R.F. Mikesell, *Financing World Trade*, New York: Thomas Y. Crowell Company, 1969, p.34.
18 For an interesting discussion on this subject see Cheryl Payer, 'The IMF and the Third World,' in Steve Weissamn *et al. The Trojan Horse*, Palo Alto: Ramparts Press, 1974. See also *The Debt Trap*, Penguin Books, 1974, by the same author.
19 See J. Keith Horsefield, *The International Monetary Fund 1945–1965*, Washington: IMF, 1969, pp.403–404.
20 Quoted in Brian Tew, *op. cit.* pp.104–105.
21 See, for example, Conrad J. Oort's presentation in *Steps to International Monetary Order*, Federation of Bankers Association of Japan, Tokyo, 1975.
22 The first major amendment to the Agreement was made in 1969 with the creation of Special Drawing Rights (SDRs).
23 See, for example, Robert Triffin, *Europe and the Money Muddle*, Yale University Press, 1957. See also his *Gold and the dollar Crisis*, New Haven: Yale University Press, 1960.
24 Mikesell, *op. cit.* p.64.
25 Sterling has also served a similar function for some countries with close economic and political ties to Britain. Sterling's role in this respect, however, has been considerably less significant than that of the US dollar. The same could be said of the French Franc, another of the major reserve currencies.
26 See for example, Peter G. Peterson's Report, *A Foreign Economic Perspective*, Washington D.C. 1971.
27 France has been a leading proponent of this view.
28 The ratio of official liabilities to gold reserves increased from 0.28 in 1949 to 6.12 in 1971 and to 11.9 in 1975.
29 The Article is vague in many respects. What it attempts to do broadly is to spell out the general principles members should observe in their exchange rate policies and to define the guidelines for surveillance and the procedures that would be followed. Under the Article 'each member undertakes to collaborate with the Fund and other members to assure orderly exchange arrangements and to promote a stable system of exchange rates'. The principles for the guidance of members' exchange rate policies are stated as follows:
    (a) A member shall avoid manipulating exchange rates or the international monetary system in order to prevent effective balance of payments adjustments or to gain an unfair competitive advantage.
    (b) A member should intervene in the exchange market if necessary to counter disorderly conditions which may be characterised *inter alia* by disruptive short term movements in the exchange value of its currency.
30 See IMF, *Survey*, Jan. 19, 1976.

31 See, for example, Fritz Machlup, 'Between Outline and Outcome the Reform was Lost', in Edward M. Bernstein *et al*. *Reflections on Jamaica*, Essays in International Finance, No. 115, Princeton University, 1976.
32 See R. Triffin, 'Jamaica: Major Revision or Fiasco', in Reflections, *op. cit.*
33 See *Outline of Reform*.
34 *Ibid*.
35 *Ibid*.
36 As we point out later, for various reasons, the floating system has not succeeded in eliminating the deficit position of certain countries. It is important to note, however, that though in absolute terms the level of reserves have increased in many cases, the reserves to import ratio of major industrial countries (Austria, Belgium, Canada, Denmark, France, Germany, Italy, Japan, Netherlands, Norway, Switzerland, UK, the US) taken together dropped from 37% in 1971 to 20% in 1973 and to 17% in 1977.
37 Oort, *op. cit.*, p.27.
38 One provision in this respect, perhaps, relates to the scarce currency clause. Article VII empowers the Fund to declare a currency 'scarce' and in such an eventuality other members could (after consultation with the Fund) temporarily impose limitations on the freedom of exchange operations in the scarce currency. This clause hardly appeared to have been used, or when used proved highly ineffective.
39 See IMF, *Annual Report*, 1977, p.25.
40 *Ibid*.
41 See CIAP, *Latin America and the Reform of the International – Monetary System*, Washington, D.C. 1972, p.24.
42 Speaking with respect to exchange rates in 1972, the Governor of the Fund and the Bank for Jamaica, Mr D.H. Coore said: 'Like all developing countries we wish to see an early return to a stable system of exchange rates, one not as rigid and inflexible as we have seen in the past, but one which would give developing countries that measure of certainty in their trade and financial operations which is conductive to maximum development'. (See IMF *Summary Proceedings*, Annual Meeting, 1972, p.192.)

Speaking in 1974 (on behalf of Jamaica, the Bahamas, Guyana, Barbados and Trinidad and Tobago), Mr Coore expressed support for the principles set out in *Outline of Reform*, which, as we said earlier, felt that the exchange rate mechanism should remain 'based on stable but adjustable par values'. (See IMF, *Summary Proceedings*, Annual Meeting, 1974, p.175.
43 The situation at the end of August, 1980 for members of the IMF were as follows: Forty countries (all LDCs including the Bahamas, Barbados, Grenada, Guyana, Jamaica and Trinidad and Tobago) were pegged to the US dollar, one to Sterling, fourteen (all LDCs) to the French Franc, and three (LDCs) to various other currencies. Fifteen nations (all LDCs), were pegged to the SDR basket while another twenty-two chose their own respective currency composites (or basket). Another three members were adjusting their rates according to a set of indicators while eight others (members of the European 'snake') were pursuing

co-operative exchange arrangements. Thirty-three countries (comprising both developed and developing nations) were placed in a miscellaneous category which included countries that were floating independently and those which could not be placed in the other groups.
44 William R. Cline, *International Monetary Reform and the Developing Countries*, Washington D.C.: The Brookings Institution, 1976, p.14.
45 See for example, Cline, *op. cit.*, p.22.
46 CIAP, *op. cit.*, p.49.
47 See Nurul Islam, in *Reflections*, *op. cit.*
48 For a more detailed discussion on some of the exchange rate options facing developing countries, see A.D. Crokett and S.M. Nsouli, 'Exchange Rate Policies for Developing Countries', *Journal of Developing Studies*, Jan. 1977.
49 See the 1973 IMF *Annual Report*, p.32.
50 Cline, *op. cit.* p.32.
51 *Ibid.* p.30.
52 See for example Arthur Lewis' 1977 Jacobson Lecture 'The Less Developed Countries and Stable Exchange Rates' in *The International System in Operation*, Washington, D.C., IMF, 1977.
53 For example, Lewis, *op. cit.*
54 Some observers have argued that IMF quotas were actually biased against LDCs. See R.G. Hawkins and C. Rangarajan, 'On the Distribution of New International Reserves', *Journal of Finance*, Sept. 1970.
55 For example, see speech by Trinidad and Tobago's Governor on the IMF and Bank at the 1977 IMF Annual Meeting in the *Summary Proceedings*, p.192.
56 The inclusion of this proposal in *Outline of Reform* did not necessarily represent a unanimity of views. This may have been done to gain time.
57 See Williamson, *op. cit.* p.144.
58 The Technical Group, Para. 6 (b).
59 Under the new decision the Fund can authorise drawings up to 75% of a member's quotas, as against 50% under the 1966 decision. Maximum drawings in any one year were raised from 25% to 50% of quota.
60 These include:
   (a) The Extended Facility set up in 1974 with the purpose of providing assistance of up to three years, in order to overcome structural balance of payments difficulties;
   (b) The Buffer-stock Financing Facility set up in 1969 provides assistance to primary producing countries in financing contributions to international buffer stock.
   Besides these, a temporary Oil Facility was set up in 1974 and 1975 to help countries experiencing balance of payments difficulties arising from the 1973 oil crisis. In 1977 a decision was also taken to establish a supplementary financing (Witteveen) Facility to enable the Fund to provide supplementary financing in conjunction with the use of (its) ordinary resources to members facing serious payments imbalances that are large in relation to their quotas. Lending under this facility, which became operational in 1979, is subject to the Fund's policy conditions.
61 See IMF *Annual Report*, 1977 p.39.
62 If gold is valued at market prices its importance would exceed that of

foreign exchange reserves. For example at the end of 1979 the value of gold at the London market price was estimated to be SDRs$361.4 billions as compared to SDRs$246.0 billions for foreign exchange.

63 See IMF *Annual Report*, 1977 p.40.
64 *Ibid.* pp.40−44.
65 See 1977 IMF Annual Meeting, *Summary Proceedings*, pp.192−193.
66 See speech 'Financing the LDCs: The Role of Public and Private Institutions' by the Fund's Managing Director H. Johannes Witteveen delivered on May 8, 1978 in London to the 1978 Euro-markets Conference.
67 See IMF *Annual Report*, 1977 p.41.
68 e.g. Japan, Canada, Singapore, Panama, the Bahamas, the Cayman Islands.
69 Susan Strange, *International Monetary Relations*, London: Oxford University Press, 1976, pp.177.
70 See IMF *Annual Report*, 1978 p.52.
71 See, for example, Tony Killick, *The Impact of IMF Stabilisation Programmes in Developing Countries*, London: Overseas Development Institute, 1982, working paper No. 7.
72 See, for example, Michael Manley, *Up the Down Escalator*, London: Andre Deutsch Ltd., 1987, chapters 8 and 9.

CHAPTER 10
The framework of development: Some theoretical perspectives

The approach to development by developing countries: A retrospective view

One of the most important concerns in the post-war period has been the question of economic development − or to be more precise how best to raise the standard of living of the vast majority of people in the world. The issue became particularly important once the decolonisation process had begun, and the membership of the UN began to grow. The reconstruction of Europe which was of paramount importance to the US in the immediate aftermath of World War II, soon receded into the background as Marshall aid began to have its desired effect. But there was to be no Marshall aid for the developing countries, many of whom, despite the possession of valuable mineral resources, had languished in poverty for centuries. The search for development became primarily their own responsibility, and this was to spur a voluminous literature on the causes of poverty and the ways to overcome it.

An early perception was to project developing countries as going along the same historical (evolutionary) path as the developed nations. A group of ideas which came to be known as the 'big push' theories rejected the bit by bit approach to development and instead advocated large-scale planned industrialisation as the way to launch countries into self-sustained growth. A closely related approach was the 'balanced growth' argument which called for simultaneous investment in a number of industries so that the necessary demand for each others' products could be created through the provision of jobs and income. By taking for granted the very factors that were in short supply, the development problem was virtually assumed away. Other theories focused on the need to increase domestic savings, the role of foreign aid, modernisation of institutions, industrial development with unlimited supplies of labour, etc. Paradigms or models purporting to show processes of development and underdevelopment became widespread. Some of them were nothing more than academic exercises with little relation to reality. In others, the representation of real world economies was highly simplistic, if not naive.

The neat division of sectors and the behavioural patterns assumed, often betrayed a failure to understand the social and economic forces which had helped to shape colonial economies and societies. The implications for practice were downplayed as mathematical elegance and internal consistency took ascendancy. There was a tendency to treat developing countries as a homogeneous group of nations whose problems could be approached with a common set of solutions. Despite this, theories and models were to have a deep influence on policy. In many cases the fact that the intellectual options with respect to strategy were very narrow may explain the overwhelming influence of certain paradigms or ideas, rather than their inherent worth gleaned through the analysis they provided.

In the study of poverty a widely accepted assumption was that developing countries suffered from a capital problem. If only financial resources could be provided, it was widely felt, development could proceed smoothly. The international environment was assumed to be favourable to any development effort, and domestic conditions would adjust instinctively to the process. This approach took critical parameters as given. No wonder the growth question was simplified in terms of capital-output ratios. It assumed that all that was required to attain a given level of output was a certain amount of capital. The exact relationship was taken from the experience of the developed countries.

The problem of capital shortage had two dimensions. Generally, it was assumed that developing countries were poor because they were not saving enough, and they were not saving enough because they were poor. It was a kind of vicious circle. The low savings ratio could be viewed as the domestic dimension. To break out of this circle, foreign savings were needed to supplement the local effort. This could be viewed as the external dimension.

Let us begin with the first dimension. It was not generally accepted that savings were low in developing countries. The problem tended to be viewed in different ways. Some argued that because of statistical difficulties, it was difficult to guage the actual level of savings taking place in the community. A large proportion of savings never entered conventional savings institutions normally located in urban centres. Even the savings that entered these institutions tended to be sent abroad on the grounds that there were not enough local opportunities for their deployment. The foreign ownership of financial institutions and financial arrangements with the metropole made the movements of funds a simple matter. While it was being argued that developing countries had a capital problem and needed foreign assistance, such local savings as there were were being exported abroad. The position was often taken that in relation to the level of income, the level of savings was quite high, and therefore the problem was not about thrift or the savings instinct. The problem was mobilisation and deployment. The potential savings ratio was far in excess of the actual savings ratio.

The possibility of access to foreign resources meant little attention was paid to the development of the local capital market, which was seen as a longer term measure. The view was also taken that domestic resources were not a complete substitute for foreign finance. In other words, if available local savings could be increased, foreign exchange would still be needed since essential goods needed by developing countries still had to be obtained from abroad. A common approach was to project a certain rate of growth over a period, and using a capital-output ratio, assess financial needs. Once an estimate could be made for local savings, the foreign component could be easily established.

Against this background, it was not surprising that during the 1960s and even in the 1970s, foreign aid emerged as an important issue in international economic relations. The 1960s was dubbed by the UN as the 'first development decade' and developed countries were urged to transfer to developing countries 1% of their national income. In the 1970s which was dubbed the 'second development decade' the industrial nations were again urged to transfer 1% of their GNP. In both decades major developed countries failed to meet this target.

An early misconception was that the growth of the domestic product was tantamount to development. Experience was quick to show that GDP could grow without any serious development taking place. Countries, for instance, with valuable natural resources tended to experience high rates of growth. Mineral sectors often represented islands of high technology and income surrounded by poverty and primitive techniques. There was little linkage with the rest of the economy, except perhaps in terms of the contribution to government revenue and expenditure of workers. Experience has shown that total income can grow while an increasing proportion of the population becomes pauperised. With growth, income can become more highly concentrated in the hands of a few. And this would be taking place while per capita income (which is an average figure) is increasing.

This question of the distribution of income is one of the most contentious issues in the literature. There is one school of thought which argues that in the early stages of development, policy should aim at pursuing a highly skewed distribution of income, and that greater equity in distribution should become a policy objective much later. In other words, the cake should be made before it is distributed. The reasoning in the latter case is that by the time redistribution becomes an important issue, there may be nothing to distribute. A corollary of this concern is at what stage should redistribution begin. A deliberate policy of encouraging skewed income distribution can create an instability which may affect growth in the long term. People who are deprived will not generally give of their best. For them there is no long term.

Another concern which has led to a questioning of GDP growth as an indication of development is the fact that very often a substantial part of the domestic product accrues to foreigners, depending on the degree of foreign involvement in the economy. In developing countries, because foreign income accruing to residents tends to be smaller than that paid to non-residents, GNP tends to be lower than GDP. Even GNP (and particularly average GNP) could project a wrong impression if a significant proportion of income accrues to residents who are non-nationals. This is more likely to be the case in small states which tend to be highly dependent on foreign skills.

Upon independence, most developing countries found themselves with key sectors of their economies in foreign hands. Despite constitutional independence major decisions regarding the economy were outside the control or influence of national governments. Taking control of what has been called the 'commanding heights' of the economy or regaining the 'national patrimony' became an important objective. This however, was easier said than done. In some cases the process of takeover was badly conceived, or undertaken at a time when neither financial resources, nor available expertise warranted it. In certain cases where agreement could not be reached between the foreign owners and the local government there was a resort to expropriation. The pressure to assert independence through nationalisation often led to the takeover of non-economic enterprises which had run their course. Generally, there was a failure to perceive the need for a political framework which could generate the support for a policy of nationalisation in the context of the post-nationalisation climate and the scarce skills required to run the state-owned concerns.

In recent years unsatisfactory growth rates, increasing unemployment and persistent balance of payments problems have led to a critical re-examination of past development strategies and economic thinking. In many cases private foreign capital flows have not been of the level and form desired. Concessional aid has also been disappointing. Technology transfer has been minimal and costly. While a few countries have been able to develop an industrial sector of some significance, and to increase the proportion of manufactured goods in total exports, generally diversification objectives have not been realised. Dependence on a narrow range of activities still characterise a large number of developing countries. Many states which in the early post-independence years adopted a very cautious, if not hostile attitude towards private foreign investment have now moved towards a more open foreign investment policy in the hope of attracting foreign savings and technology. In this connection, as indicated earlier, the adoption of foreign investment policies and investment guarantee arrangements with foreign governments have become common. There is now also a growing concern with economic efficiency in the light of the need to increase exports, and given the fiscal problems facing many governments. This exercise has not only given rise to a critical examination of the policy framework of development used since the 1950s, but has also raised questions about the intellectual basis on which they were founded.

Has development economics failed?

During the 1950s and 1960s it was widely felt that conventional economics was not particularly suited for studying the problems of developing countries, and this spurred the emergence of a wide range of theories offering insights and guidance as to how to overcome poverty. These eventually came to form a corpus of 'development economics', and the basis of this was the rejection of certain premises and assumptions which underlay conventional thought. The major objection related to the price mechanisms which, because of certain institutional defects, could not be relied upon to promote development. This called for major government intervention in the economy.

In recent years a view has emerged that because of false assumptions, development theories of the 1950s and 1960s led to the adoption of policies which, far from solving anything, created further problems.[1] The deep government involvement which these theories encouraged is seen as a major cause for many of the difficulties facing developing countries today. The emergence of increased dependence and neo-colonial relationships are often attributed directly to the development strategies which were inspired by early post-war thinking. There has, of course, been a great deal of controversy with respect to the role played by internal and external factors in the creation and perpetuation of poverty. Reacting to the internal determinancy theories of the 1950s and 1960s, the dependency school which has emerged in Latin America and the Caribbean tends to stress the external factors.

In some cases too much emphasis may have been put on industrialisation at the expense of agriculture. There are also instances where inadequate incentives have led to low savings ratios resulting in excessive government borrowing to help finance domestic capital formation. Too much stress on import substitution have in some cases resulted in uncompetitive production structures that are unable to produce for export. In some cases lack of planning or too much planning of the wrong kind has affected economic growth. There are instances also where unrealistic exchange rates have been suspected of hampering sectoral objectives. Lack of balance in investment in infrastructure and directly productive investment has also drawn some complaints.

It is easier, of course, to see mistakes in hindsight. These 'mistakes' are not always the result of government's intervention in the economy. It is also necessary to point out that in some economies which have experienced exceptionally high growth rates, governments are known to have played a crucial role. At the same time, it does not follow that in economies which have experienced moderate growth or no growth at all, government is to be blamed. The fact is government's intervention is often necessary to create the framework and conditions which can stimulate development. Private sector activities often depend on government initiatives and encouragement. Governments are often forced to become involved in ownership of enterprises to save jobs, or where such activities represent key sectors of the economy. It cannot be argued that because problems exist, there has not been progress. As Streeten has pointed out, 'many of the difficulties encountered in the path of development (and perhaps in all human endeavour) are neither the result of ideological errors nor attributable to vested interests, they are the offspring of the successful solution of previous problems. Scientific confidence asserts that there is a solution to every problem, but experience teaches us that there is a problem to every solution, and often more than one.'[2]

There has been a great deal of misunderstanding about the role of theory in shaping economic policy, and this has no doubt helped in providing a basis for the view that development economics has failed. Theory often abstracts a great deal from the real world in order to focus on essential processes. In evaluating a theory as a basis for policy, the assumption on which it is based has to be taken into account. Experience has shown that this is often not done. Also, in implementation only the parts of it which are considered to be politically acceptable may be taken, even when it is recognised that its success may depend on comprehensive implementation of its major aspects.

Despite progress in certain directions, the Commonwealth Caribbean has failed to develop a vibrant economy which could meet the challenges of the 1980s and beyond. This is so despite the presence of a highly literate and resourceful people. These countries have imposed constraints on themselves which in some cases have nothing to do with size. The institutions inherited from colonial times and those that have been set up subsequently have generally lacked a development orientation. The political institutions conceived with a view to preserving and developing democratic tradition, have in some cases been manipulated with the aim of stifling expression and creativity. The political power inherited upon the attainment of constitutional independence has often been exercised with a high degree of partisanship, thus precluding full use of limited human resources. This has also been responsible for the absence of a framework in which trade unions could make a more positive contribution to the development process. Information in many cases, has not been seen as important, and so statistical departments have tended to receive little funding. Even where they exist, certain types of data (e.g. unemployment, distribution of income) are not produced for lack of resources, or because of fear that they may reflect unfavourably on government policies.

In the Caribbean it is difficult to view economic problems apart from the political experience. There are certain clichés such as 'structural factors' or 'lack of resources' which are often offered as objective reasons for an unsatisfactory rate of progress, or for the particular type of development that has taken place. Small countries have to live by their wits and this means the mobilisation of all available human and other resources. National priorities and objectives ought not to be determined by small groups of bureaucrats or by politicians alone, but need to reflect a broader consensus. Caribbean countries have been independent long enough to have developed a sufficiently high level of maturity to see history in perspective and, therefore, to prevent historical experience from discouraging rational assessments of problems of development. This calls for the need for a more open approach towards policymaking and greater dialogue among the various sections of the economy. The phobia of secrecy is inconsistent with the education of a society that has to compete with the rest of the world.

Economic policies, poorly conceived and implemented, often produce consequences which are difficult to reverse. This has to be seen not only in terms of resources, but in terms of the mental attitude created. In trying to hold on to political power too little attention is often paid to the latter. In the process, expectations are formed which cannot be sustained by the level of public revenue or the growth of the economy. There is sometimes a tendency to excuse irresponsible policies on the grounds of politics. Development is as much about reforming economics as politics. Individuals and institutions often do not see their position in relation to the larger interest and sometimes adopt postures which retard development and weaken the national state. Progress also involves development of an ability to examine the past rationally and build upon it. Yet for reasons of politics and self interest in exercises of appraisal, indolence is often condoned, meagre achievements are excused on the grounds that others have accomplished less and mediocrity is exalted. Self-criticism is essential to forging a strong society and economy.

The framework of development

Despite reservations about the constraints which size could impose on economic development, Commonwealth Caribbean countries entered political independence in an atmosphere of hope. There was a genuine belief that colonial status was an obstacle to economic development. Independence had its political rationale. The economic imperatives, however, were dominant. In the fashion of the times a short or medium-term development plan was deemed necessary as a statement of policy and objectives. A plan was not only symptomatic of the presence of a development attitude, but was seen to be a necessary document in negotiations for foreign aid and finance, since they gave not only an insight into government strategy, but also an indication of financial requirements.

In the Caribbean a great deal of effort went into the writing of plans, and this reflected the seriousness with which the exercise was viewed. The documents contained a wide variety of statistics and analyses of problems that were being targeted. They also tended to be quite detailed as far as the public sector investment programme and government policies were concerned. The technical sophistication was, however, minimal. Preoccupation with projects, too, often consumed more energy and time than articulation of strategies.

In practice the process of planning did serve some useful purpose, even if many objectives were only partially attained. The plans generally aimed high, and were often overly ambitious, given prevailing constraints. A major problem was implementation. One aspect of this related to inadequate financial resources. In practice there tend to be serious problems in forecasting foreign exchange earnings and aid flows. Another aspect has to do with the administrative machinery necessary to implement the plans. The importance of this was often under-rated. The urge to write development plans has now largely subsided, and planning no longer has the urgency that it once had. The former Prime Minister of Trinidad and Tobago, Dr Eric Williams, summed it up well when he said that 'planning has lost its mystique'.

There are a lot of misconceptions surrounding the role of development planning in a developing society where the means of production is largely in private hands. In such a context planning is largely of an indicative nature, with the government articulating the problems of the society, proposing solutions to these problems and formulating the necessary macro-policies and projects for attainment of the goals outlined. An indication of the public sector investment programme tends to be an integral part of these plans. Monetary and fiscal policies are expected to be mobilised in this effort. One of the major purposes of plans in the past, as indicated before, was to determine financial needs over a given period of time, therefore they were an important document in aid seeking. In the private enterprise economy the market tends to be the major force determining output. Here, prices, incomes and preferences play a major part in what is produced. In a centrally planned economy the output of each enterprise or industry is determined by a central authority in relation to overall output goals.

In a market economy the profit motive is the driving force, and producers tend to produce what consumers want. The wishes of the latter dictate what is produced. This may be true up to a point. In an age of mass advertising it is easy for producers to influence the desires of consumers. The problems of planning in a free enterprise economy are compounded by factors which are outside the control of the government. Caribbean countries, for instance, are dependent on a narrow range of products or activities for their export earnings. Such activities are also significant contributors to government revenue. Foreign exchange earnings and government revenue, therefore, can easily be affected by weather conditions, a fall in export prices or, in the case where production is under the control of a transnational enterprise, an arbitrary reduction in production levels, dictated by the strategy of the corporation and formulated in relation to corporate goals.

Despite the difficulties which face planning in mixed economies of the kind we have in the Caribbean, some degree of planning is necessary if the society is to prepare itself for future social and economic changes. The budget itself is a one year plan, since it gives an indication of what is to be accomplished in the forthcoming year and how it is to be accomplished. But longer term planning is also necessary. As the population grows the increases and needs have to be projected and catered for. If this is not done, not only do pressures build up, but resources can also be wasted. There can be over investment in particular areas while others which require expansion are neglected. Projects may also not be properly related to each other if there is no clear idea of where the economy is going in terms of structure and orientation. The absence of planning in development often leads to *ad hoc* growth which may prove detrimental to development ends. Planning, it should be pointed out, does not necessarily mean the writing of a plan. What it does mean is the pursuit of policies and the adoption of projects in a framework consistent with stated goals. The private sector is brought into the process through incentives rather than compulsion.

A major difficulty with many of the plans that were drawn up in the 1960s was the question of implementation. It appears that not enough attention was directed to this issue. Executing a plan requires a particular type of administrative set-up with a clear structure of authority and delineation of decision-making areas. Absence of this condition results in evasion of responsibility. While the civil service has been enlarged in the post-independence period, there has been little change in terms of innovation where its structure and role is concerned. The public service has tended to be more routine bound rather than development oriented. Numbers have been added to it (to provide jobs) without any clear objective of increasing productivity in terms of post-independence objectives. In the process, manpower and financial resources have been wasted. Small countries cannot afford this kind of wastage. Manpower resources, in particular, need to be fully utilised. This means undertaking training and the proper channelling of professional skills. Human resources are often wasted when people are not properly allocated to jobs related to their skill, even when such jobs are available. This is common practice in the region.

The state and the private sector

Commonwealth Caribbean countries have committed themselves to a mixed-type economy. In this kind of arrangement, the private sector is conceived as having a key role to play in the economy. In most of the economies the means of production is in private hands. Governments in the region tend to see themselves as guiding the development process. This they do by providing the legal and administrative framework and the necessary infrastructural requirements. To do this, some governments find it necessary to own the public utilities such as water, port, telephone and electricity services. In certain cases governments are engaged in directly productive activities.

In recent years the role and performance of the private sector have come under critical review in the context of general economic problems facing these countries. To understand the role of the private sector in the Caribbean, it is necessary to understand its historical background. A significant part of today's private sector is a legacy of the colonial period — descendants of the plantocracy and the commercial elite of that era. The import-export economy has not really changed in essential respects. The buy and sell know-how gained in the colonial period, and the overseas connections cultivated by traditional business houses was a critical factor in the advantage taken in the context of the nationalistic development strategies adopted. Today's manufacturing sector in the Caribbean centres largely around the production of simple goods and assembly type operations involving products previously imported in finished form. Even the conglomerates tend to be commercially oriented organisations dealing in foreign products rather than original lines of their own. This type of operation necessitates little or no research and development (R and D). The risks faced in terms of recovering R and D expenditures, therefore, are minimal. What these assembly-type enterprises face is the possibility of a significant drop in the level of operations arising from a fall-out in local and regional demand, since they are so heavily dependent on these markets. The shortage of foreign exchange to pay for imported inputs can also pose a problem.

The entrepreneur as a risk-taker in terms of pioneering new products or experimenting with new technologies is a feature largely absent from these economies. Most of the new businessmen have followed in the footsteps of the traditional business houses, getting involved in the easy operations of buying and selling, either directly or through some intermediate channel.

Upon the attainment of political independence, it was hoped that the ownership of production and commercial activities would become more widely dispersed as development proceeded. To this end many foreign enterprises were encouraged to localise their operations. To prevent concentration of ownership, limits were sometimes placed on the amount of shares a single person or enterprise could acquire. Despite this, decision-making has remained highly concentrated.

The paucity of risk takers, investors, and entrepreneurs has a great deal to do with government policies. The education system was not related to development objectives, and very little was done to correct this. The emphasis in the 1960s and 1970s was in providing more school places and free secondary education. Curriculum reform received scant attention. The need to make science more widely available and to strengthen the links between it and the development process is now being increasingly recognised. Exactly how to do this, however, continues to evade regional governments. Simply adding laboratories to secondary schools, or making computers available to school-children or setting up science parks appear to be highly inadequate. It is becoming increasingly apparent that children have to be introduced to the subject and its practical uses at a very early age. As yet there is little effort in this direction.

The framework for the systematic study of international developments in technology and the effects of these on production processes is also generally absent. As far as the private sector is concerned, the perception is that if someone is making a profit in a protected market, why should he bother about innovation or technological changes. He is under no pressure to take additional risks or incur additional expenditures.

There is some controversy on the extent to which governments should intervene in the economy. It is often argued that the market, left to itself, allocates resources in the most efficient way. In every economy, government intervenes in some way either through ownership or through the use of administrative instruments. In many developed countries the government intervenes when locally vested interests are threatened by foreign competition. Agricultural protection in the US and the EC has existed for years. Governments in these countries have also intervened from time to time to assist certain industries directly, or to protect them from foreign competition threatening their existence. Intervention by developing countries, however, tends to be seen in a different light. The economic argument is that this intervention interferes with resource allocation and efficiency. There is also an underlying political objection. State intervention is often tantamount to 'socialism' where the freedom of the individual is at stake.

In a developing context the role of the state is a special one. The state often has to act as a catalyst to development. This role becomes increasingly important in a situation where there is a shortage of entrepreneurs and inadequate private savings. Because it has certain social responsibilities, the state often has to get involved in the ownership of the means of production or to save jobs or to create them. The investment involved in many enterprises facing liquidation may be so large as to be beyond the capacity of local entrepreneurs. To secure certain political objectives may also be a factor motivating government involvement in the economy. For instance, the need to have the 'commanding heights of the economy' under national control has often led governments to take ownership of key enterprises in the economy.

The view is sometimes taken that government ownership is synonymous with poor management and inefficiency. This is not inherently so. Very often government intervenes at the last minute to save an enterprise on the brink of collapse – one which may have been badly run for years. It may take considerable time, money and effort to get such an operation back into a profitable position. The situation, however, is often worsened by putting incapable political appointees in key positions.

With respect to the public utilities, the charge to consumers may be deliberately subsidised to make their services available to as wide a range of people as possible. It is often difficult to discriminate between those who could afford to pay economic costs and those who cannot. This is not to say that the problem of management of the public utilities and other government-owned enterprise is not an issue of concern in the Caribbean. In a number of cases these enterprises have become havens providing 'jobs for the boys' of the ruling party. As a result of the failure to attract or appoint competent professionals, many government-owned operations have simply failed to perform both in terms of the quality of services provided and in covering the costs of operations. In some cases, people who might be professionally competent in their own particular field are often put in charge of operations for which their training does not qualify them and they are not capable of managing. The problem is often compounded by one person often being given the task of managing several diverse enterprises at the same time.

Against this background, it is easy to see why the issue of privatisation has become such a sensitive one. Because of fiscal problems various governments in the region have been brought to a point where they either have to close or sell some or all of their state enterprises to the private sector, local and foreign. In some quarters there is a tendency to view state enterprises as assets held in trust by the government on behalf of the people. The fear is that the sale of these enterprises represents a 'loss of patrimony' in that control of key sectors of the economy is seen as being given back to traditional power groups in the society. One suspects that if the private sector were more broadly based and representative of the society, the perspective on this issue would be different. However urgent the need is for divestment, the issue of having ownership shared by a large cross section of the population is not an irrelevant one. There is therefore a need for approaches which could relieve the fiscal pressure on government and at the same time discourage the concentration of economic power in the hands of traditional cliques.

Commonwealth Caribbean governments are generally committed to having the widest possible participation in the economic process. Various types of financial and technical assistance facilities have been put in place to assist small businesses. Stock markets have also been established with a view not only of raising capital, but to encourage an expansion in the ownership base of established enterprises. It is true to say that these mechanisms have met with only limited success, and this is partly responsible for the dilemma in which governments are caught in the context of the privatisation question. A reduced role of government in the economy must of necessity go hand in hand with policies that could effectively transform the traditional ownership and income distribution patterns, if concentration of economic power is to be discouraged, and the creation of an inherently unstable situation avoided. In the event of the latter materialising the very objective that is being aimed at, namely encouraging a greater volume of local and foreign investment, would be affected.

Notes

1 See, for example, Deepak Lal, 'The Misconceptions of "Development Economics"' in *Finance and Development*, June, 1985.
2 Paul Streeten, 'A Problem to Every Solution,' in *Finance and Development*, June 1983.

CHAPTER 11
Small states and development strategies: Some further issues

Small states are not a new phenomenon on the world stage. Some of them are even known to have played a leading role in world affairs.[1] The presence of countries such as Iceland (1985 pop. 241 000) and Luxembourg (1985 pop. 366 000) in the UN caused no great stir in the 1940s and 1950s. The emergence of a number of small states as independent nations in the 1960s as a result of the decolonisation process, however, gave rise to various types of concern which have not yet subsided. In some quarters the concern was the effect that a large number of mini or micro states were likely to have on the voting structure and decision making machinery in international organisations where every member was entitled to one vote, irrespective of size or financial contribution. With the accession of increasingly smaller states to the UN and its various agencies in the late 1970s and early 1980s, this concern in some quarters was to become more acute. In the absence of any limits on the size of countries which could enter the UN, various proposals and suggestions have been put forward from time to time to provide for qualified membership for mini-states in terms of status or voting power. The principle of one country one vote, however, still holds in the UN.

A broader and more fundamental concern was the ability of small states to survive as independent political entities in view of the economic pressures they were likely to face in the world community. Given limited economic resources and certain constraining factors, surely political independence and self-determination would be a farce, it was suggested. Not surprisingly, the implications of size for development have been a major subject for study at the international level. The security issues raised have also drawn increasing attention in recent years. Of the fifty-one nations that signed the UN Charter in 1945, only five had a population of less than one million. At 31 October 1986, UN membership had grown to 159. Out of this number, 34 had a population below one million (*See* Table 11.1). Included in this 34 were five states with populations under 100 000 and 22 in the range between 100 001 and 500 000. Out of the 34 states with less than one million people, there were ten Commonwealth Caribbean nations. In the latter group the two largest countries

Table 11.1 UN Members grouped according to population[1] size

Population classes			No. of countries
Less than	–	100 000	5
100 001	–	500 000	22
500 001	–	1 000 000	7
1 000 001	–	5 000 000	37
5 000 001	–	10 000 000	32
10 000 001	–	25 000 000	24
25 000 001	–	50 000 000	12
50 000 001	–	100 000 000	11
Over 100 000 000			7
			157[a]

[1] 1985 estimate.
[a] The figure does not include the Byelorussian SSR and the Ukranian SSR which are integral parts of the USSR and not independent countries, but which have separate UN membership.
Source: Based on population data from the World Bank Atlas, 1986.

in terms of population were Jamaica with a population of 2.2 million (1985) and Trinidad and Tobago with 1.2 million (1985). Among other Commonwealth Caribbean states the population varied from 12 000 in the case of Montserrat (which is still a colony of Britain) to 806 000 (1985) in the case of Guyana. Given Montserrat's population and a physical size of 102 km^2, the political future of the country appears to be uncertain, particularly in the context of the fears which have arisen about political and military security in the region, following the Grenada débâcle in 1983. The renewed call by some OECS' politicians for a federation of these states offers a way out of colonialism for Montserrat.

Among developing countries, there are some that face special problems which are being increasingly recognised. Landlocked states, for example, face a transport disadvantage which could affect their development. Some states are located in areas which make them easy targets for earthquake or other natural disasters, or subject them to extremes in weather conditions. Yet others are what can be termed island economies consisting of one or more islands. Among

Commonwealth Caribbean countries there are twelve such states. The exceptions are Belize and Guyana which are situated on land masses, but have direct access to the sea.

While it is recognised that there are certain features which may be peculiar to island economies,[2] many of their characteristics tend to be shared by other small developing countries. We shall therefore confine ourselves to problems faced by poor, small countries generally.

In a 1984 study,[3] the UN noted certain characteristics which it concluded were the consequence of small size. These are worth repeating here:

1 small countries tend to be more dependent on foreign trade than large countries; many of them are price takers rather than price makers in the markets for their exports and imports;
2 the smaller a country in terms of physical area, the narrower is its range of resources and, generally, the more specialised its economy;
3 a small country is more likely than a large country to be heavily dependent on one external company, which may not only monopolise its trade but may have control over its resources;
4 a small country normally has a narrower range of institutions than a large country, and often is significantly dependent for certain services on institutions outside its borders. Thus, monetary arrangements or educational and small health services may be dependent on institutions and systems outside the country;
5 a small country is likely to have a narrower range of skilled manpower than a large country and may experience particular difficulties in providing necessary skills, or in providing jobs for their skills which are available;
6 there may be diseconomies of small scales in the provision of infra-structure or administrative services, and there is a critical minimum size below which certain services cannot be provided at all;
7 a country which is small in terms of GNP will have a narrow local market, and will normally experience particular difficulties in the development of import substitution manufacturing industries. Statistical evidence suggests that small countries are likely to be less industrialised than large countries at equivalent levels of income, although there are important exceptions.

The smaller the country, the more acute some of these problems would be. While the constraint of small market size may be overcome by developing export markets, or local resource availability can be augmented by importing, the problem of diseconomies of small scale in the provision of infrastructure or administrative services is not so easy to overcome.

While small countries face certain constraints with respect to development, it is felt that there are certain advantages which flow from their size. For instance, because small countries may have small production volumes they are often able to expand their exports without encountering adverse reactions. Of course, if all countries were to do this at the same time the impact is unlikely to go unnoticed. Smallness should also facilitate the planning process since a government may find it easier to get across its policies to the population at large and to mobilise them in support of its programmes. Surely, a large country affected by communication and transport problems would find such a task much more daunting.

Size and development

In the late 1950s/early 1960s there were serious doubts with respect to the ability of the British colonies in the Caribbean to survive as independent nations. The British government saw the solution in terms of a political federation with a central government assuming responsibility for the destiny of these islands. The experiment eventually failed, and as indicated earlier, the countries of the region, starting with Jamaica in August, 1962 decided to seek independence as individual units. This did not, however, dissipate doubts about the economic future of the islands, and the idea of closer political association — at least among some of the units — has lingered on into the present. A federation of all the previous participants remains a dream in some quarters, cropping up from time to time as a possibility which may have forestalled some of the political and economic difficulties which have emerged in the region. Awareness of the limitations posed by their respective sizes did, however, manifest itself in steps for economic integration and continued co-operation in certain areas which pre-dated independence.

The emergence of a large number of small countries as independent nations has drawn attention to the development choices and possibilities faced by such states. Small states face certain peculiar economic problems. Small domestic markets and a highly skewed resource base make them particularly dependent on international trade. While exports, as we have seen, may be confined to a few commodities, imports may include a wide range of essential consumer and capital goods. It may be argued with some justification that many of the problems being experienced by small states can be found in large states. This, however, does not negate the fact that small areas and small populations do create certain constraints which may militate against development.

There is considerable controversy in the literature with respect to what constitutes a small state. Writing in the context of the 1950s and early 1960s Kuznets found it useful to describe a small nation as an 'independent sovereign state with a population of ten million or less.'[4] He was quick to point out, however, that setting the 'dividing line at ten million is a rough decision, made with any eye to the distribution of nations by size as it exists today and has existed over the last fifty to seventy-five years.'[5] He took the view that just as 'the dividing line is relative to the distribution of nations by size at a given historical epoch, so it is relative to differences in the economic and social potentials that we wish to emphasise. For some industries, even a fifty million nation is too small to provide a sound economic base; for others, a community of five million may, under reasonable assumptions supply an adequate long-term market.'[6] The criteria for determining small can, therefore, be quite arbitrary, depending on one's analytical focus and historical horizon.

In a purely economic context, the question of size takes on importance when we seek to discuss the potential for development. Does a large area offer greater possibilities for development? Generally, one associates a greater variety in large area with respect to mineral resources, topography, climate, etc. Large areas also tend to carry large populations to support, though there are certainly exceptions to this general rule. A small country tends to have fewer resources, but this is not necessarily an impediment to development. Countries such as Hong Kong, Singapore and South Korea with limited natural resources have made substantial economic progress in the post-war period. Development is not simply a function of available natural resources; it has a great deal to do with the development of a capability to exploit such resources. Development need not be constrained by resources obtaining within a country. Inputs can be bought from other nations. Until quite recently, the role of the human factor seems to have been missing in the economics literature which tended to emphasise non-human resources and institutional development. Natural disadvantages can be overcome with the creation of an environment that encourages initiative and enterprise. In a trading situation production need not be constrained by market size. Exports to foreign markets can spur the creation of a wide range of industries which may not have been possible if only the local market was available.

There is no correlation between size and growth. Some small

nations are known to have grown faster than larger ones. Some have even attained standards of living equal or superior to that of larger and better endowed countries. A country, however, can grow, as Demas[7] pointed out some years ago, for a variety of reasons. It may have a high growth sector (e.g. oil, bauxite, tourism) that dominates the total economy. Substantial foreign capital inflows may also spur a rate of growth not warranted by domestic savings. Growth, Demas was at pains to show, was not synonymous with development. 'It is my view that the fundamental criterion of underdevelopment is the extent to which an economy has undergone structural transformation and has acquired the continuing capacity to adapt and to apply innovation.'[8] He went on to state that while structural transformation is usually associated with a continuous increase in real income per capita, the converse was not necessarily true, for reasons indicated earlier. Concern with the basic conditions permitting a situation of self-sustained growth led Demas to define 'development' not in terms of per capita income but in terms of a structural transformation of the economy so that:[9]

1 the degree of dualism between the productivity of different sectors, and at a later stage, different regions, is reduced;
2 surplus labour is eliminated and drawn into high productivity employment;
3 subsistence production is eliminated and a national market is established for goods and services;
4 the share of manufacturing and services in Gross Domestic Product is increased in response to the changing composition of demand;
5 the volume of inter-industry transactions increases, mainly as a result of the growth of the manufacturing sector;
6 the ratio of imports to GDP falls in the long run — although the volume of imports increases absolutely — and the composition of imports shifts away from consumer to intermediate and capital goods; and
7 the economy becomes not only more diversified, but more flexible and adaptable as a result of underlying political, social and institutional changes.

The concept of development used by Demas was posed more in terms of a final configuration, rather than as a process and it provided a great deal of speculation about the choices open to the small countries in the Caribbean with their small markets and narrow resource base. Certainly, the establishment of a wide range of industries, particularly heavy ones could not be a realistic objective. The natural variables of population and physical size are facts of life.

The view was to emerge that, given their natural constraints, small countries could not conceive their development in terms of the experience of the larger industrial states. For instance, with respect to inter-industry linkages, there is certainly limited scope for such a development, as would be the case for the variety of goods that could be produced. In restructuring their production base from extreme dependence on primary production, it is not only domestic demand that would have to be taken into account, but foreign demand as well, since it is trade (in both product and services) that holds the key to the survival of these countries. The composition of demand never remains the same, and, therefore, the production base that serves it must be responsive not only to this fact, but to the changes in international costs of production.

Available data indicate countries that have developed dynamic export sectors have also tended to experience a rapid growth in imports which often exceed the volume of exports. Without these imports, exports could not be produced, and without exports it would be difficult to sustain the desired level of raw materials, capital equipment, etc. Since export success can result in a situation where a successful country is singled out for 'special treatment', this means that even though small countries may reduce their weaknesses in certain senses, they are always likely to remain vulnerable, given their limited capacity to retaliate.

This vulnerability is reinforced in other areas. Small countries that have experienced high levels of activity resulting from commodity booms have shown a strong tendency not to be able to retain capital. Given the frequent changes in fortunes there is an inherent instability which may have no relationship to political realities and which encourage residents to seek the safety of financial systems of the developed nations. This practice often has less to do with financial returns, and more to do with insecurity stemming from a perception of transience in booms. This process of capital export takes place even while the government may be seeking resources from foreign sources. If funds held by residents outside the country are taken into account, many developing countries might end up being net lenders rather than net borrowers from abroad.

The emigration of skilled people (who are often trained at the state's expense) is another factor that has affected the development of small countries, the latter often have to rely on foreigners to fill key positions necessary for the functioning of the state apparatus and in the private sector.

Even though many of the development plans drawn up by developing countries in the post-independence years have fallen by the wayside, government's intervention in the economy is still seen as a critical element in the development process. In these countries questions have remained about the extent to which governments can influence development with or without plans, given the crucial variables which are outside their control. The frequent divergence between objectives and strategies underscore the point. Though the experience of the 1960s and 1970s points to shortcomings in certain kinds of policies, the way ahead in the light of developments in the world economy is not as clear as is often stated. The paths open to developing countries and particularly the small ones are still fraught with controversy. Some ideas are more appealing than others. 'Economic development', Best pointed out in a review of Demas' book in 1965 was 'a problem of management, of timing, sequencing and manipulation of an unending effort to perceive or create, and in any case, to exploit a multiplicity of little openings and opportunities.'[10] This meant that given limited natural resources, capital and skills, small countries could not afford to approach development like the larger, better endowed states. There was smaller room for mistakes. Countries had to choose carefully not only against the background of available resources and skills, but against trends in the world economy. Comparative advantage changes over time. Resilience has to be built into the production structure if it is to respond to changes in demand and new opportunities.

It is often argued that one of the advantages of small size is that it forces 'a country towards stronger export orientation and hence greater openness, with all the benefits associated with these. A country's basic economic position in the broadest sense, including size, location and resource endowment often dictates the orientation of its policy, and small countries are more often than not inclined towards outward orientation, while large countries with more diverse potential tend to stress import substitution. Among the small economies in the world those with export-oriented policies have achieved the highest rates of growth such as, for example, Malta, Botswana and Mauritius. Robust empirical evidence suggests that open trade policies are associated with higher growth rates, more efficient adjustment and more national resource allocation.[11]

The experience of Caribbean countries has shown this is not inevitable. Here policies have tended to be very inward looking, with heavy emphasis on import substitution. High levels of protection have resulted in high cost production structures producing largely for the domestic and regional markets. Official policies have been directed not towards increasing efficiency or improving resource allocation, but towards replacing imports by domestic production with employment creation as a subsidiary objective. Traditional industries (sugar, oil, bauxite, bananas and tourism) have been the driving force in these economies providing the foreign exchange for the import substitution strategy. The availability of protected foreign markets for the high cost sugar and banana industries have served to discourage a more rational allocation of the resources tied up in these industries. Declining production in some areas, and problems in international markets are inducing new approaches to development with an increasing emphasis on exports of non-traditional goods. This, of course, would require not only changes in policies, but a transformation and reorientation of attitudes.

Whatever may be the pressures on policy makers to deliver, a fundamental fact that has to be recognised is that the standard of living must be related to what the country can afford, and must move in line with the national effort. If consumption has to be perpetually sustained with foreign savings, then the standard of living is artificial, and could not be maintained for long. To have any impact, external resources must be directed towards improving the productive capacity of the country, if future servicing is not to become a burden. Domestic incomes must also be related to productivity. There is a feeling in some quarters that the latter is simply a function of labour performance. Far from it. Productivity in any enterprise reflects management prowess, organisation and technology. All these in turn are influenced by government's macro-policies and the efficiency of its servicing arms. As indicated earlier, because of its traditional role, the possible impact of the civil service on economic performance is often ignored or forgotten.

Also as noted earlier, Commonwealth Caribbean countries are now generally regarded in international circles as middle income countries. Since the International Development Agency (the soft loans window of the World Bank) now lends to countries with a per capita GNP below US$791 (in 1984 dollars), it means that almost all Commonwealth Caribbean countries have become ineligible for funds from this source. Certain countries (e.g. Trinidad and Tobago) are also excluded from the ordinary resources of the Bank because of their high per capita incomes. In recent years concessional funds have played an important part in helping to develop the infrastructure of the OECS countries and Belize. These countries would not only find it burdensome to service hard loans, but would find it extremely difficult to borrow in international markets, given their size and the structure of their economies. In such a situation it would be difficult to sustain the momentum of recent years. In the less developed countries, the development of their infrastructure is crucial to their economic growth. Even the more developed countries such as Barbados, Jamaica and Trinidad and Tobago have expressed dissatisfaction over the use of per capita income as a criterion for economic assistance.

Against this background, it is easy to see why Caribbean politicians generally tend to look for Marshall-type plans to solve the problems of the region. The small amount of aid funds made available under the US Caribbean Basin Initiative was a source of great disappointment to those who have been campaigning for a massive aid plan for the region. The preoccupation with foreign aid and the tendency to view it as perhaps the most critical factor in stimulating growth and development has resulted in a lack of action in a number of crucial areas, which no doubt has affected the rate of progress in the region. In many instances the failure to modernise tax systems and to enforce tax laws are partly responsible for the relatively slow growth of government revenue. Governments have also allowed current expenditure to grow faster than recurrent revenues with the result that public sector savings tend to be small or non-existent. A major item in current expenditure is wages and salaries which have been allowed to grow faster than productivity. The growth of wages and salaries has resulted not only from employing increasing numbers (sometimes even when they are not needed), but also from increases in wages and salaries stemming from cost of living changes and union pressure. Because of poor management and inefficient operation, the public utilities in many cases have had to pitch their rates far below the cost of operation with the result that the central governments have to provide heavy subsidies to these enterprises. There has also been a tendency to operate welfare services at a scale that public revenues cannot afford. These services themselves have been poorly administered in that very often the objectives have not been realised.

Failure to reorganise the public service to meet the challenges of independence has had serious implications for the implementation of government policy. The heavy politicisation of the public service in the early post-independence years has tended to discourage thinking and professionalism. The policy of promotion by seniority rather than by qualification or performance has played a major part in the rut that now besets the public service in the region. Failure to mesh training and qualifications with assignment or duties has also helped. Training itself has suffered because of failure to take advantage of opportunities offered and to reward achievements properly. The education system has also lagged in terms of the requirements of economic development and it has taken a long time for policy makers to recognise the important role of education in attaining economic goals. The content of programmes is only now receiving serious attention in the context of the shortages of certain types of skills and the serious unemployment problem. The region is paying a heavy price for this neglect.

Though governments were quick to establish foreign representation abroad, generally at very high costs following independence, these offices have not been staffed or structured to meet any clear objectives with respect to promoting or protecting the countries' economic interests. Commonwealth Caribbean countries have also been slow in taking advantage of their membership of regional and international organisations, with the result that opportunities for training and other types of assistance have often been lost. Years after independence, agricultural development is still affected by land tenure and marketing problems, access roads, inadequate credit and technical assistance facilities, institutional reorganisation, etc. Adequate and relevant research is also lacking. As a result of the latter factor, there is still a great deal of ignorance with respect to soil potential, optimum size of farms in various lines of production, treatment of prevalent disease and marketing problems.

The fact is that while the persistence of certain problems can be explained by structural factors stemming from size, attitudes, approaches and policies do have a bearing. In these latter areas financial resources are not the most important constraints. Political will and the articulation of problems in a way which specific policies could target are often missing. It is not often realised that timely action could prevent small problems turning into large ones, or that decisions in what are seen as minor areas could have a profound impact on growth and output. While foreign capital does have a role to play, there are problems in these societies which no amount of foreign resources could resolve. In fact, in some ways the problems can be exacerbated, if the country saves less, pays no attention to productivity, misallocates resources, spends excessively and operates policies detrimental to sectors vital to the economic wellbeing of the country. Vulnerability is as much the product of structural factors as economic policy and political management.

Commonwealth Caribbean countries have inherited political arrangements whose relevance in the context of the prevailing social and economic structure has often been questioned. Failure of these arrangements to work in the desired way has sometimes resulted in violence and social tensions which have led to cleavages and fragmentation in the societies. In this situation, the full mobilisation of human resources in the development effort has not taken place.

Commonwealth Caribbean societies (as distinct from officialdom) have lacked a development consciousness which needs to be developed and nurtured if government policies are to be supported and effectively implemented. In this exercise, there is need for institutional reorganisation and innovation of a kind which could facilitate the implementation of development policies and increase the participation of the population in the political development process.

In the printed media, competent and frequent analyses of developments in the various fields are lacking. News is generally reported with sensationalism determining the extent of coverage and conspicuousness. Foreign news coverage is minimal and is generally relegated to some obscure corner of the newspapers. This, to some extent, explains why the population of these countries have difficulty understanding and interpreting events which have implications on their lives, and this failing tends to condition their reaction to policies. Undereducation has helped in perpetuating underdevelopment. The general education system itself has contributed immensely to this situation. With respect to television (which is generally state-owned and monopolised), the heavy emphasis on entertainment has precluded a larger explicit role for education. After more than twenty-five years of operation in some cases, television is still essentially a conduit for foreign programmes. There has been little attempt to use this powerful medium as an educational tool without eliminating its entertainment function. The excuse that the costs involved in such a policy would be exorbitant reflects essentially an insular perception of the question, and does not take into account the economies that may be derived from using a regional approach.

In the development process the impact of effective communication has been greatly underrated, and this no doubt explains the lackadasical approach taken to the question. That calls for reform and critical assessment of the role of the printed media should be taken as a threat to the freedom of the press, or in the case of television as an intent by the ruling parties to intensify political propaganda, not only seriously underrates the perception of the public, but perhaps even more importantly, reflects the lack of faith in institutions aimed at protecting freedom of speech and expression. If this freedom is to be exercised with responsibility, as is intended, it has to be continuously assessed and criticised.

There are certainly some advantages in smallness, but attention has generally focused on the disadvantages. Smallness, as indicated earlier, not only facilitates the communication of ideas and the movement of goods, but should also make the planning of economic activity less difficult in terms of execution and balance. Very often it is not the size of a project that matters, but its efficiency, and this often depends on conceptualisation and management. Rather than rely on traditional concepts of development, small countries have to think out carefully what they can do best, and the kind of organisation best suited for doing this. The sharp separation, for instance, between firms and households may be totally irrelevant for these countries in the context of the need to keep fixed costs low and to utilise traditional skills. Mesmerised by big technology, Commonwealth Caribbean countries have allowed their artisan trades to die a slow death. The fact is that many small countries have been 'intimidated' by technology and the transnational corporations, and have receded into an inferiority mode in which all things local are seen to have little or no value, and all things foreign, including irrelevant technology, are deemed to have the germ of future development. Self-contempt is pervasive. The recent economic crises, if nothing else, have forced a re-examination of traditional approaches to development, particularly in the light of the fact that some small countries have done well in the international economy. Even if these countries do not provide exact models to follow, they do often serve as useful lessons. In the following section we review the experiences of certain Far East countries whose economic performances in recent years have drawn world-wide attention.

The relevance of the Far East experience

Developing countries are a very heterogeneous group. They are to be found in all parts of the world. They differ in size, in resources, in physical make-up, in cultural traits, in the degree of state intervention, in political systems and in historical experience. All these factors tend to affect their approach to development. In practice, countries that have made progress or have retrogressed cannot be classed in any particular paradigm. Nations can follow roughly similar paths and still end with a different experience. We say roughly because while some approaches may be common to certain countries, they may differ in certain other essential respects. Even the very fact of location may have a critical influence on countries pursuing almost identical models.

In recent years a great deal of attention has come to focus on what is called in the literature the newly industrialising countries (NICs) such as Argentina, Brazil, Mexico, India, Singapore, Hong Kong, South Korea and Taiwan. The last four are often referred to collectively as the Asian Tigers or the Gang of Four. Most of these countries have not only experienced a fast growth in output, particularly in the manufacturing sector, but have also been able to expand significantly their manufactured and semi-manufactured exports. The policies which have led to this development are being closely studied by other developing countries trying to reformulate their development strategies against a background of stagnation or retrogression. Even Japan, which one might not wish to classify as a NIC because of its relatively longer industrial experience, has also been a subject for study because of its miraculous recovery from the ruins of World War II and its becoming one of the most dynamic exporters in the world. The fact that Japan has few natural resources makes the Japanese performance all the more significant. Hong Kong, Singapore, Taiwan and South Korea also share this feature in different degrees. The performance of these countries has not only cast new light on the question of development, but they are now looked upon as examples to emulate. What these Asian states have demonstrated is that policies are a critical variable in the growth process. In the following section we take a brief look at the experience and strategies of the Far East.[12]

Hong Kong

Hong Kong has been a British crown colony since 1844. It consists of a small part of the Chinese mainland and a scattering of offshore islands, the most important of which is Hong Kong island. The area of the colony is about 400 square miles (1045 km^2), of which only 14% is cultivable. 80% of the food supply is imported. The colony is almost entirely devoid of natural resources. Its 1985 population was estimated to be around 5.4 million. With a density of over 10 000 people per square mile, Hong Kong has one of the highest population densities in the world.

Hong Kong was declared a free port in 1841, and until World War II, when it fell into Japanese occupation, served as an entrepôt for British trade with southern China. After the war trade picked up again, but was interrupted by the outbreak of the Korean War in 1950 and the subsequent UN embargo on exports of strategic goods to China and the US restriction on any trade with China. In order to survive, the population turned to domestic manufacturing for export markets. In nominal terms exports grew by twenty-nine times between 1960 and 1980 at an average annual rate of over 18%.

The transformation of Hong Kong's economy from a trading to

an industrial economy in the post-war period was assisted by several fortuitous factors. 'The Communist revolution in China produced a massive influx of refugees, but most importantly, it also resulted in Shanghainese capital and entrepreneurial skills moving to the safe haven of Hong Kong. Hong Kong's industrial revolution is thus attributed to three resources brought with the Chinese political refugees: a surplus of labour, new industrial techniques from the north and new capital-seeking employment and security. Additional circumstances favouring investment in industry included the relatively high adaptability and diligence of this labour force, the weak trade union organisation, the lack of legislation fixing minimum wages and limiting working hours, and the extremely low taxation on business profits. In the absence of strongly established trade unions, it became customary for individual bargains for employment to be struck, which tended to keep wage costs low. As there was also little objection to night work, or to relatively long working hours, machines could be run very economically. Leniency of labour regulations contributed to labour supply being highly competitive and thus kept labour costs low.'[13]

In recent years the economy has been among the fastest growing in the world. Between 1973 and 1985 real GNP is estimated to have grown by an average rate of 8.7%. Per capita GNP grew by almost 7% over the period. This growth has been accompanied by a high rate of employment despite the influx of immigrants. Unemployment was estimated to be about 4% in September 1982. One of the most important factors in the performance of the economy in recent years has been the growth of exports, particularly light manufactured goods. While Hong Kong exports a wide range of products, the textiles and clothing industries are the largest in the economy, employing about 41% of the total industrial workforce and producing some 41% by value of total domestic exports.[14] The electronics industry is the second largest export-earner among the manufacturing industries. This industry comprises over 1300 factories employing almost 90 000 workers, and produces a wide range of products including radios, computer memory systems, calculators, micro computers, etc.[15]

Besides its industrial activities, Hong Kong is also an international financial centre. In 1983 there were about 128 licenced banks.

One of the salient features of the Hong Kong economy is the *laissez-faire* framework which is sometimes compared with the nineteenth century liberalism. Government controls on the private sector are minimal. 'There are no protective tariffs or subsidies and few efforts to direct private activities through planning. A competitive free enterprise system is encouraged and, equally important, virtually no attempt is made to distort factor prices in favour of any particular type of project or industry. There are no investment allowances, tax holidays, or government preferential treatment to small businesses other than through a slightly progressive tax system on profits.'[16] Monetary and fiscal policies are also generally not used since there seems to be limited scope for such instruments. In fact there is no Central Bank. 'The currency system in Hong Kong is an exchange standard with the currency issued by private banks against 100% reserves of foreign exchange... The use to which the reserves (foreign) are put is the outcome of a collection of decisions by individuals and institutions. It is these decisions, and not those of the government that determine what fraction of these reserves become backing for the currency.'[17]

The Republic of Korea (South Korea)

The Republic of Korea (South Korea) has an area of 98 484 km^2 and a population of 40.6 million (1985). This country, which has little natural resources and is 70% mountainous, came into being at the end of World War II by the partition of the Korean peninsula which had been occupied by Japan since the early 1900s. Partition was soon followed by the Korean War which lasted for the period 1950–55. In the 1950s primary production dominated economic activity accounting for between 40% and 50% of GNP, as compared to less than 10% for manufacturing. Exports of goods and non-factor services as a percentage of GNP amounted to less than 5% of GNP.

In the period from the mid-1950s to the early 1960s industrial activity was aimed largely at the local markets. In the early 1960s a programme of rapid industrialisation was put in hand. Though the country initially had to import almost all its raw material input (including oil) and capital goods, and also had to depend on foreign aid and borrowings, it was able to lay the basis for a significant export capacity in a short space of time. By the mid-1960s, exports of goods and non-factor services were amounting to almost 10% of GNP, by 1970 15% and by 1975 to around 30%. Manufactured goods and certain specialised services have played a crucial role in this development.

South Korea has acquired a world reputation in electronic components, steel, ship-building, automobiles and civil engineering. In the mid-1970s the country embarked on a further programme of heavy and chemical industries. As a percentage of GNP, manufacturing increased from 14% in 1965 to around 20% in 1970 and to over 30% in 1975. Manufactured goods which accounted for less than 50% of exports in 1965 grew to almost 75% in the mid-1970s. GNP itself grew by an average of over 11% between 1965 and 1970 as compared to 6.2% in the period 1960–65 and 3.8% in 1955–60. In the period 1973–85 this dropped to around 7.1%. In the last twenty years the economy has grown by an average of 8% per year. Per capita GNP has also increased, experiencing a growth rate of over 5% between 1973 and 1985 as compared to less than 4% in the early 1960s. From a poor backward country in the 1950s South Korea now has a per capita GNP in excess of US$2000. This accomplishment, however, has been achieved in an authoritarian political framework in which the role of the unions has been relatively minor.

The rapid growth of exports from the early 1960s corresponded with increasing incentives to exports and liberalisation of the economy. It is important to point out, however, that the export programme grew out of an import substitution strategy which was systematically pursued from the mid-1950s to the early 1960s. The intensification of the export drive was assisted not only by interest and exchange rate policies, but by linking the granting of import licences to export performance.

Taiwan

Located near the south-east coast of the Chinese mainland, Taiwan (which comprises one large island and several smaller ones) has a land area of 36 000 km^2 (13 900 sq. miles) of which less than one-third is arable. In 1985 the population was estimated to be around 19.3 million. Under Japanese colonialism (1895–1945), Taiwan was developed as a supplier of food for Japan. In the aftermath of World War II, the island became a province of China, but this status was short-lived and political and economic separation was effected in 1949, which marked the beginning of major economic reforms.

In 1952 agriculture accounted for 90% of exports, 56% of GDP and employed 56% of the labour force. Data available for the mid-1950s indicate that in this period Taiwan was still heavily dependent on primary production which accounted for over 30% of GDP as compared to about 15% for manufacturing. In 1955 manufactured exports accounted for only 7.6% of total exports, but by the mid-1970s this share had grown to over 90%. In 1976 manufacturing's share in GDP amounted to 30%. With respect to employment, manufacturing activities have provided jobs for an increasing proportion of the labour force, employment in the sector increasing by an average rate of almost 7% per annum between 1952 and 1976. Correspondingly, there has been a rapid decline in the relative contribution of agriculture which in 1983 accounted for 7% of exports, 6% of GDP and employed 17% of the labour force. Overall, real GNP increased by an average rate of almost 7% per annum between 1952 and 1976, while real per capita GNP averaged almost 4.8% in the period. Since 1976 real GDP has grown at an average rate of 8%, as compared to over 13% for export volume.

Following the separation from China in 1949, a number of developments forced Taiwan to rethink seriously its development strategy. Among these were the rapid increase in population and the loss of major markets for its agricultural products. Even if it wanted to increase its primary production, land was a constraining factor, as was the small domestic market for a major import substitution drive. The fact that military expenditure was absorbing a significant part of the nation's output compounded the difficulties. It was obvious to the policy-makers that whatever strategy they adopted they could not afford to ignore food production which was required to feed the rapidly increasing population. In fact, the measures used to transform the agricultural sector not only succeeded in increasing food production, but also in raising income in the sector which provided some of the capital for industrial expansion. In Taiwan agricultural development assisted industrial growth both directly and indirectly.

In order to encourage industrial performance the government experimented with a number of devices in the 1950s. One such measure was the linking of foreign exchange availability to export performance. This was used for a very short period and was replaced by a quota system of commodity imports. A multiple exchange rate system bolstered by tariff and non-tariff measures were also used during the 1950s to encourage import substitution. 'Implementing a complicated system of multiple exchange rates imposed considerable administrative costs. Also, the system of foreign exchange allocation discriminated among categories of commodities without an economic rationale, induced entrepreneurs to compete for licences rather than to lower production costs, and encouraged corruption. At the same time, the preferential allocation of under-valued foreign exchange for imported raw material and capital equipment created incentives to expand capacity even when existing capacity was not fully used. The squeeze on agriculture through the allocation of foreign exchange also depressed the incomes and consumption of farmers.'[18]

The decline in growth rates during the late 1950s encouraged the authorities to adopt more outward looking policies. The overvalued currency was brought down to more realistic levels in ordôt to encourage exports, and the multiple exchange rate system was replaced by a basic official exchange rate and an exchange certificate rate. Tariffs were reduced and the import quota system was removed. Other import controls were gradually liberalised. Protection for domestic producers was not totally abolished. To receive protection, however, they 'had to show that the quantity and quality of their products were adequate to satisfy domestic demand and that the cost of imported raw material did not exceed 70% of total product costs. Also, the ex-factory price of the controlled commodity was not allowed to exceed the prices of comparable imports (inclusive of all duties) by more than 25% in 1960. In 1964 this ratio was reduced to 15%, in 1968 to 10%, and in 1973 by 5%.'[19]

Side by side with these measures a range of incentives to encourage exports was introduced. These included rebates of customs duties and commodity tax on imported raw materials, exemption from business and related stamp duties and income tax reduction based on export performance, export insurance and low interest loans for working capital. A number of export promotion facilities were also set up by government with the aim of providing managerial, technical and trade consultation. To facilitate the assembly industries a number of export processing zones were set up. Besides the measures taken in the real sector the policy-makers also saw the need for financial growth. To encourage savings, for example, savers were offered a positive real rate of return.

Singapore

With an area of 581 km^2 Singapore is slightly smaller than St Lucia and about one-eighth the size of Trinidad and Tobago. Jamaica is almost twenty times as large. Singapore's 1985 population of 2.5 million people was larger than that of Trinidad and Tobago (1.187 m) and Jamaica's (2.2 m) respectively.

Singapore, like Hong Kong, is a city state located on a small island at the southern tip of the West Malaysian peninsula. Its location and harbour contributed to its emergence as an entrepôt centre in the nineteenth century. For the first half of the twentieth century, entrepôt trade continued to play an important part in the economic life of the country, but changing trading habits by countries in the region and increasing domestic unemployment, as a result of a high population growth rate, led to increased uneasiness about the ability of the entrepôt trade to provide jobs, so encouraging the intensification of the industrialisation effort.

The period from 1959 to the mid-1960s witnessed the introduction of a series of measures (tax relief, financial and technical assistance, etc.) designed to encourage production for the home market or for export. The system of protection was strengthened in this phase, but was reviewed regularly in relation to the production performance of particular industries. Merger with Malaya in 1963 was intended to widen the domestic market. Failure to realise an intended common market and the separation of Singapore from Malaysia in 1965 shifted the emphasis increasingly from import substitution to export orientation. These policies were bolstered in the early 1970s by measures aimed at attracting higher technology industries aimed at regional and world markets.

The impact of Singapore's strategy is readily apparent in certain major economic indicators. Between 1960 and 1970 real GNP more than doubled, while real per capita GDP increased by 92% in the period. Growth continued into the 1970s and early 1980s. Between 1973 and 1985 GNP is estimated to have grown by almost 8% per annum as compared to 6.5% for real per capita GNP. Domestic exports as a percentage of GDP increased from 10% in 1960 to 50% in 1973. The rate of unemployment dropped from 13.5% in 1960 to 4.5% in 1973 with manufacturing providing jobs for 26% of the employed labour force in 1973, as compared to 7.5% in 1960. As a percentage of GDP, manufacturing's share increased from 12.0% in 1960 to over 20% in the early 1970s. The share of entrepôt trade dropped correspondingly by about 50% in this period. Gross National Savings as a percentage of GNP has shown a remarkable increase since 1960, reaching around 25% in the early 1970s compared to less than 10% in 1960.

The rapid expansion in exports has encouraged a high level of imports. The trade balance has tended to be consistently negative. Singapore's foreign exchange earnings have come not only from merchandise exports, but from a wide range of services, including tourism and finance. Overall, the current account has tended to be negative, a major financing item being inflows of direct foreign investment. Total foreign reserves stood at US$12846.6 million at the end of 1985 as compared to US$3363.8 million at the end of 1976.

The role of the state has varied in the four countries. 'Public policy towards primary input markets, especially labour, assisted the export effort indirectly by providing education and vocational training, offering incentives to upgrade labour skills, and allowing wages to be determined largely through the interplay of supply and demand. Minimum wage legislation was shunned, employee benefits were seldom mandated, and barriers to labour mobility were not erected. As a result, firms chose labour intensive production methods that put to work large numbers of urban unemployed and migrants from agriculture plus the flood of refugees in the case of Hong Kong.'[20] In Singapore 'The government took major equity positions in companies and sought repeatedly to influence investment and other business decisions. To guide industrial development, the South Korean government worked closely with about a dozen private sector conglomerates. Taiwan's government has kept its ownership of commercial banks. The Hong Kong authorities, by contrast, followed *laissez-faire* policies. But in none of these countries were state-owned companies allowed to distort labour and other markets or burden public finances excessively.'[21]

Generally, macro-economic policies were aimed at discouraging consumption and boosting savings. Exchange rates were managed in line with objectives of competitiveness. With respect to the role of foreign capital and technology 'Hong Kong, Singapore and Taiwan actively sought out multinational direct investment. Modern technology was acquired through licensing, technical agreements, and imports of the latest machines; also many US companies were enticed to contract out component parts or finished goods. By contrast, South Korea relied mainly on foreign loan capital, maintaining restrictions on foreign ownership, profit remittances and capital repatriation. The government encouraged local firms to analyse and supplement the elements of imported technology – a policy that has put the country well ahead of the other Asian NICs in technological self reliance.'[22]

Concluding observations

In the case of Taiwan, South Korea and Singapore export performance grew out of an import substitution phase. In the case of Hong Kong, which has a fairly large home market compared to a number of other developing countries, this was not the case. The question of strategy has often been posed in terms of import substitution or export orientation. Experience has shown this need not be the case, if short term policies are fashioned in relation to longer term objectives. In the Caribbean where the emphasis has been on national import substitution, policies for increasing efficiency have largely been absent. Most industries established as 'pioneer' or 'infant' are unable to compete with imports (thus requiring continued protection) and generally have been put under no pressure to export. The foreign exchange required to pay for inputs have tended to come from tourism and the traditional export sectors. The export incentives used have largely been ineffective. High levels of unemployment have tended to encourage policy-makers to continue to afford protection, even in cases where industries show no signs of growth or development after many years of establishment.

It is often argued that the objective factors of size, lack of resources, small domestic market, etc. may force a country to be very dependent on the outside world. Size itself (or what some people may call the structural factor), however, may not be sufficient to compel the adoption of policies designed to lead to a rational allocation of resources. It is policies to a large extent that determine the nature of the relationship with the international economy. These policies relate not only to incentives or to the regime of protection, but to the selection of the kind of industries on which one is going to tie one's sail. In this selection process comparative advantage may be a factor, but since this in itself changes over time, it has to be done in the context of development and trends in the world economy. The production structure aimed at must be one that is resilient and able to respond to changes in international demand.

Hong Kong, South Korea, Taiwan and Singapore have not only achieved remarkable growth rates in recent years, but have become major exporters (*See* Table 11.2). In 1984 Brazil's exports totalled US$27.0 billion as compared to US$24.1 billion for Singapore, US$29.2 billion for South Korea, US$28.3 billion for Hong Kong and US$30.2 billion for Taiwan.

The question has often been asked whether Caribbean countries can emulate the examples of the Far East. Certainly as far as the use of policies are concerned there are important lessons to be learnt. Lack of resources and size are not serious impediments to development in an open world system. Taken together, Caribbean countries may have a better resource endowment than some Asian countries. It is worth pointing out, however, that the export performance of the Far East countries was made possible by a world that was less protectionist than at the present time. High levels of unemployment in the industrial countries have made them more conscious of the need to protect many of their industries from the effects of foreign

Table 11.2 Data on selected NICs

	Average annual % change 1976–86		Value of exports US $ million	
Countries	Real GDP	Export volume	1970	1984
Hong Kong	8.6	8.4	2 514	28 317
South Korea	7.2	13.5	835	29 245
Singapore	6.5	8.3	1 554	24 108
Taiwan	8.0	13.2	n.a.	30 185
Argentina	0.4	9.0	1 773	8 107
Brazil	3.4	12.8	2 739	27 005
Chile	4.6	7.7[a]	1 234	3 657
Mexico	3.7	6.6	1 311	23 602

[a] 1978–86
Source: Morgan Guaranty, *World Financial Markets*, January, 1987; UN, *International Trade Statistics Yearbook*, 1985.

competition.[23]. Even countries exporting insignificant amounts of particular products have been affected by the protectionist surge in major industrial countries. One may choose to see the present attitudes to protect as part of the global restructuring process. International trade will continue to grow. The strategy for small countries is to find niches, exploit little openings, and generally put themselves in a position to seize whatever opportunities come their way. In the case of the Caribbean, the US Caribbean Basin Initiative and the Lomé Convention provide market outlets which are yet to be taken advantage of.

The strategies on growth, employment and exports often do not tell the whole story about the development experience of the small Asian countries. Military threats (in two cases) and population pressures have produced a degree of industriousness which may be difficult to find elsewhere. The *laissez-faire* framework found in Hong Kong may have no counterpart anywhere else, and certainly Caribbean policy-makers may find that environment difficult to emulate. Hong Kong is a very special case which is partly the result of its history and its location. In the case of Taiwan, Singapore and South Korea, there has been a high degree of autocracy in their political arrangements. The heavily supply-weighted market has been left to determine wages. The role of trade unions has been limited and the indications are that despite a great deal of social progress, wage levels and working conditions in certain cases leave a great deal to be desired. Many writers who have drawn attention to the 'success stories' of the Far East often emphasise that their concern is the economic policies used, and not the socio-political framework within which growth has taken place. Very often little is said about the distribution of income, regional developments, or general social conditions. In the Caribbean where the right to strike, to agitate, and to criticise is deeply embedded in the national psyche, 'leaving the sharing of the cake until it is completely baked' is not an easy proposition, particularly in the absence of consensus on strategy and national priorities.

The considerable controversy which the setting up of Export Processing Zones (EPZs) or Free Trade Zones have generated demonstrates some of these points. Despite the existence of a great deal of unemployment in the region, the perception that EPZs are based on the payment of exploitative wages and poor working conditions has resulted in a certain amount of opposition to their establishment. In an area grown accustomed to a fairly high standard of living, the lowering of wages tends to meet with strong resistance. The link between trade unions and political parties in some cases reinforces this tendency.

Notes

1. See UNITAR, *Small States & Territories, Status and Problems*, New York, 1971, p.11.
2. See Edward Dommers, 'Some Distinguishing Characteristics of Island States', in *World Development*, Dec. 1980. The other articles in this special volume also highlight this issue.
3. UN, *Developing Island Countries*, New York, 1984, p.9, Sales No. E. 74.11.D.6.
4. See R. Kuznets, 'Economic Growth of Small Nations', in Austin Robinson (ed.) *The Economic Consequences of the Size of Nations*, London: Macmillan and Co. Ltd., 1963.
5. *Ibid*.
6. *Ibid*.
7. W.C. Demas, *The Economics of Development in Small Countries with Special Reference to the Caribbean*, Montreal: McGill University Press, 1965.
8. *Ibid*. p.6
9. *Ibid*. pp.11–20.

10 See Lloyd Best, 'Size and Survival', in *New World Quarterly*, Vol.2, No.3, Guyana Independence Issue, 1966.
11 Barend A. de Vries, 'Industrial Policy in Small Developing Countries', *Finance & Development*, June, 1984.
12 The data used in this section came largely from Bela Belassa and Associates, *Development Strategies in Semi-industrial Economics*, Baltimore: The Johns Hopkins University Press, 1982.
13 Alvin Rabushka, *The Changing Face of Hong Kong*, Washington, D.C.: American Enterprise Institute for Public Policy Research, 1973, p.12.
14 M.J. Parson (ed.), *Hong Kong 1983*, Government Information Services, Hong Kong, 1984.
15 *Ibid.* p.20.
16 William F. Baezer, *The Commercial Future of Hong Kong*, New York: Praeger Publishers, 1978, p.5.
17 *Ibid.* p.6.
18 Belassa & Associates, *op.cit.* p.315.
19 *Ibid.*
20 'The Asian NICs and US Trade', in Morgan Guaranty Trust Company of New York, *World Financial Markets*, January 1987.
21 *Ibid.*
22 *Ibid.*
23 Cline has argued that 'generalisation of the East Asian model of export-led development across all developing countries would result in untenable market penetration into industrial countries.' See W. Cline, 'Can the East Asian Model of Development be Generalised', *World Development*, Vol.10, No.2, 1982.

CHAPTER 12 | Concluding observations

The heavy dependence of the Commonwealth Caribbean countries on the international economy for trade, capital and technology makes these countries extremely vulnerable to external developments. The drop in the price of a single commodity easily puts these economies in a tail spin. Foreign exchange is the fuel that makes these economies function. Without it almost all activities grind to a halt. This problem was recognised long ago, and diversification of production and exports has long been on the development agenda of Caribbean governments. To do this, it was felt that national control had to be exercised over the 'commanding heights' of the economy – an object that has been relentlessly pursued in some countries of the region, not only because of the economic rationale underlying it, but because of the psychological imperative. Development plans have come and gone, and though both aggregate and per capita income have grown, in several important respects Commonwealth Caribbean countries have become more dependent on the outside world than before. In a real sense development continues to elude regional states who now find themselves not only having to cope with the consequences of an increasing population, but with a more complex external environment that calls for new approaches, more versatile skills and a greater understanding of the forces providing the dynamic to changes in the world system.

The strategies of development pursued by Commonwealth Caribbean governments in the post-war period has clearly not produced the kind of results that were anticipated. The industrialisation programme has been essentially an adoption of the Arthur Lewis strategy at the insular level. This has resulted in a new type of dependency which now literally pits Caribbean states against each other, notwithstanding the political rhetoric and the frequent commitments to regionalism. It is being increasingly recognised that there is a need for a new development strategy in the region, elements of which are still far from articulated. The increasing concern with dependency and its consequences is putting greater focus on the conception of self-reliance, though the policies necessary to give effect to this are still lacking. The need for food security programmes and for attaining self-sufficiency in food production have long been recognised as objectives by Caribbean governments. The fact is that although Caribbean countries are basically agricultural in nature, the region's food import bill has been increasing, and this in the face of foreign exchange problems. The use of agricultural resources is yet to be rationalised. Macro-economic policies used to encourage industrialisation have generally been biased against agricultural development. Industrial development, too, has suffered from the absence of a regional framework and a basic commitment to the complementary use of the region's natural resources. Integration projects have been conspicuously lacking.

The nature of the link between individual economies and the international economy would depend a great deal on the commitment to a regional strategy of development. Economic integration cannot be pursued in a *laissez-faire* fashion, or structures could emerge which reinforce dependency. There is need for careful long-term planning, a proper conceptualisation of the economic structures desired, and the kind of strategies necessary to effect these. Economic integration needs to be put at the centre of national and regional planning, if it is to serve as an effective instrument in Caribbean development.

Even if Commonwealth Caribbean countries were to achieve a high level of integration, they would still need to trade extensively with the outside world, given the small size of the regional market. This means the adoption of policies which could lead to the creation of competitive production structures. It also means participation in the persistent efforts by developing countries to lower or remove trade barriers affecting products of interest to them.

Co-operation with other developing countries needs to extend beyond trade. In some cases initiatives have been taken in the field of transport, technology, investment and resource exploitation. Considerable scope, however, exists for an intensification of South-South relations. If developing countries are to have a more effective voice in international negotiations, action must replace rhetoric. A large number of studies and reports have been done by various bodies pointing to areas where poor countries could strengthen their position by collaborative action. Bickering, distrust, boundary disputes, and political squabbles, however, have often served to prevent a full or even partial exploration of some of the possibilities to which attention has been drawn. The weakness of the South is not solely the result of policies pursued by the North. A great deal of it stems from their own lack of initiative, division among themselves, failure to help each other, poor internal social, political and economic policies and an inability to take full advantage of opportunities that crop up from time to time.

That they have often allowed themselves to be manipulated and played against each other by transnational corporations is symptomatic of the degree of division underlying the unity of position on many issues in international fora. The traditional rhetoric is wearing thin and becoming increasingly ineffective. There is a tendency by the South to view inputs from the North as necessary to the success of all their undertakings, and this has led to a great deal of inaction and delays in implementing programmes. The process of reducing dependence on the North must of necessity involve an approach by which the South begins to move quickly to identify and implement undertakings within its own capacity to do so.

Index

ACP states: and EC trade, 135−9
agriculture, 11, 22, 38−42, 271, 287; decline in, 11, 25, 36−7, 43−4; domestic, 37; exports, 139; and GDP, 1; and imports 121; and Lomé Agreement, 138; production of, 158; rationalisation, 161, 170, 175−6, 287; trade, 9
aid: concessions, xv, 249, 250; EC, 139; and foreign policy, 2; and middle income states, 269−70; policies, xiv; provision of, 5; and trade, 115, 163; US, and CBI, 139−42;
alumina, 40, 42−3, 77
aluminium, 76; demand for, 78
Anguilla: and offshore banking, 96, 106; 107, 108, 110
Antigua: economy of, 37; exports, 117; external debt, 196; GNP of, 51; investment, 193; and offshore banking, 96, 106; sugar in, 66−7; tourism in, 36, 86, 87; trade balance, 183
artisan trades: importance of, 273
Aruba: oil in, 80, 81
assembly-type industries, xiv, 26, 45, 141, 257; exports, 117; and imports, 125; in Montserrat, 40; in St Lucia, 41
authorised: agents, 98; dealers, 98, 99, 104

Bahamas, xiii, 27, 34; banks in, 100−1, 112; and drug trade, 110−11; economy, 37; exports, 117; GNP in, 33, 51; offshore banking, 96, 97, 98−102, 103, 106, 108; oil storage in, 81; tax haven, 97, 98, 111; tourism, 36, 86, 87; trust companies in, 100−1
Baker Plan, 190−3
balance of payments, 233; deficits, 109, 116, 144, 162, 192, 208, 210, 238, 250; and IMF, 214, 238; and

integration, 169; and US, 218; *see also* debt
bananas, 36, 41, 61, 69−76
banks: in Bahamas, 100−1, 112; commercial, 237; and external debt, 190, 191; *see also* loans; 'shell' banks
Barbados, xiii, 35; economy of, 38, 51; exports, 117; external debt, 194; imports, 120, 121; manufacturing in, 44; and offshore banking, 96, 106, 108; oil in, 82; size, 27; sugar in, 66−7; tax haven, 110; tourism in, 36, 86, 87; trade balance, 181
bauxite, 76−80, 183; decline in, 76, 78−80; in Grenada, 39; in Guyana, 40, 76; in Jamaica, 36, 42−3, 76−7; and prices, 61; as resource, 80
Belize: bananas in, 71; economy of, 38; exports, 117; external debt, 196; imports, 121, 125; size, 27; tourism in, 86, 87; trade balance, 183
Bermuda: as tax haven, 97
bi-lateralism, 145, 154, 169, 177
Bradley Plan, 190
Bretton Woods, international monetary system, 1, 3, 153, 213−15, 220, 225, 240; and exchange rates, 215−17; reform of, 211−13, 217−19

Canada: trade with, 128−30
capital: corporate, 16; and development, 104, 248, 281, 286; goods, imported, 36; and integration, 167; mobility, 217; movements, 180−209, 216, 222; and unemployment, 15; *see also* foreign investment
Caribbean Basin Recovery Act, 139, 140
CARIBCAN, 128−30, 159, 176
CARICOM, 43, 52, 169−70, 227;

289

assessment of, 172–8; imports, 121; and trade, 130–1, 160
Cayman Islands: offshore banking, 106, 108, 110; as tax haven, 97, 102, 111
CBI, US, 139–42, 159, 176, 204, 270, 283; criticism of, 140–2
Centrally Planned Economies, 7, 60, 153, 255; and trade, 12, 13
citrus growing: in Dominica, 38–9
colonialism: legacy of, xiv, 25, 159, 257, 271; and sugar, 65–6
Committee of 20, 211, 213, 222–3, 234
commodity: agreements, 57, 61–2; booms, 267; dependence on, 230; depression in, 116; and exchange rates, 228; exports, 56, 117, 183; prices, 52, 116; *see also under* prices
Commonwealth Caribbean: bananas in, 71–6; exports, 36, 122–3, 136–7; and external debt, 193–200; GNP, 30; integration in, 133, 142, 165–78; and international monetary system, 210–41; middle-income, 33; offshore finance in, 95–113; oil in, 82–3; population, 30; size of, 27, 30; sugar in, 65–9; tourism in, 86–91; trade, 115–42; unemployment in, 34
communication: and development, 272
conditionality: and funding, 237–40
costs: comparative, 150; high production, 26, 45, 75, 151, 268; offshore banking, 102–5; of tourism, 90
counter-trade, 22–3
credit-worthiness: and funding, 237
Curaçao: oil in, 80, 81
currencies: basket of, 229; blocs, 228; convertibility, 231; floating, 221, 222, 230–2
customs unions, 154, 166

debt, external, 1; accumulation, 186; in Commonwealth Caribbean, 193–200; crisis, 187; growth of, 180–209; international, 184–93; nations, 17, 188–9; pattern, 230; service ratio, 197; servicing, 6, 22, 51–2, 84, 156, 158, 186–7, 195, 204, 208, 224; and trade policies, 192
dependence, 286, 288; changes in, 36–7; and high import prices, 62; and integration, 177–8; and openness, 35–6; on tourism, 91
devaluation, 162, 232
developed countries, xiv, xv, 2, 116; and developing countries, 3–13, 135
developing countries, 1; and developed countries, 3–13, 135, 145; and development, 247–60; and exchange rate, 226–7; external debt of, 184; growth of, 2; influence of, 158; integration in, 168–9; in IMF, 241; and unemployment, 16–17
development, xiii, 247–60; capital, 104; changes in, 36–7; concept of, 266; economics, failure of, 251–4; framework of, 254–6; and IMF, 224–5; orientation, 253; planning, 150, 171, 252, 254–6, 267–8, 286, 287; policy, xiv, 26, 44, 95, 163, 184, 200; problems of, 2, 4; programmes, 193; and small states, 261–84; theories, 247–8, 251, 252–3; and tourism, 90, 91; and trade, 115
diversification: and exports, 120, 183; need for, 54, 56–7, 75, 91, 161, 286
Dominica: bananas in, 71; economy, 38–9; exports, 117, 120; external debt, 196; GNP of, 51; trade balance, 183
drugs: and offshore banking, 110–13
duty-free goods: and CBI, 139–40

economic: growth, and debts, 192–3; management, 53–4, 178; policies, 254; viability, xiii
economy: control of, 53; data on, 28–9; fragility of, 207–8; free enterprise, 255; interdependence, 145, 190; international, 1, 7; and offshore financial centres, 109; of scale, 160, 167, 175, 263; underground, 39; *see also* diversification; island economies; *and under* individual countries
education: and development, 258, 272
emigration, 17, 40, 267
employment: need for, 160; and offshore banking, 103, 104
energy: alternatives, and oil, 84–5; costs, 84, 125

entrepreneurship: development of, 167, 257–60
Euro-currency: operations, 98, 106; market, 99, 104, 106
European Community, 60, 165; financial assistance, 137–8; and foreign investment, 205; GNP, 165; as market, 69; and sugar quotas, 65; and trade, 15, 16, 126, 133–39, 157
European 'snake', 226
exchange controls, 214
exchange rates, 26, 104–5, 162, 187, 210, 215–17, 219, 220–1, 223, 225–32, 252; fixed, 217; floating, 223, 224, 226; forward market, 229; mechanism, 215; relations, 231; stability, 231
exports: of bananas, 71, 72–3; bias, 160; and CARICOM, 173; of Commonwealth Caribbean, 36, 117, 120, 122–3, 136–7, 159; domestic, 117, 120; and GDP, 35; invisible, 86; of oil, 83; and openness, 34, 36, 268; of sugar, 67; and UK, 126–7; to US, 140; volume, 9, world growth in, 7, 8

Far East: development in, 273–84
federation: political, 264
financing: facility, compensatory, 56, 60
floating exchange rates: *see under* currencies; exchange rates
food crop production, 160–1, 168, 287
food imports, 121, 287; cost of, 89; increase in, 11, 36, 50
foreign exchange, 160, 257, 286; crisis, 39, 208; earnings, 36, 37, 50–2, 88; and exports, 120; and imports, 121; lack of, 115, 116; and tourism, 86–8
foreign investment, xv, 25, 49, 167, 171, 175, 178, 182, 200–8, 251
FPDI, 182, 237; increase in, 184–5
fraud: and offshore banking, 110–11
free: market system, 144–5, 255, 276; trade, 152, 154, 158, 165, 166, 284
FSCs, 141
fuel: import of, 121, 125, 184
functional co-operation, 168, 175

gambling, casino, xiv, 89, 91
GATT, 5, 14, 153–5, 214–15

GDP, real, xv, 1, 17–18, 36–7, 194; and development, 249, 250; equation, 34; and service industries, 11, 37
Generalised System of Preferences, (GSP), 5, 137, 139, 140, 154, 159
GNP, 1, 22, 28–9, 30, 155, 186; development, 250; distribution of, 30–2; of EC, 135; growth of, 20–1, 33
government: and development, 251–2, 256–60; intervention, 159, 271; investment, 193, 200; revenue, 103; and trade, 152
Grenada: and bananas, 71; economy of, 39–40; exports, 117; external debt, 196; GNP of, 51; tourism in, 87, 88; trade balance, 183
Guyana, xiii, 156, 162, 173, 184, 193; bauxite in, 76–80; economy, 40, 50; exchange rate, 227; exports, 117; external debt, 194; GDP in, xv; GNP in, 33; imports, 121; investment, 193; manufacturing in, 45; size, 27; sugar in, 66–7; trade balance, 182

Heckscher-Ohlin theory, 147–8
HFCS, 65; and sugar prices, 64
Hong Kong: economy of, 265, 274–6; offshore banking in, 103
hurricanes, 40, 74; Gilbert, in Jamaica, 181; and production, 116

IBFs, 111–12
IBRD, 3, 153, 214
IMF, xiv, 3, 60, 153, 158, 196, 204, 208, 210, 213; Agreement, 3, 214–15; and Commonwealth Caribbean, 212; credit, 184, 216; intervention, 238–9; quotas, 237, 238; reform, 246; role, 220; voting in, 240
immigration controls, 17, 52
imports: growth in, 117; and living standards, 116; and markets, 36; ratios, 34; restrictions, 214; and SDRs, 235; structure of, 120, 124–6; and UK, 127
import substitution strategy, 43, 45, 120, 152, 160, 161, 167, 176, 252, 268, 281–2
income: average, 33; from bananas, 71; and development, 249; distribution, 249–50; groups, xv; increasing, 11; middle, 33, 269;

and population growth, 20; and tourism, 88
independence, political, xiii, 1, 3, 25, 54, 204, 254, 257, 264; and foreign control, 250; and integration, 169
industrialisation: in Commonwealth Caribbean, 25, 45, 252, 286, 287; and integration, 175, 167; and trade protection, 144, 155–60
industries, 45; light, 43; state ownership, 53; *see also* assembly-type
inflation, 223; and trade, 15
infrastructure, 207, 252, 264, 269; and external debt, 193, 200; and offshore banking, 105; and tourism, 88
insularity: problems of, 54–5
Integrated Programme for Commodities, 57, 60
integration, 133, 142, 165–78, 287; regional economic, 144, 264; theory, 166–8
interest rates: and foreign debt, 190
international monetary systems, 210–41; and LDCs, 210–11, 223–5; reform of, 211, 219–23
international organisations, 3–4
investment: and external debt, 193; international, 5; under CBI, 141; volume, 200; *see also* foreign
invisible earnings, 86, 156, 180
island economies, 27, 262; problems of, 263–4

Jamaica, xiii, 156, 173, 184, 193; Agreement, 219–21; bananas in, 71; bauxite in, 76–80; economy, 42–3, 50–1; exchange rate, 227; exports, 36, 117, 120; external debt, 186, 195, 208; GDP, xv; GNP, 30; and IMF, 210–11, 213; imports, 117, 121; investment, 193; manufacturing in, 44–5; size, 27; sugar in, 66–7; tourism in, 86, 87; trade balance, 180–1
Japan, 274; and foreign investment, 205; GNP, 166; and trade, 1, 13, 130, 157, 218–19

labour: low cost, 125, 141; and oil, 83; productivity, 147; and sugar, 69; supply, 49, 256; and trade theory, 150–1
land: demand for, 105; and tourism, 89; use, 43–4
Latin America: external debt, 186–7; trade with, 131–2
LDCs, 170, 173, 178; exchange rates, 227–32; external debt, 196–200; GNP in, 155; international monetary system, 210–11, 232–5, 238, 241; and monetary reform, 223–5; and SDR, 232–5
Lewis: Sir Arthur, 49; model, 25, 49, 286
licence fees: and offshore banking, 103, 109
loans: and external debt, 191, 195–6, 197; and middle income states, 269
Lomé Convention, 133–5, 159, 176, 177, 207, 283; III, 135–8

Malthusian model, 20
manufacturing, 11, 36, 41, 160, 257; capacity, 13, 14; diversification, 54; emergence of, 43–50; failure of, 161; and GDP, 48; production, 9, 14, 25; sectors, 46–7; trade, 9, 132; types of, 45
market: access, 5, 167; and bananas, 74; for bauxite, 79–80; diversification, 43; economies, 13, 255; effects of, 36; foreign, 160, 190; integration, 170, 176; protection, 45; regional, 130–1
Marshall aid, 247
MDCs, 173, 178; external debts of, 194–6, 198; and floating currency, 222–3, 227; imports, 121, 124
mining, 9, 25; in Jamaica, 42–3
Montserrat, xiii; economy of, 40; exports, 117; external debt, 196; GNP in, 30; and offshore banking, 96, 106, 108, 110; size, 27
multilateralism, 5, 22

nationalisation, 53, 204, 250, 286; and bananas, 71; and bauxite, 79; and oil, 82–3; and sugar, 67–8
New International Economic Order, 6–7
NICs, 273; data on, 283
non-tariff barriers, 14, 15, 16; *see also* protectionism

OECS, xiii; average income, 33; debt servicing, 108–9; external debt in, 196–200; imports, 121, 125; tourism in, 86, 87; trade

balance, 182–3
offshore banking centres, 96–7, 99; benefits, 102–5; competition, 110; costs, 105; secrecy of, 108, 110
offshore finance, xiv, 37, 89, 95–113; in Bahamas, 98–102; centre, 96–8
oil, 80–85, 183; in bauxite production 78, 80; boom, 57; companies, 83; and debt crisis, 187, 190; exporting, 6, 19, 36, 187; importing, 6, 116, 187; prices, 6, 13, 19, 33, 42, 50, 52, 53, 82, 83–5, 121, 125, 157–8, 173, 181, 184; products, 83; refining, 80, 85; transhipment, 80, 85; in Trinidad and Tobago, 42, 82–3, 181, 184
onshore financial centres, 97–8, 112
OPEC, 5–6; and prices, 61, 85; production, 83; and world trade, 12, 13
openness: of Commonwealth Caribbean, 34, 36, 268

Panama: and drug trade, 112–13; as tax haven, 110–111
par value system, 215–16, 218, 219–20, 222, 225–6, 227, 230, 231
petroleum: *see under* oil
plantation: economy, 26, 43
politics: and CBI, 142; and development, 253–4; and monetary system, 241; and protectionism, 15, 161; and trade, 158
population, xv, 28–30, 262, 265, 283; increasing, 11, 20, 21, 49
poverty, 2–3, 5; and development, 247, 251
preferential trade, 144, 170; with UK, 126, 137
prices, of commodities, 58–9, 183, 286; instability, 56–7; and trade, 150; *see also* oil: prices
private sector development, 256–60
privatisation, 259–60
product cycle theory, 149
production: of bananas, 69, 71, 74; of bauxite, 77–8; declining, 269; factors, 147, 151; levy, 79; of oil, 83; structure, 144–63, 162; sugar, 70; world, by volume, 9, 10, 116
protectionism: and industry, 49, 50; regional, 167; and sugar quotas, 64–5; in trade, 14–17, 22, 23, 116, 126, 145, 154, 155, 157, 160, 193, 200, 224, 283; and US, 15, 16
public: policies, 26; sector, role of, 6, 270–1

quotas: IMF, 237, 238; oil, 85; sugar, 64–5, 141, 161; trade, 14, 154

recession: international, 19, 84, 224; and trade, 116
regional trade, 130–1, 172–8
regulation: of offshore banking, 106–10
reserve currency countries, 219
reserves: foreign, 230, 232–3, 236; and SDR, 233–5; world, 236
resource flows, 201, 202–3, 250
resources: effective use of, xiv, 54, 265; foreign, 249; and IMF, 224–5; and integration, 167, 171, 175, 176; lack of, 282; and tourism, 89, 90
Ricardo, David, 146–7

St Kitts-Nevis: economy of, 40–1; exports, 120; GNP of, 51; sugar in, 36, 66–7; trade balance, 183
St Lucia: bananas in, 36, 71; economy of, 41–2; exports, 120; external debt, 196; GNP of, 51; and oil, 81; sugar in, 66–7; tourism in, 87, 88; trade balance, 183
St Vincent: and bananas, 71; economy of, 41; external debt, 196; GNP of, 51; and offshore banking, 96, 106, 108, 110; trade balance, 183
savings: and development, 248, 252; export of, 248–9
SDR, as reserve, 220–2, 226, 233–5; and LDCs, 232–5; pegging to, 228–9
service industries, 11, 38; as export, 117, 162; government, 37, 41; and trade, 155–6
'shell' banks, 99, 102, 106, 107
Singapore: economy of, 265, 279–81
size, physical: of Commonwealth Caribbean, 27, 30; and development, 261–84; and growth, 265–6; vulnerability, 267
skills, 54; and development, 256

South Korea: economy of, 265, 276–7
South-South co-operation, 6, 287
STABEX, 60; and agriculture, 138
standard of living, 115–16, 207, 247, 268; and external debt, 192
state: role of, in development, 256–60; size of, 261–84
subsidies, 270; for sugar, 69
sugar, 36, 37, 38, 40–1, 63–9; acreage of, 66; decline in, 67; exports, 64, 67; production, 70, 183; rationalisation, 68; types, 63–4; viability, 69

Taiwan: economy of, 277–9
tariffs: concessions, 154; non-barriers, 144, 159; trade, 13, 15, 144
tax haven services, xiv, 37, 89, 95, 96, 97, 102, 110
taxation: avoidance of, 106–7; and bauxite, 78–80
technology: and aid, 250–1; and development, 258, 273, 281, 286; gap, 149; and integration, 167; and trade, 151
tourism, xiv, xv, 25, 26, 37–9, 42, 85–91, 121, 182; development of, 90–1; direction of, 126–33; domestic, 86; as employment, 103; as export, 36, 86, 162; growth of, 36–7, 88; and integration, 171; international receipts, 85–6; intra-Caribbean, 91; profits from, 89; type of, 91
trade, 74, 166; barriers, xiv, 144–5, 162, 171, 215, 287; by barter, 22, 23; changes in, 13–21; concessions, xv, 2, 159; direction of, 129; and economic relations, 115–42; growth, Commonwealth Caribbean, 117–19; /income ratio, 117; institutional framework, 153–5; and integration, 168; international, 5, 19, 85, 144–6, 148, 286; intra-regional, 52, 130–1, 160, 171–2, 178; policies, xiv, 145, 159–63; regional composition, 12; restrictions, 5, 52, 116, 145, 154; and state size, 267; theory, 145–53; world growth in, 7, 10, 11, 218

trade deficit: US, 11, 13, 17; *see also* debt
trade liberalisation, 1, 22, 156, 211
trade unions, 26, 184
transnational corporations, 26, 27, 49–50, 102, 204, 205, 288; and bauxite taxation, 78–9; and oil production, 81, 85; and prices, 62, 63, 150
trust companies: in Bahamas, 100–1
Trinidad and Tobago, xiii, 34, 156, 162, 173; economy of, 42, 50, 52–3, 172; exports, 120; external debt, 194–5; foreign reserves, 161; GDP, xv; GNP, 30, 33; imports, 121; manufacturing in, 45; oil in, 36, 42, 82–3, 85; size, 27; sugar in, 66–7; tourism, 86–7; trade balance, 181–2
Turks and Caicos Islands: and offshore banking, 96, 108

UK: oil in, 84; sugar quotas, 65; and trade, 126–7, 219
UN: small states in, 261–2
UNCTAD, 4, 57
unemployment, xv, 3, 15, 16, 23, 52, 200, 250, 282; in Commonwealth Caribbean, 26, 34, 37; data, 52; and manufacturing, 49; and tourism, 89
US: and Commonwealth Caribbean trade, 127–8; economy of, 1, 218–19; exchange rate, 225; and foreign investment, 205–7; GNP, 166; market, 157; Marshall Plan, 3; and oil, 81; sugar quotas, 64–5; trade decline, 219; trade deficit, 11, 13, 17, 102, 218

wage levels, 26, 270, 284
West Germany: trade growth in, 219
Windward Islands, 71, 72–3, 74, 75
World Bank, xiv, 3, 15, 153, 158, 184, 192, 204, 208; loans, 196
world: economic policies, 153–5; tourism, 86

Yaoundé Convention, First, 134, 136